the TRUE SAGE

BHAGWAN SHREE RAJNEESH

---

talks on hassidism

Compiled by
Ma Yog Prem

Edited by
Swami Christ Chaitanya

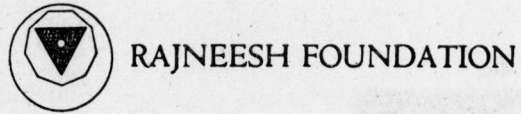

RAJNEESH FOUNDATION

© 1976 by Rajneesh Foundation

First Edition

Published by
Ma Yoga Laxmi
Rajneesh Foundation
Shree Rajneesh Ashram
17, Koregaon Park
Poona 411 001
India

Printed by
P. P. Bhagwat
Mouj Printing Bureau
Khatau Wadi
Bombay 400 004
India

Art Work by
Swami Anand Visuddah

Design by
Swami Anand Yatri

Printed in India

ISBN 0-88050-159-6

the TRUE SAGE

CONTENTS

INTRODUCTION

I

To Walk With One's Own Light   3

Questions and Answers   37

Ideology: a part of language? ... There is only the right question. ... What is grace? ... Do you love me? ... Why am I less aware now than ever?

II

The Watchman   79

Questions and Answers   117

So new yet so revealing. ... The difference between being an introvert and being aware. ... Why am I afraid of others? ... After the ego goes, what then? ... Mind as a beloved servant .... The sky penetrates me. ... Life: predestined or not? ... Was woman before man?

III

The Perfect Swimmer   157

Questions and Answers   191

I have neither eyes to see nor ears to hear. ... Is there an opposite to Buddha? ... Boredom. ... How can I be authentic? ... When do we come to know love?

IV

The Light Behind The Window   237

Questions and Answers   269

Neither in the world nor the watcher on the hill. . . . Can you be in total anger? . . . Why don't you laugh while telling jokes? . . . Where are you Bhagwan? . . . Death for an enlightened being. . . . Do we take the cake? . . . What about silence? . . . Alertness without tension. . . . Is real authenticity possible? . . . The most stupid thing Mulla Nasrudin ever did.

V

True Wisdom   309

Questions and Answers   353

The difference between passivity and flowing with the river. . . . Is it lonely up there? . . . Do you ever despair of us? . . . Before you, I am bathed in sweat. . . . When the watcher turns into the judger. . . . When you speak, do you read my mind? . . . Should I watch the wave or ride on it? . . . What is Hassidism?

INTRODUCTION

THE HASSIDIC MOVEMENT was founded in Poland in about 1750. It consisted of Jews who were no longer interested in head-oriented theories or even Kabbalistic doctrines (esoteric doctrines) — but in direct, spontaneous, religious experience.

It is said that the chief characteristic of the Hassidic movement was the emergence of different communities around a true sage or zaddik. The presence of a zaddik served as an inspiration to the people in the community, for here was living proof of everyone's possibility to live in God. In the midst of the world, yet in the midst of God.

As I find out more about Hassidism, I feel tremendous parallels between this 18th and 19th century existential movement and what is happening in Poona around Bhagwan Shree Rajneesh today.

Says Bhagwan Shree:

I am not teaching you an ideology,
and I am not teaching you an anti-ideology.
I am not teaching you anything
that belongs to the world of concepts and ideas.
I am teaching you 'me'.
I am teaching you a way of being,
a different quality of existence.

There is a Hassidic saying: 'If a man of Israel has himself firmly in hand, and stands solidly on the earth, then his head reaches up to Heaven.' Hassidic sages and those around them never left the world; they worked deeply in the world. They had their feet planted solidly in the earth and they brought a bit of Heaven into their every activity.

Bhagwan Shree's ashram community has its feet also planted on the earth. Bhagwan Shree creates situations in which one sees what one has been continuously avoiding: fears, loneliness, power-trips, all sorts of ego-games. The mirrors that he uses are many: meditation, therapies, work relationships, love relationships. Initiation into sannyas, into discipleship, means the surrender of one who is asleep to one who is awakened. It's like saying, 'Look, I know I'm escaping all that existence is trying to show me. So I will use you, my zaddik, as my mirror — and I promise not to look the other way.'

> Wherever you are,
> use all situations to awaken yourself.
> And every situation can be used.
> Hassids live in the world
> in an ordinary way,
> and they use all sorts of situations
> to make themselves more and more aware and alert.
> That's why when I give sannyas to you,
> I am doing a Hassidic work.

Anecdotes and stories represent the greatest expression of Hassidism. Many zaddikim laid down the whole treasure of their ideas in such tales. Their Torah took the form of an inexhaustible fountain of story-telling.

The 'True Sage' is five Hassidic stories. Bhagwan responds to them with more stories. Bhagwan Shree is a storyteller. He is not concerned with history, dates, places; he is concerned with understanding. His anecdotes, like those of the zaddikim, or the Sufis, or the Zen Masters, are a major tool to transmit a deep understanding.

> These words are alive.
> They have the throb of my heart.
> I bring them to you as a gift.
> They are not doctrines.
> At the most
> you can call them poetries.
> At the most most
> you can call me a good storyteller,
> that's all.

Introduction

*My words are nothing
but knockers on your door,
so that you can come home.
Accept my gift.*

This book is a gift to you from a true sage. Accept his gift.

Swami Christ Chaitanya
April 9, 1976.

the TRUE SAGE

11th October 1975

A young rabbi
    complained to the rabbi of Rizhyn:—
'During the hours
    when I devote myself to my studies,
I feel life and light,
    but the moment I stop studying,
it is all gone.
    What shall I do?'

The rabbi of Rizhyn replied:—
  'That is just as when
a man walks through the woods
    on a dark night,
and for a time
    another man accompanies him
who has a lamp,
    but at the crossroads they part
and the first
    must grope his way on alone.
But if a man
    carries his own light with him,
he need not be afraid
    of any darkness.'

To walk with one's own light

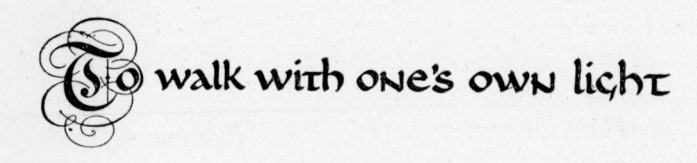

There are religions —
Hinduism, Christianity, Buddhism, Judaism —
and many more.
But they are religions, not *the* religion.
They are the reflections of the moon
in many kinds of minds.
They are not the real moon.

The moon is one
but it can be reflected in millions of lakes.
Reflections differ, but the reflected is one.

Mind is a mirror.
When religion is reflected through the mind
a Hinduism is born, or a Mohammedanism or a Judaism.

When the religion is not a reflected one,
when one comes face to face with reality
without any mind whatsoever,
when there is no mind between you and the truth,
then there is born *the* religion.

Hassidism is *the* religion.
Sufism is *the* religion.
Zen is *the* religion.

They differ only in names;
otherwise they are all the same.
Their language is different but not their content.
They all have looked at the moon,
but they call it different names.
Obviously, that is natural.
But they have not been looking at the reflections.
They don't believe in creeds, ideologies,
scriptures, dogmas, doctrines.
They know the truth, and when you know the truth
there is no need of scriptures.

You carry the scripture on your head
when the truth is not known.
Theories are substitutes, dead.
Truth is always alive, eternally alive.
It cannot be confined in words; the message is wordless.
And you cannot come to it by somebody else
because whenever there is a medium,
it becomes a reflection.
When your own mind creates a reflection,
what about other minds through which you come to know it?

One has to come in immediate contact,
direct, heart to heart.
Nothing should be allowed between the two:
your heart and the heart of reality.
They should respond in a deep resonance.
They should meet and mingle and merge
and there should not even be a curtain
of words, knowledge, concepts.
Only then, you know what religion is.

Hassidism is religion, Judaism is just a reflection.
Or you can say the same thing in other words:
Judaism is just the periphery and Hassidism is the core —
the very core, the living soul, the very center.

Buddhism is the periphery, Zen is the core.

Islam is the periphery, Sufism is the core.

And the core is one; peripheries are millions.
On one center you can draw many concentric circles.
You can go on drawing them; the center remains one.

We will be talking about Hassidism.
Before we enter into the spirit of it,
a few remarks are needed as an introduction.

Whenever the problem arises
of how to talk about *the* religion,
it becomes very difficult
because whatsoever you say about it
is always going to be less than the truth.
Whatsoever you say about it
is always going to be a reflection.
It can indicate; it cannot explain.
It can show but it cannot say.
So from where to begin, to indicate, to show?

I would like to start
with Samuel Beckett's beautiful play, *Waiting for Godot*.
It is absurd —
as absurd as life is —
but the very absurdity of life, if understood deeply,
becomes an indication towards something
which is beyond and meaningful.

That which is beyond you is meaningful.
And only the beyond is meaningful.
That which is beyond mind is meaningful.

Waiting for Godot can be a good beginning
for Hassidism, Zen, or Sufism —
a very indirect indication.
Because to say something direct
about such intimate, deep phenomena
is to violate them.
So be cautious, move slowly. It is holy ground.

The True Sage

The curtain rises:
two vagabonds are sitting and waiting for Godot.
Who is this Godot?
They don't know; nobody knows.
Even Samuel Beckett, when once asked:
'Who is this Godot?' said:
'If I had known, I would have said so in the play itself.'
Nobody knows.
This is a Zen gesture.

The word Godot sounds like God. That is significant.
Who knows God? Who has ever known?
Who can say? Who can claim that he knows?
All knowledge is foolish
and one who claims that he knows God
is simply stupid.
Godot sounds like God, the unknown.
It may be all, it may be nothing.
They are waiting for Godot.

When they don't know who this God is,
then why are they waiting?
Because if you don't wait for something
you fall into the inner emptiness.
If you are not waiting for something to happen,
you have to face your inner vacuum, the inner nothingness.
And it is scary, it is death-like.
To avoid it, to escape from it,
one projects a dream in the future;
that's how future time is created.

Future is not part of time, it is part of mind.
Time is always present.
It is never past, never future. It is always now.
Mind creates future because then one can avoid the 'now'.
One can look ahead into the clouds, wait for something
and pretend that something is going to happen —
and nothing happens.

To Walk With One's Own Light

One of the most basic truths about human life
is that nothing ever happens.
Millions of things seem to happen
but nothing ever happens.

One goes on waiting and waiting and waiting:
waiting for Godot.
Who is this Godot? Nobody knows.
But still one has to project to avoid one's inner emptiness.

There is a Hassidic saying that man is made of dust
and returns to dust.
Dust unto dust.
Between and betwixt, a drink comes handy.
It's really beautiful:
made of dust, falls one day back unto dust.
Between and betwixt, a drink comes handy.

That drink is the desire, the projection,
the ambition, the future, the imagination.
Otherwise, suddenly you will become aware
that you are just dust and nothing else.
Hoping for the future, waiting for the future,
the dust has a dream around it.
It partakes of the glory of the dream; it illuminates.
Through the dream you feel you are somebody.
And dreaming costs nothing, so you can dream.
Beggars can dream to be emperors;
there is no law against it.
To avoid being, a dream of becoming is projected.

Those two vagabonds are the whole humanity personified.
Man is a vagabond.
From where do you come? —
you can't say.
Where are you going? —
you can't answer.
Where are you right now, this moment? —
at the most you can shrug your shoulders.

The True Sage

Man is a vagabond, a wanderer,
with no home in the past, with no home in the future —
a wanderer on a continuous wandering, endless.
Beckett is right:
those two vagabonds are the whole humanity.

But to create a dream, one is not enough; two are needed.
Because one will be less than enough.
The other's help is needed.

That's why those who want to get out of dreams
try to remain alone, start becoming silent.
They meditate, move to the Himalayas. They try to be alone.
Because when you are alone it is difficult.
By and by, again and again,
you are thrown back to your reality.
The prop is not there, the excuse is not there;
the other is needed.

That's why whenever somebody falls in love,
suddenly, dreams explode in the being.
The other is there; now you can dream together
and you can help each other to avoid oneself.
That's why there is so much need for love:
it is a dream need.

Alone, it is very difficult to dream.
Again and again the dream is broken
and you are thrown to the bare naked reality,
the emptiness.
A lover is needed:
somebody to cling to, somebody to look to,
somebody to share with, somebody who will patch the gaps,
who will bring you out of yourself
so that you don't come face to face
with your naked reality.

Two vagabonds are sitting.
The curtain rises.

They are waiting for Godot.
They don't ask each other:
'Who is this Godot anyhow, anyway?'
Because to ask will be dangerous.
They both know deep down that they are waiting for nobody.

It is dangerous, risky, to ask who Godot is.
To raise the very question will be dangerous,
the dream will be shattered.
They are afraid so they don't ask.
One question they avoid continuously:
'Who is this Godot?'
That is the basic question which should be asked
the very first moment one becomes aware.
You are waiting for Godot: ask who this Godot is!

But they are touchy about it,
they talk about many other things.
They say: 'When is he coming?
Are you certain he will keep his promise this time?
Yesterday he deceived.
The day before yesterday he never came.
And today also, the promised time is passing by
and he seems not to be coming.'
They look again and again at the road; the road is empty.

But they never ask the basic question.
They never ask: 'Who is this Godot?'
They never ask: 'When did he promise you to come?
Where did you meet him?
How do you know he exists?'
No, they never touch that.

This is how all worldly people live:
they never ask the basic questions.
It is risky, it is absolutely dangerous.
One has to hide. One has to pretend
that one knows the basic questions;
one goes on always asking secondary questions.

The True Sage

Remember, when you come to me it rarely happens
that anybody asks a primary question.
And if I try to bring you to the primary,
you become scared.
You ask futile things which can be answered,
but even if answered, you are not going to gain anything
because they are not basic.

It is as if your house is on fire and you ask:
'Who has planted these trees?'
The question may look relevant, it can be answered,
but what will be the outcome of it?
Ask the fundamental.

The house is on fire; you have to do something.
But they never ask.
Again and again they say:
'This day is again passing and he has not come.'
And they help each other:
'He must be coming, he must be delayed.
There are a thousand and one hazards,
but he is a man you can rely upon.
He is reliable.'
And this 'he' is simply empty.

One day more has passed and he is not coming
and they get fed-up and start saying:
'Now it is enough. Enough is enough!'
They are going to leave, they cannot wait anymore —
but they never leave.

Next day again they are there,
sitting in the same place, waiting for Godot again.
And yesterday they had decided,
very vehemently they had decided
that now they will leave, that it is finished.
One cannot wait for the whole life.
'If he is coming, it's okay;
if he is not coming, that too is okay.'

To Walk With One's Own Light

Why don't they leave?
They again and again say that they are leaving.
The problem is: where to go?
You can leave but where to go?
Wherever you go, you will again wait for Godot.
A change of place won't help.

You can come to India.
You can be in England.
Or in America.
Or you can go to Japan —
but what will be the outcome?
You will be waiting for Godot.
Japan, England, India — it is the same.
The change of geography won't help.

That's why, whenever humanity is in deep turmoil,
people become travellers.
They go from one country to another.
They are always on the go.
They are always going somewhere.
They are not reaching anywhere,
but they are always going somewhere.
In fact they are not going anywhere,
they are only escaping the place where they are.

If they are in America they are going to India.
If they are in India they are going to Japan.
If they are in Japan they are going to Nepal.
They are not going anywhere!
They are simply trying to escape
from the place where they are.
But everywhere they remain the same.
Nothing happens.
Because geography has nothing to do with it.

In a way, those vagabonds are truer, more honest.
They decide in an angry mood.
They curse, they swear, and they say: 'Now enough!

Tomorrow morning we are not going to be here,
waiting for Godot.
We will leave.'

Tomorrow again, the sun rises
and they are in the same place, and waiting.
And again, asking when he is coming.
They have completely forgotten
that last night they had decided to leave.
But where to go?
There is nowhere to go:
this is a second basic truth about humanity.

First, nothing ever happens.
Things appear to happen, but you remain the same.
Look into your being —
has anything ever happened there?
You were a child and you dreamed a lot,
and then you became young and you still dreamed a lot.
Then you became old and you still dreamed.
You dreamed about the riches of this world;
now maybe you are dreaming
about the riches of another world.
But has anything ever happened to you?
And don't be scared — because if you are scared
you start asking secondary questions.

Religion is to ask the fundamental question,
the very basic question,
and to ask it courageously is very significant
because in the very asking
you are coming nearer to the center.

The second truth:
you have been going and going and going
from one place to another,
from one mood to another,

from one plane to another,
from one level to another level.
You are not reaching anywhere.

Have you reached any place?
Can you say that you have arrived anywhere?
It is always a departure; an arrival never happens.
Trains are always leaving, planes are always leaving,
people are ready in their waiting rooms.
Always departure — never arriving anywhere.
The whole absurdity of it.
But you never ask these two basic questions.

And then the third automatically bubbles up:
Who are you?
Because it is not really meaningful
to ask who Godot is.
That is your creation; your gods are your creations.
Forget what the Bible says —
that God created man in his own image.
It is just the reverse: man created God in his own image.
It is Godot.
It is your creation.
It is your dream.

Somehow to feel that you are significant, meaningful,
you have created a God in the skies.
God has not created the world, God has not created man.
Man has created the whole concept.

A real religion, an authentic religion,
does not ask who God is.
It asks: 'Who am I?'
I have to fall upon my basic source.
There, and there only — the revelation.
Jesus, Buddha or Baal Shem Tov —
they ask the fundamental questions.

The second thing to understand
about fundamental questioning is:
fundamental questions have no answers.
The question is itself the answer!
If you ask it authentically,
in the very asking it is answered.
It is not that you ask: 'Who am I ? Who am I ? Who am I ? ...
and one day you come to know that you are a, b, c, d. . . .
No — you never come to know a, b, c, d.
By and by, the more you ask it, the deeper it goes.
One day, suddenly, the question disappears.
You are standing face-to-face with your own being,
you are open to your being.
The question has disappeared and there is no answer.

Take it as a criterion: if a question can be answered,
it is not fundamental.
If, by asking, a question disappears — it is fundamental.
And in the very disappearance you have arrived,
and for the first time something happens.
For the first time you are no more the same.
Godot has not come, but waiting disappears.
You don't wait, you have arrived.
And once you have arrived
the quality of your being is totally different.
Then you can celebrate.

How can you celebrate when you have not arrived?
You are sad, miserable.
How can you dance when the goal is very far away? —
so distant that there seems to be no possibility
that you will ever be capable of reaching it.
How can you be happy?
How can you enjoy?
How can joy happen to you?
You are still on the way.
The seed is still a seed and the flower is far away.
No, it is not possible.

When the seed becomes the flower
there is joy, there is delight.

Once you understand who you are,
once you go deep into your emptiness and are not scared,
once you accept the inner death
and you are not trying to escape
through dreams and projections,
once you accept that you are dust unto dust
and between these two happenings
there is nothing but a deep emptiness,
you have arrived at what Buddha calls 'nirvana'.
And this is what Hassids call 'God'!
It is not your Godot.

Jews have insisted always
that the name of God should not be uttered,
because once you utter it you falsify it.
It is not utterable; it is inexpressable.
You can contain it in your heart but you cannot relate it.
You can become it but you cannot express it.

And Jews are perfectly right in their feeling about it.
God is not a being; it is a phenomenon —
so vast, so infinite, that no word can contain it.
Only the infinite heart can contain it.
Only the infinite inner emptiness can contain it.

When you enter within yourself,
you will feel you are entering into a space
where you are going to be lost —
just as a drop of water
entering into the ocean is lost.
You will be lost: that is the fear.
That is why you become afraid of death
and you start dreaming — future, projections.

Entry into your being is always like death.
It is a crucifixion. It is a cross.

But if you are courageous enough. . . .
And cowards can never become religious.
Only very rare courageous souls
who can take the risk of being lost, arrive.
You have to pay for it
and nothing less will do.
You have to lose yourself to gain it.

Once you are ready to enter into the emptiness,
suddenly the fear disappears.
The same energy becomes a celebration.
You can dance, because that which appeared as emptiness
was an interpretation of the mind.
It was not empty.
It was so full that the mind could not understand
the fullness of it!

Mind is impotent. Mind is negative. Mind is empty.
It understands the language of emptiness.
If something is very full then mind cannot understand it.
It is just like you have lived in darkness
for your whole life.
Then suddenly you are brought out into the sunlight
and your eyes go blind.
It is so dazzling, the light is so much.
You cannot open your eyes. You see darkness.
Standing before the sun you are standing in darkness.

You have lived up to now with the mind.
Mind means future.
Mind means that which is not.
Mind means dream, appearance, illusion, maya.
Maya means a magical world.
You create your own world and you live in it.
You create your hallucinations and you live in it.
Your hell and your heaven — all are mental.

To Walk With One's Own Light

Once you enter into your inner being
the mind cannot understand.
It is totally unaware of the new language,
the new territory.
It is absolutely unknown to it.
The mind cannot cope with it.
It simply goes empty; the thing is too much.
The light is so bright and dazzling —
the mind goes empty and blank.
You become afraid and you escape.
Then you create a false god, a Godot.

A Godot is a false god.
It may be wealth.
It may be prestige and power.
It may be politics.
It may be ego.
It may be a god in heaven.
But it is all Godot. You created it.
You don't know what is.
Not knowing what is, you create your own dream around it.

Authentic religion is an inquiry into what is.
Inauthentic religion is inventive.
Authentic religion is a discovery.
Inauthentic religion is an invention.
Mind invents. And mind is the barrier.
And once the mind invents, it creates great philosophies:
Christianity, Hinduism, Judaism.

All the great mystics —
Hassids, Zen Masters, Sufis — they are rebellious.
They have to be.
A religious man is a rebellious man —
there is no other way.
Religion and rebellion are two aspects of the same coin.

The True Sage

There are religions of Godots:
churches, mosques, temples,
organized around a creed,
organized because of the fear of man,
organized because of the mind escaping
from inner emptiness.
Doctrines, dogmas, to fill you.
These are all barriers.

A Jesus, a Buddha, or a Baal Shem Tov
are by necessity rebellious.
I don't call them revolutionaries;
I call them rebellious —
and the difference has to be understood well.

A revolutionary is one
who wants to change the society,
who wants to change the government,
who wants to change the structure —
economical, political, religious.
A revolutionary is not spiritual.
He is not concerned with his own change.
He thinks if others change
then everything will be perfectly okay.
A revolutionary lives in an illusion.
All revolutions have failed, failed utterly.
And ultimately a revolution cannot succeed.
The very attitude is wrongly oriented:
it is an effort to change the other.

A rebellious man is not concerned
with the structure of the society, state, government, no.
He is concerned with his own being. He is individual.
Revolutionaries make parties.
A rebellious man is alone; he is his own revolution.
Wherever he moves, a revolution moves around him.
His very being is a transforming force.

A Jesus, a Buddha, a Zarathustra —
these are rebellious people.
They have changed their own being, they have arrived.
Even if you watch them from the outside
you can see the serenity, the calm, the subtle joy —
the way they breathe, the way they move.
You can watch, you can feel,
you can hear the sound that surrounds them —
the subtle ripples of their inner calm.
If you open yourself it will be reaching you.
A rebellion has happened —
the state of being is totally new.
The old is dead and the new is born.
This is the meaning of the story
of Jesus' crucifixion *and* resurrection.
It is a metaphor. Don't try to find history in it.
Once you take metaphors as history,
you are behaving very foolishly.
It is a beautiful, poetic metaphor.
Christ is crucified
and on the third day he is resurrected.
A new life — immortal now, eternal now.

If you move withinwards
and come across the inner emptiness,
you will die.
And there will be a gap.
The three days are symbolic.
There will be a gap.
You will lie dead for three days
just like Jesus in the cave.
Just a passage is needed
so the old can disappear completely.
Remember — completely, totally —
not even a single fragment of it should remain,
because that can poison the new.

That's why a gap is needed: so the old is completely gone
and the new enters.
There is no continuity in them.
There is no continuity at all.
This is a discontinuity.
Jesus, the son of Joseph and Mary, died
and then after three days Christ revived —
the Son of God, the new.

Ordinary religion is a pseudo phenomenon.
Beware of it!
You can study and while you study you may feel good.
While you study, you may forget yourself.
You can get into subtle theories
and there may be a certain intellectual enjoyment,
an intellectual delight.
You can move into rituals
and there may be a certain intoxication in it.

If you repeat a mantra continuously
you will feel intoxicated.
It is creating an inner alcohol through sound.
Or you can move into drugs;
then you change your chemistry,
and for a few moments
you attain to a height which is false,
which is not a real height
because you have not grown towards it.
The chemistry has pushed you.

This has to be understood well:
the chemistry of the body can be changed in many ways.
It can be changed by drugs:
LSD, marijuana, and others.
It can be changed by old methods,

by too much oxygen in the body.
You can inhale too much oxygen;
it will change your chemistry.
If you fast, it changes your chemistry.
Even by standing on your head, it changes your chemistry
because the blood now circulates more in the brain.

You can change the chemistry in many ways.
Drugs are the latest.
But all these methods are also drugs
which change your chemistry.
They may be better than psychedelics,
but still the same.

By rituals, by study, by belief, by auto-hypnosis,
you can attain to a few glimpses which will be false—
as if you are fast asleep,
and in a dream you see the sun rising.
In a dream the sun is not real,
the whole phenomenon is hallucinatory.
When you awake it is a dark night.

The false religion, the church, the organization,
they have always been supplying intoxicants, drugs.
They may be against the modern drugs,
but they are not against drugs.
They are always for the old;
the old is always better for them.

I am against all drugs, old and new.
I am even against yoga —
because that too is a way to change the chemistry.
Then what to do? —
because unless you attend to your own growth,
this story will remain true.
I will read it.

To Walk With One's Own Light

*A young rabbi
complained to the rabbi of Rizhyn:
'During the hours
when I devote myself to my studies,
I feel life and light,
but the moment I stop studying,
it is all gone.
What shall I do?'*

It is possible.
If you listen to me, it may happen.
Listening to me you may sometimes feel light and life,
because even listening changes the chemistry of the body.
Listening to my voice, the rhythm,
continuously, attentively alert,
your body chemistry is being changed.
You go on looking at me; a subtle hypnosis happens.
You go on listening to me; your own thinking stops.
You feel life. You feel light.
But don't depend on it.
And don't take it as something that you have achieved.

I ask people : 'Which meditation is suiting you more?'
Many of them say : 'The morning lecture.
When we listen to you, that meditation goes deepest.'
But that is a sort of hypnosis.
Beware!
This may have happened to the young rabbi.

'During the hours
when I devote myself to my studies,
I feel life and light,
but the moment I stop studying,
it is all gone.'

To Walk With One's Own Light

When you leave this hall and you move on your own,
how long will be the deep meditation
that you felt with me?
It will be gone.
Before you have reached to the gate
it is no more with you —
and it is good that it is gone.
Otherwise you will remain always illusioned.

It is good that you cannot carry it home.
It is good that you cannot depend on it.
Otherwise, you are *such*
that you will make a treasure of it,
and you will forget that this is not your own.

Unless religion is your own, it has not happened.
And this is one of the greatest things
to be continuously remembered,
because there is every tendency in the mind to forget it —
because it is so cheap and easy.

Listening to me, reading the Gita, or the Talmud, or the Bible,
you are taken out of your mind.
A foreign element has been functioning on you.
Maybe the foreign element is Jesus, Buddha, or me —
but somebody outside you has been pulling you up.
Once he is not there,
you are thrown back to your reality.
And almost always it happens
that you fall back even deeper than before.

It is just as if you are passing down a road.
The night is dark and a car passes by.
For a moment, a strong light;
the headlight of the car dazzles your eyes.
Then the car is gone.
The darkness is even darker than it was before.

The True Sage

Listening to me, reading the Gita, the Koran, the Talmud,
a car passes by with strong headlights.
You are dazzled for a moment,
you are taken out of the vast dark night
that is surrounding you.
But when the car has gone by,
when the Buddha passes, when Jesus passes,
suddenly you are in a deeper darkness than before.

By the way,
I would like you to know that in India
the greatest number of mystics have been born.
That's why India is in so much darkness.
So many people dazzled the mind —
a Buddha, a Mahavir, a Krishna —
thousands of them, a great procession, again and again.
And they enchanted people; people became hypnotized.
And when they passed,
people fell into a darker night than ever before.

Go and watch the Indian mind:
you will not find a more rotten thing
anywhere in the world.
It is completely rotten to the roots.
And the reason is: so much light
and not that much capacity to absorb it —
because the capacity to absorb light
comes only when you have grown.

Don't look at the sun; you can burn your retina.
One has to learn it,
and by learning, I mean one has to become capable.
The eyes have to become stronger and stronger and stronger —
and then you can look at the sun and it will be helpful,
it can be tremendously helpful.

Now even scientists agree that the third eye center . . .
they have their own scientific names — that doesn't matter —
some gland, pineal or something, that feeds on light.

To Walk With One's Own Light

If you look at a lamp, a flame,
your third eye starts functioning.
It feeds on light.
That's why it is difficult to sleep in the day,
because the light is there
and the third eye goes on functioning and trembling.
That's why it is difficult to sleep in the night
when the light is on.
You would like darkness;
otherwise the third eye goes on functioning —
and the third eye's function is consciousness.
Hence the Hindu methods of *tratak*,
of looking at a flame.
If you look at a flame for a long time,
for a few months, one hour every day,
your third eye starts functioning perfectly.
You become more alert, more light-filled.

The word *tratak* comes from a root which means tears.
So you have to look at the flame
until tears start flowing from the eyes.
Go on staring, unblinking,
and the third eye will start vibrating.
But don't look at the sun!
One has to come by and by to the sun.
If one can look at the sun for thirty or forty minutes
without burning his retina,
immediate enlightenment is possible,
because the third eye feeds on the light.

When you look at me,
suddenly there is a little light inside.
You listen to me, you become attentive.
When you become attentive your third eye becomes focused.
You look at me, you watch me, or you read a book . . .
not an ordinary book —
a book which has come from a man who has attained:
a Torah.

The True Sage

Thousands of years have passed,
but the man who uttered those words
or wrote those words,
if he had known . . .
a certain vibration still continues.
You become attentive, you feel light,
and whenever you feel light you feel life.
This combination has to be remembered.
Whenever you feel dead you will feel dark.
Whenever you feel life you will feel light.

There is a saying of Jesus:
'Come follow me. My burden is light.'
Ordinarily, Christians have been interpreting it:
'My burden is not heavy' — that's not true.
When Jesus says: 'My burden is light,'
he simply means *light*.
He does not mean 'not heavy'.
'Come follow me. My burden is light.'
'That is the only burden I carry: the light.'

And light has no weight.
That's why the secondary meaning: 'not heavy'.
Light has no weight.
It is the most weightless thing in the world,
the most immaterial matter.
And whenever you feel light within,
suddenly you feel an upsurge of life energy.

The young rabbi said:
'*During the hours
when I devote myself to my studies,
I feel life and light,
but the moment I stop studying,
it is all gone.
What shall I do?*'

The rabbi of Rizhyn replied:

To Walk With One's Own Light

*'That is just as when
a man walks through the woods
on a dark night,
and for a time
another man accompanies him
who has a lamp,
but at the crossroads they part
and the first
must grope his way on alone.
But if a man
carries his own light with him,
he need not be afraid
of any darkness.'*

I meet you on the road; I have a lamp.
Suddenly, you are no more in the dark.
But the lamp is mine.
Soon we will depart,
because your way is your way and mine is mine.
And each individual has an individual way
to reach to his destiny.
For a while you forget all about darkness.
My light functions for me as well as for you.
But soon the moment comes when we have to part.
I follow my way; you go on your own.
Now again you will have to grope in the darkness
and the darkness will be darker than before.

So don't depend on another's light.
It is even better you grope in darkness —
but let the darkness be yours!
Somebody else's light is not good;
even one's own darkness is better.
At least it is one's own, at least it is your reality.
And if you live in your own darkness,
even the darkness will become less and less dark.
You will be able to grope.
You will learn the art, you will not fall.

Blind people don't fall.
Try walking with closed eyes; you will be in difficulty.
Even a hundred feet you cannot walk
but the blind man can walk the whole distance.
The blindness is his.
With closed eyes, you are borrowing blindness.
It is not yours.
Even darkness of one's own is good.
One's own errors are better than other people's virtues,
remember this —
because the mind is always tempted to imitate, to borrow.
But that which is significant cannot be borrowed.
No, you cannot enter the kingdom of God
with borrowed money; there is no way.
You cannot bribe the guards because there are no guards
and you cannot enter from a thief's door
because there are no doors.

You have to walk and through walking create your path.
Ready-made paths are not available.
That's what the false religion goes on teaching to people:
'Come. Here is a superhighway.
Be a Christian and you need not worry.
Then we take all the burden, then *we* are responsible.'

Jesus says: 'Be yourself.'
The Pope of the Vatican says: 'Follow Christianity.'
All Christianity is against Christ,
all churches are against religion.
They are the citadels
of anti-religion and anti-Christ,
because those who have known have emphasized
that you should be yourself.
There is no other way of being.
All else is false, dishonest, insincere, imitation, ugly.
The only beauty possible is to be yourself,
to be yourself in such purity and innocence
that nothing foreign enters in you.

To Walk With One's Own Light

Walk in your own darkness —
because through walking, groping,
by and by, you will find your own light also.
When you have your darkness
the light is not very far away.
When the night is dark, the morning is close —
just reaching.

Once you become dependent on borrowed light, you are lost.
Darkness is never so dangerous as borrowed light.
Knowing is good, but knowledge is not good.
Knowing is yours, knowledge is others.

*'That is just as when
a man walks through the woods
on a dark night,
and for a time
another man accompanies him
who has a lamp,
but at the crossroads they part
and the first must grope his way on alone.'*

Buddha was dying.
He walked for forty years with a lamp
and thousands followed him.
Now he was going to die.

One day in the morning he said: 'This is my last day.
If you have something to ask, you can ask.'
The moment had come, the crossroad had come;
now he would go on his own way.

Suddenly, infinite darkness surrounded everybody.
Ananda, Buddha's chief disciple,
started crying like a child —
beating his heart, tears coming down — almost mad.

Buddha said: 'What are you doing, Anand?'

Anand said: 'What will we do now?

You were here, we followed in your light.
Everything was safe and secure.
We have completely forgotten that darkness exists.
Following you, everything was light.
Forty years, and now you are leaving —
and you are leaving us in total darkness.
We were better before we met you
because at least we were attuned to darkness;
now that tuning is also lost.
Don't leave us in darkness!
We could not attain to enlightenment
while you were here;
now what will happen when you are gone?
We are lost forever.'
He started crying and weeping again.

Buddha said: 'Listen.
Forty years you walked in my light
and you could not attain to your own light.
Do you think if I am alive forty years more,
you will attain to your own light?
Even four thousand or four million years?
The more you walk in a borrowed light,
the more you imitate, the more you will lose.
It is better I should go.'

The last words on Buddha's lips were:
'Be a light unto yourself.'
He died with this uttering: 'Be a light unto yourself' —
'Appo deepo bhava.'

The story is beautiful.
The next day Ananda became enlightened.
He could not become enlightened for forty years
and he loved Buddha tremendously;
he had almost become a shadow of him
and he could not attain.
The borrowed light: he relied too much on it.

To Walk With One's Own Light

And it was so beautiful, and so effortlessly available —
who bothers about anything else?
And within twenty-four hours he became enlightened.
What happened?

Twenty-four hours of deep crying
and facing the darkness,
and the reality,
and one's own helplessness.
Those twenty-four hours must have been so long for him.
It was the darkest period — painful, deep anguish and agony.
He passed that hell.
It is said that for twenty-four hours
he was lying down under a tree as if dead,
the whole body shaking, tears continuously flowing.
People thought that he had gone mad
or that he wouldn't be able to survive without Buddha.

But after twenty-four hours
he was a totally different man.
He opened his eyes and people could not believe it —
those eyes had the same glimmer as Buddha's eyes.
His body had the same beauty, the same fragrance.
He walked like Buddha.
He had attained to his own light.

The Rabbi of Rizhyn replied:
'But if a man
carries his own light with him,
he need not be afraid
of any darkness.'

The whole world need not be filled with light
for you to walk —
just your own heart.
A little flame, and that's enough,
because that will light
enough of a path for you to walk.

Nobody walks more than one step at a time.
A small flame in the heart of awareness,
mindfulness, *dhyana,* meditation.
A little flame and that's enough.
It lights your path a little.
Then you walk, then again the light goes further.

Says Lao Tzu : 'By taking one step at a time
one can walk ten thousand miles.'
And God is not that far away.

Godot is very far away. You will never reach him.
You will have to wait and wait and wait.
It is a waiting, Godot is a waiting, infinite —
because it is just imagination.
It is not there, it is just like the horizon.
It appears, just a few miles away,
that the sky is meeting the earth.

You think : 'A few hours journey
and I will reach the horizon.'
You will never reach.
The earth never meets the sky anywhere.
You can go around the earth again and again,
you can encircle it millions of times ;
you will never come across the horizon.
And it will always be there,
just ahead of you, waiting for you.

Godot is a horizon ; it is a waiting.
It fills your emptiness, deceives you. That is the only deception.
But God is not far away.
God is exactly where you are right now!

In the Upanishads there is a saying :
'God is far and God is near also.'
If I am to translate this, I will say :
'Godot is far. God is always near.'
He is here–now.

To Walk With One's Own Light

Right this moment who surrounds you?
Right this moment who throbs within you?
Right this moment who is talking to you?
And who is listening to it?

God is life, God is this oceanic energy.
Somewhere it is a tree and a flower
and somewhere a stream and a song.
Somewhere a bird.
Somewhere a rock.
Somewhere you and somewhere me.

William Blake was asked once: 'Who is God?'
He said: 'Jesus, you, and me.'

All is God. God is just a name for all.
God is not someone sitting there,
the supreme-most manager or something like that.
God is all.
You are in it. He is in you. God is near.
Only a little flame, a little light inside is needed.
Then you live for the first time.
Otherwise you simply desire, you never live.
You simply hope to live somewhere, sometime,
when Godot comes.

Living is possible only in this moment
because there is no other moment.
And when I am saying these things,
don't start thinking about them,
because thinking is a process
and leads you into the future.

Listen to me and realize it.
It is not a question of thinking.
I am not talking about any hypothesis;
I am simply telling you a fact.
I am not giving you a doctrine;
I am just indicating what is the case.

The True Sage

You need not think about it
You can listen to it,
and if you have listened to it well, attentively,
immediate is the realization of it.

You will lose track again and again
because it will be my light,
but once you know that light is possible,
you become confident that your light is also possible.
If it can happen to this man, why not to you?
My bones are just like yours,
my blood just like yours, my flesh just like yours.
I am as much dust as you.
And this dust will fall unto dust
as your dust is going to fall.
If something of the beyond
has become possible to this man,
you can be confident.
There is no need to hesitate. You can also take the jump.
With me in these days, while you will be with me,
I will try to walk with you with my light.

Remember, delight in it, but don't depend on it.
Read the Torah, read the Bible, delight.
They are really beautiful, but don't depend.
Delight, so that your own urge, your own desire,
takes an urgency, an intensity to arrive,
to arrive where you already are.
It is not going somewhere else,
it is being there where you are.

Religion is not a goal; it is a revelation.
Religion is not a desire; it is a reality.
Just a little turning is needed
and I say : 'Just a little' —
and everything becomes possible.
Life becomes possible.
Otherwise you will live empty and waiting.

Don't be the vagabonds of Samuel Beckett's play,
Waiting for Godot.
As it is you have already waited long.
Now be finished with it!

Start living!
Why wait? For whom are you waiting?
Who is this Godot anyhow?

This moment, the whole existence crosses you.
This moment, all that is in this existence
culminates in you.
This moment you are a crescendo.
Delight in it.
If you can understand that you are the goal
then it will be very simple
to understand this small anecdote —
very significant and penetrating.

You are the goal.
You are the way.
You are the light.
You are the whole.
That is the meaning when we say : 'You are holy.'

If you have come to me, remember,
let me be just an encouragement,
an encouragement to lead you to yourself.
Allow me and help me so that I can throw you back
to your own innermost being.
That is the meaning of a Master.
A Master helps you to be yourself.

I have no pattern to give you, no values, no morality.
I have only freedom to give to you
so that you can flower and you can become a lotus, a light.
And life eternal.

12th October 1975

Questions and answers

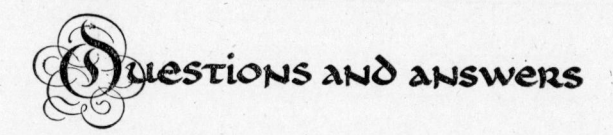

*Even the words of someone
as totally against ideology as yourself,
contain a continuous if subtle ideology.
Is it impossible to talk seriously without it?*

It is not only impossible to talk seriously about it —
it is impossible to talk about it at all.
Seriously is not the question.
Just to talk about it is impossible
because then talk implies language.

Language has a pattern, language itself is an ideology.
To use language is to fall into the trap of it.
Language has a logic, a system, a substratum.
Once you talk about something,
you have entered into the world of ideology.

But to talk is a necessary evil. It has to be tolerated.
I would like not to talk; I would like to convey
and commune directly without language,
but then it will not reach you.
The silence will not be understood.

The True Sage

So I have to use language,
knowing well
that this is a necessary evil,
knowing well
that you have to transcend it,
knowing well
that that which is worth saying
cannot be said in it,
knowing well
that the moment you utter a truth
the very uttering falsifies it.
But before you become capable
of understanding silence,
that communion from heart to heart has to happen.

So I talk to help you towards silence.
By my talking you will not understand silence,
but by my talk you may have a taste, a fragrance.
By my talk you may be able to listen to the silence
that is bound to be there between two words,
the silence that is bound to be there
between two sentences.

Whatsoever I say is not important;
the gap between is important.
Don't pay too much attention to what I say.
The words are like two banks of the river;
the banks are not the river —
don't get too attached to the banks.
They won't quench your thirst.
Forget the banks; just look in between.
The gap, the silence between two words is the river.
That's what I am trying to convey to you.

I know you listen to the words,
you don't listen to the silence.
The gestalt has to be changed.
But one day it happens.

If you go on listening, one day it happens.
Suddenly, one day, unaware, you are caught.
Suddenly, for the first time, words are no more important,
but the being that I am touches you.
The ears go on listening to the words
but the heart is moving in some unknown direction.

It cannot be planned to happen, but it happens.
That's why in the East *satsang* has been praised so much.
Satsang means to be with a Master.
When he speaks, to be with him.
When he sits, to be with him.
When he looks at you, to be with him.
When he does not look at you, then also, to be with him —
just to have a feeling flow between the one who knows
and the one who is seeking.
One day something tunes in —
and that day is unpredictable; nothing can be done about it.
The more you do anything about it
the more you will be missing it.

So just go on listening to my words,
but by and by shift your emphasis to the silent gaps.
Sometimes I am not saying anything.
Sometimes I just look at you.
There exactly, precisely there, is the message.
And if you listen to that message, it is not ideology.
It is not even anti-ideology!
Because if something is anti-ideological,
it is again an ideology.
To be anti is to be in the world of the idea.

I am not against ideology. How can I commit that sin?
I am beyond, not against.
Ideology, anti-ideology — both are left in the valley.
I have moved to a different world, a peak which is beyond.
And I am not teaching you anti-ideology.

The True Sage

I am not teaching you anything
that belongs to the world of concepts and ideas.
I am teaching you 'me'!
I am teaching you a way of being,
a different quality of existence.

Listen to my words.
But don't only listen to my words — shift.
One day you will understand even *that*
which cannot be said through words.

Even through words there may be glimpses.
Once you can feel my silence,
my words will take another significance.
Then they will not be just words, just sounds — no.
Then they become a flowering.
It is a very difficult job : to talk about silence.

In Zen they say it is like selling water by the river.
The river is flowing, but you are blind
and I have to sell water.
And, of course, you pay for it —
and the river is absolutely free.
It is like watering the garden when the rain is falling.
Or, as in old Indian scriptures it is said :
'It is putting legs on a snake to help him walk !'
Foolish, stupid —
because the snake walks perfectly well without any legs.
In fact, legs will hinder.
But what to do ? The snake goes on saying : 'Help me.'
Or as it is said in old Taoist scriptures :
'To talk about truth is as if to put a hat on a man
who is already wearing one.'
To put another hat on top of the hat — useless.

So what am I doing here ?
I am just giving you patience, the capacity to wait, watch.

It is an effort to be with me;
in the beginning it is like an effort,
but one day suddenly it happens
and it is no more an effort.
Effortlessly you are here.
Then you understand me —
whether I say something or not.
Then you will understand me —
whether I am here in this chair or not,
whether I am in this body or not.
But before that happens,
that supreme flowering of your silence,
I have to go on beating the bush, around and around.

And the second thing about the first question:
I am not a serious man.
I look like one but the appearance is deceptive.
I'm not a serious man; I'm absolutely non-serious —
and that is the only way
the enlightened consciousness can be.

Seriousness is mundane, it is of the marketplace.
You find it in the churches — in fact, too much —
because your churches are nothing
but part of the marketplace,
part of the world of commodities.

I have heard one Jewish joke:
a Jew came to the synagogue with a dead cat,
and he asked the rabbi if he could bury it
in the Jewish burial ground.
The rabbi was aghast, horrified.
He said: 'What! You, a good Jew,
and asking your rabbi to bury a dirty, dead cat
in the holy grounds?
No! Never! Certainly not! Absolutely not!'

The True Sage

The man stood up and said:
'Then I will not be able
to give you the ten thousand pounds
the cat has left in the will.'

Suddenly the rabbi jumped, and he said: 'Wait!
Don't try to go out.
You fool! Why didn't you tell me before
that the cat was a Jew?'

Your synagogues, your churches, your temples —
they belong to the marketplace;
they have to be serious.

The world is too serious, and it has to be
because death always hangs over.
You may avoid, you may not look at it,
but in the world, death is always around.
You have to be serious.
Even if you laugh, your laughter has tears within it.
Even if you smile, your smile is not total;
it is painted, forced.
It is not an inner flow and glow.
No, it is not.

In the marketplace
you have learned too much seriousness.
Then your churches become serious.
Your gods cannot smile.

Christians say Jesus never laughed —
looks absolutely foolish, the whole idea.
Jesus never laughed? Then who will laugh?
If even Jesus cannot laugh,
then laughter becomes a sheer impossibility.
In fact, *only* he must have laughed;
only he can laugh, and enjoy it.

In India we don't take the world seriously.
We call it God's *leela*, God's play;
a joke at the most, a story, a drama —
told beautifully, but nothing serious about it.

I am not serious,
and whatsoever I am saying
I am saying in a very non-serious mood.
Of course, I am sincere, but not serious.
Whatsoever I am saying,
I really want to convey it to you,
but if it is not conveyed I don't feel frustrated.
If it is conveyed I don't feel proud.
If I fail utterly or if I succeed absolutely —
both are the same.
That's why I say I'm not serious.

You may be here seriously,
but by and by I will persuade you not to be serious,
because seriousness is the shadow of the ego.
Without the ego you can't be serious.
Simply without the ego, seriousness disappears,
because without the ego, death disappears.
Only the ego has died — not you.
You have never died; you have never been born.
You have been eternally here,
and you will be eternally here.
You are part of this whole existence.
You cannot be separated from it.

Sometimes you may have been in the trees,
you may have been a tree.
Sometimes in the birds,
and you may have been a bird.
And sometimes a rock,
and sometimes a stream falling from the Himalayas.

The True Sage

Millions of ways.
Millions of forms.
Millions of names.
Yes, you have existed in many many ways.
It was never that you were not;
it will be never that you will not be.
The form changes; the formless goes on and on and on.

There is nothing to be serious about.
But the ego is afraid, apprehensive. Death is coming.
The ego is a weight. The ego cannot laugh.

My whole effort
is to create such a deep laughter in you
that the laughter remains but you disappear.
The dance remains but the dancer disappears.
Then life is tremendously beautiful —
and only then life is beautiful.

So don't think about me like other religious people
who are very serious.
If they are serious they cannot be religious:
that is *my* criterion.
If your saints cannot laugh,
they may be suppressed sinners at the most.
Because a suppressed person cannot laugh,
he is always afraid.
With laughter many other things may escape.
He has to suppress everything:
the anger, the sex, the greed, the hatred, the love.
Now he cannot allow only laughter to escape.
And this is a deep secret:
either you are totally expressive or you are not.
You cannot be partially expressive.

Your so-called saints
have to suppress themselves totally.
And to me, a saint is one

who has no suppression in his being.
When he laughs, he laughs.
His whole being is involved — ripples of laughter.

Remember this —
and this will be very very meaningful to remember
in reference to Hassidism.
Hassidism has created
the greatest tradition of laughing saints;
that is one
of the most beautiful contributions of Hassidism.

A Hassidic sage
is not one who has renounced the world.
He lives in the world,
because to renounce it looks too serious.
He does not go away from the marketplace —
he goes above.
He lives where you live,
but he lives in a different way.
He exists by your side,
but simultaneously exists somewhere else.
He has joined the *sansar*, the world —
and sannyas, the renunciation.

When I give sannyas to you, I am doing a Hassidic work.
I don't tell you to move to the Himalayas
because that would be a choice,
and a choice is always serious —
because you would have to leave something,
you would have to cut a part of your being,
you would have to cripple yourself.

When you choose you move in a certain direction —
then the whole is not accepted.
If you live in the world,
then you reject renunciation, sannyas,
then you reject meditation.

You say: 'They are not for us. We are worldly people.'
Then one day you get fed up with the world,
you leave the world.
Now you are afraid to come into the world.
Now you say: 'We are unworldly people.
We live outside the world!'
But in both the cases, you remain half-hearted,
you are never total.

A Hassidic sage is total.
He lives in the world,
he lives as ordinarily as everybody else.
He has no madness, no megalomania
about his extraordinariness.
A Hassidic rabbi is absolutely ordinary —
and that is his extraordinariness.
He has no need to show it. He is!

There are other saints
who have a need to show that they are special.
That very need shows
that deep down they are very ordinary,
because this is part of the ordinary mind:
to be always in need, always expecting,
always wanting people to feel and think
that you are not ordinary.
This is a very ordinary need.
Only somebody who is really extraordinary
can be ordinary —
because he has no need to convince others:
'I am special.'

Once I was travelling in a train.
In my compartment three persons were also there.
They talked about a thousand and one things.
The journey was long and they needed to be occupied.
Then their talk drifted
towards the subject of happiness.

One of them was a very rich man and he said:
'I am happy because I have attained
all the riches that I need.
I have succeeded, I have arrived.'
I looked at the man's face —
no sign of any arrival, a sort of nervousness.
In fact, the way he was saying it —
with such confidence —
was nothing but to hide a deep nervousness.
I could see he was trembling inside
like a leaf in a strong wind.
He was pretending.
He said: 'I have attained to happiness.'
But his eyes were desert-like,
no happiness, no greenery.
He was almost a dead person, shrunken, wasted.

The other man belonged to a political party
and he said:
'I am also happy because the party needs me.
Without me, they cannot win the coming election.
I am needed. That's my happiness.'

One thinks that because he has accumulated much riches,
he is happy.
What have riches to do with happiness?
Riches are outside;
happiness is an inner flowering.
A poor man can be happy;
it has no intrinsic relationship
with poverty or riches.
A beggar like Buddha can be happy.
And a man who says he is happy
because he has attained to many riches
is just befooling himself, pretending.

The other man said: 'I am happy because I am needed.'
A certain significance comes to you
when you are needed.

You think you are essential to somebody,
to some political organization, to some religious sect.
But a man who is happy is not dependent on others.
If the political party
can find a better man than this,
or a worse man than this —
which is the same in politics —
then he will feel frustrated.
Happiness never feels frustrated.
If it does, it is not happiness —
it is a covering of the reality by a false notion.

Then there was one woman.
She said that she was also happy.
She had five children, beautiful persons, all growing.
Her hopes were fulfilled in them.
And her husband loved her deeply;
he had always remained faithful to her.
The woman must have been beautiful
when she was younger.
Now near about fifty, just a skeleton, a memory —
a memory of the past.
Eyes shrunken. The whole life gone. Death approaching.
She was clinging to the children;
they would fulfill her hopes.
She could not fulfill herself so now they would fulfill;
now she would live through their ambitions.

Happiness never lives through anybody else.
It needs nobody; it is enough unto itself.
And she insisted
that her husband had been faithful to her,
but I could see that whatsoever she was saying
she didn't believe it —
her eyes were showing something else.
In fact, whenever you say that your husband is faithful,
you are suspicious.

Or you say that your wife is faithful —
the doubt has entered.
Because faith does not know about doubt
and does not know about faith.
If faith is true faith, then you don't know it.
Otherwise, the worm of doubt
is deep down somewhere, eating it.

Then they all turned towards me.
They said: 'What about you?'

I told them: 'I have never tried to be happy
and I don't belong to any organization,
religious or otherwise.
Nobody needs me, and if somebody needs me,
that may be *his* problem — it is not mine.
I don't need to be needed; that's not my need.
And as far as success goes, I am a failure —
my hands are absolutely empty.
And the very language is alien to me —
in terms of faith —
because to talk about faith is to hide doubt.
In fact,
I have never been deeply interested in happiness,
because I am already happy.
I just am happy. There is no cause to it!'

If there is a cause of happiness,
you are ready to be unhappy any moment.
You are just on the verge because a cause can **disappear**.
Then the happiness will disappear.
Unless you are just happy
for no visible or invisible cause,
unless you are just happy —
unreasonably, irrationally, illogically, madly —
you are not happy.

And a happy person cannot be serious.

The True Sage

An unhappy person is serious
because he is missing something.
He is seeking and searching,
always tense, moving, going somewhere —
waiting for Godot.
That is the nature of an unhappy person.

I have arrived so deeply
that I don't even feel the arrival.
In fact I had never departed.
I'm not serious.
Appearances may be deceptive.
You may not find me laughing,
but that is only because when you are very serious
then you need laughter also.
When you are simply happy,
seriousness disappears, laughter disappears.

Your laughter is medicinal.
You are too serious. You need to laugh.

It may be that Jesus never laughed,
but the way Christians interpret it is wrong.
I can conceive that he never laughed.
It is possible because he was a laughter.
He was laughing so deeply and so continuously.
It was not an event, it was a process.
It was not something that happens and then dissolves.
It was ongoing.

If you are *really* happy,
there is no need to laugh and there is no need to weep.
Both will disappear.

I am not serious, I am just celebrating.
And when I talk to you, I am not giving you an ideology,
a philosophy, a religion — no.
I simply want to share my celebration.

Shift from the words to silence.
Don't listen to my words; listen to me.
There, precisely there, is the message.

*If you help me to find the question,
will it help me to find the answer?*

   There will be no need then.
If you know the question, the answer is found.
The problem is not with the answer;
the problem is with the question.
You don't know the right question —
that's why you go on and on, seeking and searching.
And the right answer never happens.
It cannot happen
because you have missed the very beginning.
The first step has gone wrong.

One needs to find the right question — your question!
The question should not be of somebody else,
it should not be borrowed.
You should not resound another's question.
You should not repeat.

You are so imitative
that even about questions, you repeat others,
you reflect others.
How can your search be true?
And how can you achieve?
Impossible — when the search itself is imitative.
Ask *your* question!

My whole effort here
is to help you to ask the right question, the fundamental,
the question of your being, of your innermost core.

And they are not many — remember.

The True Sage

The basic question is absolutely one.
That's why the basic answer is absolutely one.
You can ask a thousand and one wrong questions;
you cannot ask more than one right question —
because that right question
will have all the questions in it.
It will be the essence of all your anxiety,
of all your anguish.

And that question is not going to be theological;
it is going to be existential.
It will not come by reading.
It will not come by going to the universities.
It will come if you start encountering yourself.
If you start looking with your own being —
it will come then.
It is already there. You have brought it with you.
It is *you*, a seed inside.

And when you have found the right question. . . .
That's what I help to find, not the right answer.
That I leave to foolish people.
Then you can go to the priests; they have right answers.
You can go to the professors; they have right anwers.
I have only the right question.

Once the right question is there,
you need not seek the answer
because the right question itself carries its answer.
They are always together.
Once you can ask a true, authentic question
that comes from your being and not from the mind,
immediately you will be surprised.
Following the question comes your answer.
It has to be so.

If the question is yours,

how can anybody else's answer quench it?
The thirst is yours —
nobody else's water is going to quench it.
You have to go deep within yourself.
Find the question
and you have already found the answer.

But that is very difficult and arduous
because you are in a hurry and you say:
'When you have the answer, please give it to us.
When you have the answer, why force us to go
and inquire for the question first?'
You would like it readymade.
That's not possible.
That's how you have been deceived
and how you have been deceiving yourself.
That's how religions are born —
Christianity, Judaism, Islam, Hinduism, Jainism.

Mahavir found his question and he found his answer.
Then people gathered around, greedy people
who had not even looked into their questioning,
who had not even inquired.
Seeing the possibility
that this man had found the answer,
they gathered around.
They started clinging to the answer.
It is absolutely absurd.
You can make that answer a part of your memory
but it won't help.

Let me tell you a story.
It happened: a certain man was fascinated by the river
that flowed by his village.
And he wanted to go downstream, to the very end —
to see where the river fell into the ocean.

The True Sage

Of course, he started studying old scriptures
to find if anybody had ever gone down the river.
Many people had gone.
In many centuries many people were fascinated.
But he was puzzled because their answers differed.
He could not believe it.

One answer said that the river was straight.
But another said something else:
that after five miles
the river takes a turn to the right,
and another said that after exactly five miles
the river takes a turn to the left.

Seeing much confusion in scriptures,
he started meeting people.
Maybe somebody is alive who had gone down the river.
Many people pretended because it feels so good to advise.
To become a guru is such a deep desire in everybody
and it feels good to the ego.
Everybody becomes a wiseman
whenever it is a question to advise somebody else.
In his whole life he may have proved a fool,
but whenever somebody else is in difficulty
he becomes a wiseman with plenty of advice.
Of course, nobody takes it
and it is good that nobody takes anybody's advice.
So, many advisers and pretenders were in the town.
He visited them.
He was even more confused
because everybody had his own idea.

He gathered much material. He planned a map.
On paper everything looked perfectly beautiful;
on paper it is always so.
That's how every scripture is beautiful —
Gita, Koran, Talmud — on paper.

And he dropped all contradictory things;
he made a consistent whole of the whole thing.
Now, this consistent river was just a mental concept.
Then he was very happy with the plan, with the map,
so he started moving down the river.

Immediately problems started arising
because he had planned to move
after five miles to the left —
but the river wouldn't follow the map.
He was puzzled and he was afraid.
Now the whole effort to gather wisdom
had been futile —
and the river wouldn't listen.
No river listens to your maps.
He became so worried about moving into the unknown —
dangers may be ahead.
But he had to move with the river.
If the river cannot move with the map, what to do?
You have to move with the river.
He couldn't sleep the whole night.

Next morning he was waiting for a village
on the bank of the river.
It never turned up.
He was hungry. Now he was at a loss.
What to do?

Were all those scriptures false? —
no, they were not false.
But the river is a river; it changes its course.
Sometimes a village may have existed;
villages exist and disappear.
The river goes on changing its course.
Sometimes it may have turned towards the left;
now it turns towards the right.
Rivers are not logical, not consistent.

They are simply alive.
One never knows.

He was hungry, puzzled.
The map looked absolutely absurd.
What to do?
The river was creating trouble.

Silently alone, floating on the river,
he started to meditate: what to do?
Scriptures have not helped, advise has been useless —
what to do now?
He started meditating.
Suddenly a realization arose:
'The river is not creating the trouble; my maps are.
The river is not creating any trouble.
The river is not even aware that I am here.
And the river cannot be inimical to me.'

He threw the maps in the river. The trouble stopped.
Now he started floating with the river,
with no expectations.
He was never frustrated again.

If you float with the river of life,
you will come to find your question
and you will come to find your answer.

But the trouble is you have already found the answer.
You have maps, scriptures, advice —
and many fakers who go on advising you.
They feel good in advising.
You are just a victim, an excuse.
They want to advise.
They are not concerned with your need.
They don't look at you. They have a fixed idea.

Go to a Christian; he has a fixed idea of God.

Even rivers don't move in a fixed way —
how can you have a fixed idea of God?
He is the river of consciousness.
Maybe somewhere in the past
somebody had known the river in a certain way.
It is no longer in the same place.
Says old Heraclitus:
'You cannot step in the same river twice.'
The river is always floating and changing and flowing.
Always moving.
The river does not have a fixed route.

Life is free. Life is freedom. God is absolutely a freedom.
You cannot have any fixed attitudes, fixed ideas.
If you have, then you will be in trouble,
and you will think that God is putting you in trouble.
No — just throw your scriptures into the river.
Move with the river and everything is beautiful.

Forget the answers if you want to find your question.
You are so surrounded by the answers
that it is almost impossible
in this confusion and crowd to find the right question —
and the right question is the key.

I don't give you any answer.
If you have come to me for any answer,
you have come to the wrong person.
I don't give you any maps of consciousness, no.
I don't give you any concept of God.
I simply give you a thirst, an intense thirst.
I bring urgency to your thirst
to know your authentic question.
Then everything takes care of itself.

The answer follows the question.
There is no doubt about it. It has always been so.

That is the very nature of it.
First seek the question and the answer will follow.
But you try to be cunning.
You say: 'Why bother about the question?
Answers are available. And cheap at that!
And advisers are always there.'
So why bother about your own inquiry?
But if the inquiry is not yours,
the fulfillment is not going to be yours.

Answers won't help.
You need a different state of consciousness.
Only a different state of consciousness
can become the answer.
Through questioning you start changing.
Question everything
and don't become a prey to easy answers.
Go on questioning, go on to the very end,
so that your whole questioning quest
becomes one-pointed, concentrated.
It goes like an arrow into the heart, penetrates deep.
It is painful,
but nothing can be achieved without pain.
Suffering is part of growth.
You are seeking comfort. Then you borrow answers.
Then don't come to me
because I will force you, throw you
into the abyss of your own being.

In the beginning it will look like death,
in the beginning it will look like nothingness.
But if you are courageous,
soon the eternal ground appears.
For the first time you are at home.
It is just like the pain of birth:
a child has to pass through the birth trauma,
has to come out of the womb.

Questions And Answers

You are in the womb of the mind right now.
Meditation is nothing
but coming out of the womb of the mind —
from thought to thoughtlessness,
from unconsciousness to consciousness,
from borrowed, imitative being to authenticity.

Yes, I help you to find the question.
But there is no need then to find the answer;
it happens simultaneously,
not even a single second's gap.
The answer is not separate from the question.
The question *is* the answer.
The very inquiry *is* the realization.
The very seeking *is* the goal.

Everything that is really worthwhile
seems to happen out of grace.
What is the logic or illogic of grace?
When is one most attractive to it?

   Grace is not something that happens sometimes
and does not happen other times;
grace is always happening.
It is the very nature of existence.
The existence is grace-full.

But sometimes you get it and sometimes you miss it.
The rain is falling;
sometimes you are showered, sometimes not.
But the rain is continuously falling.
So something has to be searched within you.
Sometimes you are sheltered against it.

Grace is the very nature of existence.
And ego is the shelter.

The True Sage

You protect yourself, even against grace.
Unknowingly, you create defense measures around you,
you create an armour.
The grace is available but *you* become unavailable —
that's why rarely it seems to happen.

Whenever you are not defending. . . .
You are sitting,
just early morning, the sun has not risen.
You look at the sky, the new sun is just coming up.
Everything is silent, peaceful.
A new life arising. A new day is born.
You become part
of this infinite whole happening around you.
You are not a watcher, not an onlooker.
You participate in the mystery.
It is not that the sun is rising
and you are looking at it, no.
You and the sun have become one.
Then you are unprotected. Then the wall disappears.
Then it is not an armour.
Then it is not that the sun is rising there,
very far away,
and you are sitting here, no.

The 'here' and 'there' disappear. It is one whole.
Then you have forgotten yourself.
In that forgetfulness you are no more an island —
you have become part of the continent.
No barriers —
suddenly you are filled with grace,
suddenly you are no more miserable,
suddenly there is no darkness.
Everything is beautiful. You can bless everything.
In this moment you can have only one feeling arising
out of your heart:
a deep gratefulness, a deep gratitude.

Just to *be* is perfect; just to breathe is great.
Just to be alive in this moment, you are fulfilled.

Sometimes it happens sitting by a human being you love:
a woman, a man, a child —
sitting silently, not doing anything in particular,
because doing is always a sort of occupation
through which you go on protecting yourself.
Not even talking!
When you are deep in love
you would like to sit in silence.
Lovers don't talk much.   They convey, they commune.
A subtle communication starts happening.
They know each other so deeply
that even gestures are understood.
Words are not needed.
In fact, words look jarring; they create a disturbance,
the resonance is disturbed by them.
They sit silently and suddenly there is grace —
something which is bigger than both surrounds them.
A cloud of virgin bliss surrounds them.
They are encompassed.
They are not two, the twoness has disappeared.
They are completely oblivious of their separateness.
Time stops. There is grace.

Again they start talking, again the egos enter —
they are protected and grace is lost.

Yes, all that is beautiful,
all that is true and good happens through grace;
it never happens through effort.
All efforts are tiny. What can you do?
We are so tiny, so atomic — what can we do?
So limited — what can we do?
If we try by our own effort to be happy,
we will be getting more and more unhappy.

The True Sage

That's what is happening all over the world —
everybody trying to be happy.
The more you try, the more unhappy you become.
Your whole effort seems to be wasted.
Not only wasted —
your whole effort seems to be bringing results
that are just the contrary:
you want to be happy and you become unhappy.

I have heard about an old man.
He was one of the unhappiest men in the world.
The whole village was tired,
because he was always grumpy and complaining
and always in a bad mood, always sour.
And the more he advanced in age,
the more acidic he became,
the more poisonous his words.
People avoided him because he was so unhappy
that he became infectious.
To not be unhappy with him
would have been offensive to him.
He created unhappiness in others also.

But one day, his eightieth birthday,
suddenly the whole village could not believe it —
a rumour spread like fire:
'The old man is happy today,
not complaining, even smiling,
and his whole face has changed.'

The whole village gathered and they asked:
'What is the secret? What has happened to you?'

The old man said: 'Nothing.
I tried to be happy for eighty years
and I could not be —
so I thought it is better to go without happiness.

I tried hard to be happy and I could not be happy
so I said that now it is enough —
eighty years wasted —
now I will do without happiness.
That's why I'm happy.'

This happens.
This is what is happening all over the world.
Try hard and you become unhappy.
The more you try, the more frustration it brings.

Ask the awakened, all those who have known say:
'Ask for happiness and you will be unhappy.'
Accept unhappiness, and suddenly you are happy —
because the effort is no longer there —
and grace is always available.
Through your effort you push it away.
Don't push it.

You are the greatest enemies of yourself,
and you know it well:
that whenever it has happened
that you had a moment of happiness,
it was not because of you.
You know it, but your ego won't concede to it.

You know it,
that suddenly one day
a bird started singing in the grove
and everything became silent within you.
You listened to it,
and for a moment there was no misery, no hell —
the paradise regained.
It was nothing on your part.
The bird was singing — you simply listened.
In that listening, you were passive;
no effort was there.

What do you have to do? —
the bird was singing, the grove was green.
For a moment you became passive, feminine —
not doing anything.
Suddenly it was there.
It has always been there. You just have to stop.

Says Lao Tzu : 'Seek and you will miss.
Don't seek and it is already there.'
The treasure that you are seeking is within you.
All seeking is futile.

Just look at the facticity of it.
Existence is celebrating!
It is a celebration!
It is already dancing —
in every leaf, in every stream,
in every rock, and in every star —
it is always dancing.
And you are invited.
Otherwise you would not have been here.
You are accepted; otherwise you would not have been here.

But you resist.
You are trying something,
you are trying to do the impossible : to become happy.
An unhappy man cannot become happy,
but the unhappy man goes on trying to be happy.
Drop the whole nonsense!

People come to me and they ask me how to be happy.
I say : 'If you ask how, you will never be.
Just be! — there is no how to it.'
The 'how' is the problem.
How to be happy? — what a nonsense question!
Be happy — why ask how?
There is no science of happiness.
Notwithstanding what American books say,
there is no science of happiness.

All Dale Carnegies are just mediocre — but they sell.
Next to the Bible, Dale Carnegie sells the most;
he is a good salesman.
He knows that everybody wants to be happy.
He knows that everybody wants to be successful.
He knows that everybody wants to find love.
He fulfills the desire. He gives you the 'how'.
He gives you books like:
How to Succeed, How to Win Friends, How to be Rich.

But I tell you there is no 'how'.
The 'how' is the trouble.
You already know too many techniques to be happy;
that's what is creating the mess.
Drop it.
Remember that old man, the eightieth birthday,
and how he decided to go without happiness.
Can you be unhappy
if you decide to go without happiness?
Who can make you unhappy then? And how?
Suddenly, unhappiness becomes impossible.
Unhappiness is a by-product of the desire to be happy.
Frustration is a by-product of the desire to succeed.
A state of defeated, bored, wearied being,
is but a by-product of ambition.

This has to be simply looked into,
there is nothing else to do.
Just see the fact of it, and the *very* seeing frees you.
Jesus says: 'Truth liberates.'
I agree — absolutely right. Truth liberates.
Just see the fact of it —
that this is how
you have been creating your unhappiness.
If you want to create more unhappiness,
try to be more happy and you will succeed.
Just see the facticity of it.
Just watch how you become unhappy.

THE TRUE SAGE

Have you ever been unhappy
when you were not expecting anything?
When you don't expect, you are simply happy.
Happiness is natural; unhappiness is earned.
Unhappiness needs much effort;
happiness is simply the case.

Yes, everything that is really worthwhile
always happens through grace.
When I say 'grace'
I don't mean any theological principle.
I don't mean that there is a God
sitting on top of the roof, watching you:
that those who prove to be good-guys will be happy
and grace will shower on them
and for bad-guys there is hell.
Because of your foolishness
you even make your God appear foolish.

There is nobody sitting on top of the roof,
grace is just the nature of existence.
Nobody is giving it to you, pouring it on you.
It is not an award that it is given to saints
because they prove to be good-guys.
Nobody is preventing it from reaching you
because you are a sinner and you never listened
to the right counsel of the priests,
churches, organized religions,
because you proved rebellious.
Nobody is giving and nobody is preventing.

Grace is existential. It is simply there.
It is part of life.
Nobody gives it, but you can get it.
Nobody prevents it from reaching you
but you can prevent it.

It depends on you.
It is not a question of praising God
and praying to him : 'Be grace-full to us.'
It is simply a question
that if you don't create an armour around yourself,
it reaches.
The armour can be of a sinner
or the armour can be of a saint.
This last thing has to be understood
because the armour can be of gold
or the armour can be of steel.
The question is : if you are armoured,
grace will not reach you.

A good man has an ego —
of course, very pious, holy, sacred.
A religious man is a pious egoist.
He says : 'I have done so many fasts,
I have been donating so much money
towards philanthropic ends —
for hospitals, for poor people, for this and that,
and I have made so many churches and temples,
and I have created so many charitable trusts,
and I pray every day,
and I have not committed a single sin' —
a pride, a deep ego.
Now he will not be available to grace.

A sinner also creates his own armour.
He says : 'I don't bother about anybody else.
I live my own idea. I am against the society.'
He is rebellious,
he commits sins just to enhance his ego
so he can say : 'I am I. I don't bother about anybody.'
Now he is also creating an ego, a steel ego.
The religious man has a golden ego.

The True Sage

But steel or gold doesn't make any difference.

Whom do I call 'the true sage'?
The true sage is one who has no armour,
who has no shelter,
who is not protected by anything.

A true sage is one who is open to existence
to flow through him —
open to the winds, open to the sun, open to the stars.

A true sage is a deep emptiness.
Everything passes through him, nothing is hindered.
Then every moment is grace.
And every moment is eternity.
And every moment is God.
And then God is not something separate from you;
it is your innermost core.

Do you love me?

 No! Never!
Because I don't do anything.
If you feel my love, it is not because I love you;
it is because I *am* love.
So you can feel it, but I have nothing to do with it.

It is just like when a flower opens
and the fragrance spreads.
Not that the flower is doing anything to spread it,
not that there is any effort on the flower's part
to spread it,
not that because you were passing by the side,
the flower threw its fragrance towards you, no.
Even if nobody was passing
the fragrance would be floating around the empty path.

It would fill the empty path
It is not directed; there is no effort.
It simply *is*; the flower has bloomed.
Nothing to do.
When the flower blooms, fragrance spreads.
When you attain to your innermost being, love spreads.
Love is the fragrance.

What *you* call love is not love.
What you call love may be many more things,
but it is not love.
It may be sex.
It may be greed.
It may be loneliness.
It may be dependence.
It may be possessiveness.
It may be many more things — but it is not love.

Love is non-possessive.
Love has nothing to do with somebody else,
it is your state of being.
Love is not a relationship.
A relationship *is* possible but it is not relationship.
A relationship can exist but it is not confined to it.
It is beyond it. It is more than that.

Love is a state of being.
When it is a relationship, it cannot be love —
because the two exist.
And when two egos are there,
there is bound to be constant conflict.
So what you call love is a constant struggle.
Sometimes it happens
that when you are tired you don't fight,
but again you are ready and again you fight.

Rarely it happens that love flows.

Otherwise, almost all the time it is an ego-trip.
You are trying to manipulate the other;
the other is trying to manipulate you.
You are trying to possess the other;
the other is trying to possess you.
It is politics; it is not love.
It is the power-game.
Hence, so much misery out of love.
If it was love, the world would have been a heaven —
it is not.
In fact, you cannot find any hell
which is more hellish than this world.
And how has it become such a hell? — with good intentions.

You talk about love
and something else which is poisonous
is hidden behind it.
You talk about the love of the motherland —
and just deep imperialism, a deep disease of nationalism
is hidden behind it.
You talk about the love of the family
and nothing but the hate of others' families
is hidden behind it.
You are together in a family
because to fight alone with other families
will be difficult.
You are together as Indians,
because separately, it will be difficult
to fight with the Pakistanis.
And the same is with Pakistan.
And with China.
And America.
And Russia.
And the same is with the whole world.

You are in such a state that you cannot love.

When you come and ask me about love,
I always feel it is such an impossible thing to talk about
because you mean something else, and I mean something else.
We can go on talking for ages
and there will be no meeting, no conversation
because you have labelled something as 'love'
which is not love.

Remove that label.
Look at what it contains, look deeply at what it contains:
hatred, anger, greed, jealousy,
ambition, lust for power, destructiveness.
No, I don't love you that way.
And I don't love you in any other way.
Because love, to me, cannot be a doing.
You cannot make an effort towards it;
love cannot be done.
You can be love, but you cannot do it.
And then love has tremendous beauty
and a stillness, a silence.
And then love becomes prayer.
Then there is no need to go to any other temple;
the state of love is *the* temple.

And the Hassidic sages
have been in favour of this love.
They have loved the world.
They have loved the ordinary world
with an extraordinary love.
They have lived in the world, bloomed.
They have never escaped.
Thy were husbands, fathers.
They lived very ordinarily.

Sometimes I see that people who renounce the world
are very deep egoists.

Their renouncing the world
is really a deep failure of their love.
They have failed to love, and because they failed to love,
the world became miserable.
But they think the *world* is miserable.
They think they are unhappy because of the others.

A husband leaves the wife and goes to the Himalayas.
He thinks that because of the wife
he was in trouble, misery.
This is absolutely wrong.
He was in trouble and misery
because he was not in the state of love.
In the state of love, nobody can create misery for you.
That is impossible.

A man who has known love
remains blissful — unconditionally.
Whatsoever happens is irrelevant to his state of being.
You can kill him but you cannot make him miserable.
You can throw him in an imprisonment
but you cannot make him miserable.
His freedom remains total.
His freedom remains untouched, uncorrupted.

Through doing your meditations,
the body is getting stronger and healthier,
and awareness less than ever.
The more I jump and dance, the louder I snore.
Why is this?

Nothing is wrong in snoring;
it is as holy as anything else.
And nothing is wrong in the body.
Never think in terms of duality —
that you are not the body,

that you are separate, that you are different.
Never think in terms of duality.
The body is also you — your outermost garment.
It is through the body that you touch existence.
From the outside you touch God through the body.
From the inside
you touch the same God through consciousness.
But it is all the same, out or in.

But the so-called religions
have created a division, a split.
They have been telling you that you are not the body.
Because they have been against the world,
they have been against the body.

I am not against the world
and I am not against the body.
Let the body be healthy.
Let the body be beautiful.
Let the body be graceful.
Because only in a graceful body
will a graceful consciousness become possible.
Only in a healthy body
will inner health become possible.
Only in a peaceful, silent, relaxed body
will a relaxed consciousness happen.
Remember that, and there is no division.
It is the same wave going out and coming in.
It is just like breathing, going out and coming in.
It is just like the blinking of the eye,
opening and closing.
Out and in.
Opening and closing.
In-breathing and out-breathing.
They are two aspects of you, two wings.
So don't be worried.
The first thing to remember: the body is holy.

The second thing to remember :
if you feel that by doing meditations,
your awareness is becoming less and less,
then only one thing is certain :
whatsoever you have been thinking to be awareness
was not awareness.
Otherwise it increases.

How can it lessen ? How can it decrease ?
Whatsoever you thought of as awareness, consciousness
must have been self-consciousness, not consciousness.
It must have been ego-consciousness.
Now it is decreasing.
It is good. It should be so.
It is exactly on the right track.
Self-consciousness will be lost ;
only then consciousness arises.

Self-consciousness is ill-consciousness.
People are self-conscious.
The difference between the two is very subtle.

We are sitting here.
You come into the auditorium.
You can come with awareness ;
you can come with self-consciousness.
Awareness means you come with an inner light,
you move fully alert.
Each step is taken in awareness —
the walking, the coming, the sitting —
everything is done in full awareness.
It is beautiful. That's how a Buddha walks.

But when you are self-conscious,
there is no light inside.
You are just alert of other people ; they are there.
So you shrink.

You walk with a tense effort because others are there.
What will they say?
How will they say?
How will they react to your presence?
What will be their opinion?
That's what happens.

You can talk well, you talk the whole day,
but if suddenly you are put near the mike
and you have to address a meeting
of a thousand people,
suddenly you start stuttering, perspiring —
a nervousness happens.
You lose control.
What is happening? You are too self-conscious.
You are too aware of what others will think.
Self-consciousness is an ill state of affairs.

If you are aware, you speak with awareness.
But the awareness comes from the inward being.
It flows from the inner being towards others.
Self-consciousness comes from others' eyes towards you.
It is fear of others.
Awareness and self-consciousness are totally different.

So if meditation brings you to the feeling
that your awareness is decreasing,
it simply shows that you misunderstood
self-consciousness for awareness.
It is good. Let it go.
It will not be a loss; it is just losing a disease.

Soon, when it has gone, your energy will be transformed.
The same energy will be released
from the confines of self-consciousness.
It will be available now.
You will be more alert.

Alert — life becomes graceful.
Self-conscious — life becomes misery.
Alert — you attain to your being.
Self-conscious —
you go on seeking others' opinions, their praise.

The ego is always afraid of others
because it has to depend on their opinions —
on what they say.

If they say you are beautiful, you are beautiful.
If they say you are ugly, your ego is shattered.
If they say you are good, saintly,
you are good and saintly.
If they say you are a sinner, the ego is shattered.
Self-awareness or self-consciousness
is a very tense thing, always afraid.
It depends on others' opinions.

And the whole thing is very paradoxical:
others are afraid of you; you are afraid of them.
They are self-conscious because of you;
you are self-conscious because of them.
You help each others' illness.
A person who is aware has no self in it.

In the light of awareness
there is no flame of the self.
It is simply light with no source.
He moves, lives gracefully.
He does not bother what others say about him.
Whether they think him a saint or a sinner
is all the same to him.
He knows who is — *he is*.

And he knows so absolutely
that there is no need to ask for others' opinions.

13th October 1975

In Roptchitz,
  the town where Rabbi Naftali lived,
it was the custom for rich people
   whose houses stood isolated,
or at the far end of town,
   to hire men
to watch over their property by night.
  Late one evening,
when Rabbi Naftali was skirting the woods
   which circled the city,
he met such a watchman
   walking up and down.
'For whom are you working?' he asked.

  The man told him,
and then enquired in his turn:—
  'And for whom are you working, Rabbi?'

The words struck the zaddik like a shaft.
  'I am not working for anybody just yet,'
he barely managed to say.

Then he walked up and down
   beside the man for a long time.
'Will you be my servant?'
   he finally asked.

  'I should like to,' the man replied,
    'But what would be my duties?'

'To remind me,' said Rabbi Naftali.

The Watchman

ONCE, a Hassidic mystic, Joseph Jacov, was asked:
'What is the difference between a rabbi and a zaddik?'
A rabbi is the ordinary priest,
belongs to the organized religion,
the church, the synagogue, the temple.
And a zaddik is a rebellious master,
does not belong to any organization —
only belongs to himself.

The rabbi is a teacher, the zaddik is a Master.
The teacher teaches,
but has not gone through the transformation himself.
The zaddik is also a teacher
but he teaches by his life, by his very being —
what we call in India 'satguru'.
The enlightened Master is 'zaddik' in Hassidic terms.

So somebody asked Joseph Jacov:
'What is the difference between a rabbi and zaddik?'

The Master said:
'The zaddik remembers, and the rabbi knows.'

The rabbi knows much but doesn't remember himself.
He is lost in his knowledge.

He may be a great scholar, he may be very efficient
as far as scriptures are concerned.
But a zaddik remembers!
He may not know much, or may know —
but that is irrelevant.
He remembers — he remembers himself.
And that remembering is the difference.

It was difficult for the inquirer to understand,
so he said:
'Please explain it to me in a little more detail.'
The Hassid told him a story.

He said that once it happened:
a prince by his wrong behaviour enraged his father.
And the way the prince was behaving
was so uncourtly, so unkingly,
that the father had to banish him out of the kingdom.

But the father was thinking that he would repent
and that he would ask forgiveness
and that he would come back.
But the prince simply disappeared.
He never tried in any way to contact his father.
He never showed any desire to come back to the palace.
It appeared as if he had been simply waiting —
how to escape the kingdom
and how to escape the palace and the father.

He wandered around the kingdom
and found a group of drunkards, gamblers, prostitutes —
all sorts of evil-doing was going on.
He became part of it.
Not only did he become a member —
by and by, he became the leader.
Of course, he was a prince
and he had the charisma of becoming a leader.

The Watchman

Many years passed.
The father was getting older and older,
and he was worried,
worried for the welfare of his only son.
Seeing that death is approaching,
he sent one of his most clever ministers
to bring the son back.

The minister went in a beautiful golden chariot
with many servants, almost a regiment following him.
A great golden tent was fixed outside the village.
He sent a messenger to this prince
but he himself didn't bother to turn up.
The minister remained outside the village;
it was below him to go inside the village.
A poor village, and it was absolutely inconceivable
for him to enter the black hole
where the prince was living
with all those dirty people.
The minister tried to contact the prince
but the communication was not possible —
the distance was vast.
He failed and came back.

Then another, a more courageous man, was sent.
He was courageous and he had understood the failure
why the first messenger, the first minister
could not communicate.

So he didn't go there like a minister;
he went like a peasant in ordinary clothes,
with no servants.
He simply went and mixed with the group.
He became friendly, but by and by,
he himself started to love that freedom.
The palace was like a prison; there was no freedom.
But here everybody was absolutely free, totally free.

The True Sage

Nobody was creating any hindrance for anybody,
everybody was allowed to be himself.
They were drunkards, but they were beautiful people.
They were gamblers, but they were beautiful people.
He also failed because he himself never turned up
to report back to the king.

The king was very much worried.
Now the thing was becoming unmanageable.
He asked a third minister,
who was not only courageous, but wise also —
and that was going to be the last effort.

The third minister asked for a three months leave —
to prepare himself.
Only then could he go.
The king asked: 'What are you going to prepare?'

He said: 'To remember myself.'

Three months leave was granted.
He went to a zaddik, to a Master,
to become more mindful.
The way the first minister had behaved
was absolutely useless;
communication was not possible.
The second had done better, but he had also failed
because he could not remember himself.
So he said to the Master:
'Help me, so that I can remember myself
and can remember that I come from the palace
on a certain duty to be fulfilled.'
Three months he meditated,
a method of self-remembering —
what Buddha calls 'mindfulness'.
Then he went.

He also behaved like the second.

He went like a peasant, in ordinary clothes —
not only like a peasant, he went like a drunkard.
But he was pretending, he was not really drunk.
He lived with the group, he enjoyed their company,
he pretended to drink, he pretended to gamble —
he even pretended to fall in love with a prostitute.
But that was all pretension — he was acting.
And continuously, as an undercurrent,
he was remembering himself: 'Who am I?
Why have I come here? For what?'
He was watching himself, he was a witness.
Of course he succeeded.

The Hassid mystic said to the inquirer:
'He was a zaddik.'

The first man was a rabbi, a teacher.
You are drowning in the river,
he stands on the bank, gives you good advice,
but he never jumps in the river to save you.
He cannot save himself.
He is afraid to come in the river.
He does not know the art of swimming,
the art of self-remembering.

He is not courageous.
He clings to the bank, he clings to a far-away place,
secure, sure of his own state, of his own safety.
He talks beautifully,
he can tell you everything about swimming,
but he cannot jump and save you.
He himself does not know how to swim.
He is a rabbi, a teacher.

You can find these types of teachers
all over the world —
good as far as their advice goes, nothing more.

Their advice is borrowed;
they have not come to that advice
through their own experience.
It is not knowing, it is knowledge.
They have not gone through it,
they have not been transformed by it.
It is not their own,
it has not arisen out of their consciousness.
They are not crystallized beings.
Their minds are full of knowledge,
their hearts are completely empty.

The other man was courageous,
but his courage was more than his wisdom.
He was himself drowned.
So remember,
when you jump into a river to save someone,
don't forget that the first necessity
is that you know swimming.

It happened once:
I was sitting on a river bank.
A man was drowning, so I ran to jump,
but before I could reach the bank,
another man who was standing on the bank, jumped.
So I prevented myself.
I was almost on the brink to jump; I prevented myself.
Somebody else had already jumped.
But then I became aware
that the other man started drowning.
He created more trouble for me.
I had to jump and save both.

I asked the other man: 'What happened?
Why did you jump?'

He said: 'I completely forgot!
The man was drowning and I became so attentive to it

that just the desire to save him,
and I completely forgot that I don't know swimming.'

You can forget.
In any intense moment you can be hypnotized.
The other was courageous, but not wise enough.
You can find the second type of teacher also.
So don't just be impressed by the courage,
because courage alone cannot help.

The third type of teacher is a zaddik.
He knows from his own experience
what the first type knows
only as a borrowed knowledge.
He is courageous like the second, he takes the risk,
but he is wise also.
He remembers himself.

To remember oneself
is the whole art and science of religion.
You can condense all religion
into one word: 'self-remembering'.

Before we start to go deep
into what self-remembering is,
it is a must, it is an absolute requirement
that we should understand the unconsciousness
in which you live — the sleep.

Ordinarily, you think you are perfectly awake.
That's a misconception.
Only a Buddha, a Baal Shem, a Moses, a Mahavir, are awake.
You are completely asleep.
I can hear your snoring right now;
you are fast asleep.
Just because you can open your eyes,
don't claim that you are awake.
Just that is not enough for being awake.

The True Sage

For example, a man is in a coma.
He breathes, but because he breathes,
can you say that he is alive?
He is almost vegetating.
Just by breathing, nobody is alive,
and just by opening your eyes, you are not awake.
Even a drunkard walking on the street
moves with open eyes.
Can you say that he is awake? He is not awake at all.
Awareness is an inner quality of consciousness;
it has nothing to do with closed or open eyes.

Krishna in the Gita says:
'When the whole world is fast asleep,
then too the yogi is awake'—
'Ya nisha sarvabhutayam tasyam jagrati samyami.'
When the whole world is under dark sleep,
when the whole world has its night,
the yogi is still awake.
That doesn't mean that the yogi never sleeps, no.
He sleeps, but only his eyes are closed.
His body sleeps but he is alert and aware.
Deep down a current of self-remembering runs.
He is fast asleep as far as the body is concerned,
but the witnessing self remains alert.
Like an inner light it goes on burning.

One who remembers is not asleep
even when he is fast asleep.
And one who does not know how to remember oneself
is not awake even though the eyes are open.
You are moving in the market,
doing your job, your work, coming back home,
fighting, loving, hating, eating, sleeping,
doing all sorts of things —
but the whole thing is happening
as if you are a robot.

Everything is mechanical; you are not doing it.
You are not alert when you are doing it.
It is just happening
and you are behaving like a mechanism.

Watch any mood: somebody insults and you are angry.
Is there a gap between the insult and the anger?
Is there a gap when you meditate,
whether to be angry or not? —
whether it is worth it to be angry or not?
Or maybe what the man is saying is right
and it is not an insult,
but simply a statement of fact.

Do you give a little time
to think about the whole situation,
or do you simply react?
You react. There is no gap, no interval.
Insult . . . anger . . .
they happen as if somebody puts on the light.
Switch on. Switch off.

And the light has no freedom.
When you switch it on, the bulb cannot say:
'Right now, I am not in the mood.
I will have a little rest.
You can go on switching on;
I don't feel to be lighted now.'
No, the light cannot say anything.
You switch on, it has to be on.
You switch off, it has to go off.

Is your anger just like that?
Somebody smiles and you smile.
Is your smile just a reaction?
Or is it a response?
A response is not a reaction,
and a reaction is not a response.

The True Sage

What is the difference
between a reaction and a response?

A reaction is automatic; it is built-in.
Somebody smiles; you smile.
Somebody is angry; you become angry.
The other creates it. You simply react.

A response is conscious.
The other may be angry,
but you decide whether to be angry or not,

Buddha was passing a village.
A few people who were against him gathered
and they insulted him very deeply.
He listened silently, very patiently.
In fact, because of his patience,
the people started becoming restless.
They started feeling uncomfortable,
because if you insult a man
and he listens as if it is music, something is wrong.
What is happening?
They started looking at each other.

Then one person asked Buddha: 'What is the matter?
Don't you understand what we are saying?'

Buddha said: 'Because I can understand,
that's why I am so silent.
Had you come ten years before,
then I would have jumped on you.
Then there was no understanding. Now I understand.
And for your foolishness, I cannot punish myself.
It is for you to decide to insult or not,
but it is my freedom to take it or not.
You cannot force your insults on me.
I simply refuse them; they are not worth it.
You can take them back home; I refuse to take them.'

The people were bewildered.
They couldn't understand what the matter was.
They said: 'Please explain to us.'

He said: 'Sit down and listen to me.
In the last village I just passed,
people had come with sweets and garlands
but my stomach was full, so I told them:
"I won't be able to eat anything.
Please take your gifts back
and give them to the other people
in the town as prasad —
my gift to the people of the town."
What do you think they did?'

Somebody said: 'They would have gone into the village
and distributed the sweets.'

Buddha said: 'Now listen — what will you do?
You come with insults
and I say that my stomach is full,
and I am not going to take these.
Now, poor people, unfortunate people, what will you do?
You will have to go
and distribute them in the village.'

Buddha is responding. You react.
He simply laughed.
And the thing that he said is very beautiful.
He said: 'For your foolishness
I cannot punish myself.
You can be foolish; that is your freedom.
But why should I punish myself?
Once I take your insult, I start punishing myself.'

When you are angry,
you punish yourself for the other's fault.
Reaction is unaware.

Response is a fully alert phenomenon.
But you cannot just move from reaction to response.
It is not a decision.
Between the two,
self-remembering is needed, awareness is needed.
Otherwise, before you have known, you have reacted.

Somebody insults you, and before you have known,
you are already angry.
The anger has entered in.
It is such a subtle phenomenon.
Very deep awareness is needed, remembering is needed.

Buddha used to teach his disciples to walk,
but to walk with mindfulness.
Walking, know that you are walking.
Not that you have to verbalize and repeat inside:
'I am walking.'
If you repeat that, you are not aware.
Just have the feeling of being aware.
Walk, with awareness.
Eat, with awareness.
Breathe, with awareness.

The breath goes in;
let it be mirrored in your being
that the breath is going in.
The breath goes out;
let it be mirrored in your being
that the breath is going out.
And you will feel such tremendous silence
descending on you.
If you can see the breath going in and going out,
going in and going out,
this is the deepest mantra
that has ever been invented.

There is no need to repeat:
Aum, aum . . . Ram, Ram . . .

The Watchman

because a great natural mantra
is continuously going on —
breathing in, breathing out.
No need to create an artificial mantra.
Just watch the breath.
And by watching it, a great mutation happens.
The mutation is: if you walk, and watch walking,
you will see — the walking is there,
but the walker has disappeared.
You eat, eating is there,
but the eater has disappeared.

The ego is nothing but condensed unawareness.
When you become aware by and by
that condensed unawareness we call 'ego' disappears.
Just as if you bring a lamp into the room —
and the darkness disappears.
Awareness is the lamp,
the lamp we were talking about the first day.
Be a lamp unto yourself.

In somebody else's light,
for a few moments you can feel happy, alive,
but then you have to depart,
because nobody else's path can be your path.

Kindle your own flame.
Enlighten your own being.
In that light the first thing that disappears is ego
because ego is nothing else — remember it —
but layers and layers of unawareness.

Watch . . . .
Walking. Eating. Going to bed.
Lying down. Falling into sleep.
Go on watching.
Just the watching, and all restlessness disappears
and you feel a tranquility surrounding you —
a calm, a silence.

The True Sage

The quality of this silence
is very very different than ordinary quiet.
Sometimes you feel quiet. . . .
For example, this morning:
the trees are silent, no wind blowing,
birds silent, resting — a quiet.
But this is a quiet, this is not a silence.

Silence is something inside;
quiet is something outside.
Quiet depends on conditions outside;
silence is unconditional.
So don't mistake quiet for silence,
because if you mistake quiet for silence —
and millions have done that. . . .
People go to the Himalayas to find silence.
They can find quiet but not silence.
The Himalayas are perfectly quiet,
but whenever you will come back to the world again
you will find the quiet has disappeared.

Silence is something you can rely upon.
It is within you.
Quiet is something which depends on conditions,
which does not depend on you.
You can never be a master of quiet —
but there is no need.
If you know silence,
wherever you move, your silence fills the space.
Now you know the inner secret of it.

Quiet is possible through scientific technology —
silence, never.
Quiet is possible
in an air-conditioned room, sound-proof.
You can be more quiet than in the Himalayas,
but that quiet won't help much.

The Watchman

You will feel fed-up with it,
you will hanker to go out,
you will feel very restless.

John Cage reports in his book *Silence*
that in Harvard University
they have made an absolutely sound-proof room
for certain scientific experimentation.

Cage entered —
the greatest sound-proof room in the whole world.
It was absolute quiet,
but suddenly he started hearing two noises.
He was worried, because he had heard
that this place was absolutely sound-proof.
So he asked the technician: 'What is the matter?'

The technician laughed.
He said: 'These sounds are within you.
The first sound is just your mind functioning inside,
the nervous system.
And the second sound is nothing but your blood
running through the body, the blood circulation.'

Cage said: 'But I have never heard these sounds before.'

The technician said: 'You never heard
because there were so many sounds outside.
Now it is absolute quiet. No sound at all.
That's why you hear the inner mechanism functioning,
the brain continuously working,
millions of nerves continuously working,
and the blood circulation continuously going on —
just like a stream flowing.'

Cage said: 'Quiet won't do. Silence is needed.'

Even in the quietest room,
your inner turmoil will be there.

You will hear your own thoughts,
you will hear your own body functioning,
you will hear your own heartbeats.

Silence is something of the beyond, unconditional.
It happens only when you remember.
If you can remember yourself
while doing millions of things, ordinary things:
digging a hole in the garden, watering the trees,
talking to somebody, listening to somebody. . . .
Just go on being watchful.
Whatsoever happens should be mirrored by you.

Remember one thing: you are not to verbalize it,
because by verbalizing you will miss the beauty.
You can say: 'I am walking.
This is my left foot moving, this is my right foot,
the breath is going in, the breath is going out.'
If you start verbalizing inside
then you will be filled by your own noise again.

Just watch the breath going in;
don't think about it.
Just see it, feel it. Move inwards with it.
Then the breath stops for a second.
Then remain in quiet silence for that second —
nothing moving, no movement.
In that state of no movement
you are the nearest to God that you ever can be.

Then the breath starts moving out. Move out.
Then again, outside, for a single second,
the breath stops.
Then watch.
In that stopping, again, you are closest to God

Make it a rhythm.
Then no other meditation is needed.

The Watchman

Just this remembering
will bring you to your own treasure.

Ordinarily, we live in sleep.
We are all somnambulists —
walking, doing things in sleep.
Sometimes, catch yourself moving in sleep,
and then you will know what it means.

You are just walking on the road,
a thousand and one thoughts coming inside the mind.
You are walking like a robot,
not aware where you are going,
what you are doing,
why you are going,
what is happening in the body,
what trees you have passed,
not aware that the wind is blowing.
No, you are not feeling anything.
The flower is sending its scent; it has not reached you.
The world is beautiful; you are unaware.
You are lost deep in your thoughts,
but yet you are moving.

Give a jerk to yourself. For a moment become aware.
Look at the whole situation and suddenly you will see
the difference between ordinary sleeping life
and the life of a Buddha.
For a single moment you become a Buddha.
When you are aware,
for a single moment you become a Buddha.
The whole quality of a Buddha comes to you.
And the taste of it will create a deep desire
to attain to it as an eternal state of your being.

Make yourself more and more aware,
and use all sorts of situations.

The True Sage

There is no need to go beyond the world,
no need to go outside the market.
Wherever you are,
use all situations to awaken yourself.
And every situation can be used.

That's why Hassids are not against the world,
they are not in favour of renunciation,
they don't leave the world.
They live in the world in an ordinary way,
and they use all sorts of situations
to make themselves more and more aware and alert.

Use all situations,
because all situations can be used.

Now listen to this beautiful story.

*In Roptchitz,
the town where Rabbi Naftali lived,
it was the custom for rich people
whose houses stood isolated,
or at the far end of town,
to hire men
to watch over their property by night.
Late one evening,
when Rabbi Naftali was skirting the woods
which circled the city,
he met such a watchman walking up and down.
'For whom are you working?' he asked.*

A simple question,
but a simple question can become a very deep one.
A simple situation,
but a simple situation
can be used to awaken yourself.
The mundane is the sacred also;
it is the ordinary and the extraordinary also.

In the matter is hidden the immaterial.
The only thing is to know the secret: how to use it.

'For whom are you working?' he asked.

A simple question. A formal question.
But it became an insight.
Every moment can become a door.

The man told him,
and then inquired in his turn:
'And for whom are you working, rabbi?'

Because the rabbi was also walking on the same road,
the watchman thought that maybe he is also working
as a watchman for somebody.

'And for whom are you working, rabbi?'

An ordinary question again.
But sometimes, if you are in the right mood, in tune,
a very ordinary thing
can become a message from the divine.

The words struck the zaddik like a shaft.
'I am not working for anybody just yet,'
he barely managed to say.

A very alert man in a way.
Otherwise, he could have said: 'I am working for God.'
A rabbi, an ordinary teacher would have said that
and would not have meant anything by it.
This rabbi — a sincere man, a true man.

The question became very significant:
'And for whom are you working, rabbi?'
'I am not working for anybody just yet,'
he barely managed to say.

How can you say you are working for God?

The True Sage

He is not working for any other rich man.
He is a man of God, a priest, a rabbi —
but no ordinary priest — he is alert.

'I am not working for anybody just yet.'

Very difficult to say —
and much more difficult for a rabbi to say,
because ordinarily a priest in the temple
goes on thinking and saying that he works for God
without knowing what he is saying, what he is asserting.
Ordinarily, priests don't hesitate.

Remember, only a very sincere person hesitates.
Fools, stupid people, hypocrites —
they are all very certain, they never hesitate.
They are stubbornly certain,
they are always absolutely certain.

Only a very very intelligent being . . .
and by intelligence I don't mean intellect;
by intelligence I mean understanding.
I don't mean a trained intellectual.
By intelligence, I mean the radiance of understanding.
An intelligent being always hesitates
because life is such a tremendous mystery.
How can you be certain about anything?

Lao Tzu says: 'When others are absolutely certain,
I am the only confused one.'
Lao Tzu, a man absolutely enlightened, says:
'While others are sane, I look mad.'
He says: 'I walk, but I hesitate,
as someone walking in a winter stream.
I walk, but I am afraid,
as if someone surrounded by enemies.
But others — they simply don't bother at all.
They look absolutely certain.'

The quality of hesitating shows a very delicate mind.

He cannot assert, even in ordinary talk, formal talk,
anything which is not really true.
How can a man who has not yet known God say:
'I am working for God'?
That would be profane, that would be sacrilegious.

'I am not working for anybody just yet.'

What Naftali is saying is this:
'I am no more working for anybody in this world.
The goals of this world are lost,
and the goals of the other world are not yet clear.
I am in a transition.
Here, nothing seems to be significant,
and there, my eyes are yet closed.'

He's saying:
'I'm not working for any ambition in this world.
And the other world? — it is yet far away.
I am on the way.
I have left the old and I have not entered the new.
I am just in the middle of the bridge.
The old bank is lost forever,
the new bank is hidden in mist.
I am not working for anybody just yet.'

There comes a moment in every meditator's life
when the world is meaningless
and God has not yet become meaningful.
That is the greatest, most dangerous point to cross over,
because the mind tends to fall back —
because at least something was significant
and one was occupied.

Now the old occupation is gone
and the new does not seem to happen.
One is in a limbo, one hangs in the middle.
That is the point where patience is needed,
infinite patience is needed.

And that's the point where a Master can be helpful —
to persuade you not to fall back,
because the mind will have a tendency to do so.
A thousand and one temptations
will be there to fall back on —
because what nonsense are you doing?
The old life you have left,
but at least in it there was some meaning.
If not meaning,
at least some occupation, some business to do.
At least one did not feel empty.
Maybe things were not eternal, meaningful,
maybe they were temporary, temporal, momentary —
but at least some meaning was there,
some content was there.
That too is gone.
And the eternal seems nowhere to enter in.

This gap is an absolute necessity.
Unless the mind comes to a state
where it is no more thinking of the past,
falling back to the past,
the new cannot happen.
The temptation of the past
shows a deep bondage with the past.
When the temptation is also gone
and you remain in the vacuum,
not hurrying, not in any haste,
then you allow the emptiness to settle.
Suddenly the eternal enters.
You have become the temple.

Many are here who have been meditating long,
who have come to this state.
Then their minds will say: 'Go back home.
Escape from this man.
You have not gained anything.

The Watchman

On the contrary, you have lost much.
Your old identity gone, your old name gone,
your old image, not anywhere to be found.
And the new? — the new has not happened.
Will it ever happen?'
The mind is afraid, scared.
Is it going to happen or not?
Or have you come to a dead end?

It happens only when you have settled in the vacuum.
The whole comes only
when you have settled in emptiness.
For the whole to descend,
absolute emptiness is needed.
Even a slight clinging,
a slight temptation for the past, is a hindrance.

*'I am not working for anybody just yet,'
he barely managed to say.*

A really sincere man.

*Then he walked up and down
beside the man for a long time.*

What was he doing? — he must have been brooding.
What has happened?

This man, an ordinary watchman —
he can at least say that he is working for somebody.

Naftali says: 'I'm a religious man, a priest, a rabbi,
and I cannot even say that much.
At least this watchman is engaged, occupied,
doing something significant.
It may not be significant
but he believes he is doing some significant work.
And I, a religious man, can barely manage to say
that I am not working for anybody just yet.'

THE TRUE SAGE

*He walked up and down
beside the man for a long time —*
brooding, contemplating, meditating.
*'Will you be my servant?'
he finally asked.*

*'I should like to,' the man replied,
'but what would be my duties?'*

'To remind me,' said Rabbi Naftali.

'To remind me' —
that the world is lost,
but that God is not yet attained.
'To remind me' —
that the material has disappeared,
and the immaterial has not materialized yet.
'To remind me' —
that the known is no more meaningful,
and the unknown is far away.
'To remind me' —
that I should not forget this.
To make me alert again and again.
To strike the note within me
so that I don't fall asleep.

A beautiful story, very meaningful,
and it can become a part of your inner treasure.
Let it become, because there are many situations
in which you need to be reminded.
You fall asleep again and again.
It is natural,
because sleep is the way of least resistance.

It is convenient to fall asleep;
it is uncomfortable to awaken.
And your sleep may have many investments in it.
Sometimes, in deep sleep, you have beautiful dreams,

and when you awaken, all dreams disappear
and the naked reality has to be faced.
There is a temptation to remain asleep,
not to face the reality.
And, you can create beautiful dreams.

That's all we do in the world:
make a beautiful house, a dream in marble.
But still a dream.
Sooner or later you have to leave it.
No house can be a home here.
All houses will have to be left behind —
at the most, a night's rest.
In the morning we have to go,
so don't cling too much.

The world can be at the most a *saraya,* a *dharmashala,*
a resting place for the night.
In the morning we go.
Don't cling to it, don't get attached to it.
Don't think the dream is real.
Let it be reminded to you again and again
that this is a dream.

Every temptation is there to think it is reality,
because when the dream is beautiful,
who wants to think that it is a dream?
Of course, when the dream becomes nightmarish,
you start thinking that it must be a dream.
That's why great anguish and pain
sometimes trigger spirituality.

Your wife has died and you loved her,
you loved her tremendously.
Now you are left alone.
It is not only that your beloved has died,
something deep inside you also died with her
because you were so much involved with her.

You had penetrated into each other's being,
you had become parts of each other,
members of each other.
Now she is dead.
It is not only that somebody outside you is dead;
something of the heart within you is also dead.
You will miss many beats,
you will never be so alive again.
Maybe in this situation
the shock can trigger an awakening.

So misfortunes are not always misfortunes;
sometimes they prove blessings, great blessings.
And the blessings that you think are blessings
may be nothing but narcotics,
may be nothing but drugs.
Beautiful dreams are drugs. They help you to sleep.
Maybe you call them tranquilizers.

Misery is not always misery.
Dukkha, anguish, agony, can become a door to ecstasy.
Let me say it: 'Blessed are those
who are unfortunate enough to know anguish,
blessed are those who are in anguish
because they can be awakened.'

Use your anguish as a force to awaken yourself —
because when you are comfortable, you tend to sleep.
When you are uncomfortable,
the possibility to awaken is greater.

Continuously go on remembering
that the world that you are in
is a momentary phenomenon.
It is just a dewdrop on a grass leaf.
Any moment, a breeze passes by
and the drop slips and is gone forever.

The world is a dewdrop on a grass leaf.
This is what Mahavir has said:
'A dewdrop on a grass leaf.'
Any moment . . .
it is slipping already, you are dying already.
It is not that somewhere in the future, one day,
you will die.
Don't try to deceive yourself.
You have been dying
from the very day you have been born.
The first breath was already amidst death.
You have been dying continuously.
Seventy years, eighty years, a hundred years
you may take to die completely,
but every moment you are dying.
The dewdrop is slipping. Any moment it is gone.

Just a few days ago,
I was talking about a woman saint, Sahajo.
She says: *'Jagat taraiya bhor ki'* —
the world is just like the last star in the morning.
Go on looking.
Just a moment before it was there,
and a moment after, it is not there.
The last star in the morning,
disappearing, disappearing, continuously disappearing.

Remember that the world is a dream.
What is the definition of a dream?
A dream is that which is,
but which is not going to be forever.
A dream was not before, and will not be later on.
Between two non-existences, a fragment of a moment,
and it seems real.
'Existence between two non-existences'
is the definition of a dream.

And what is the definition of a reality? —
existence, existence, existence.
Past, present, future — existence.

Dream: non-existence in the past,
non-existence in the future.
Just in the present, existence.

How can existence
be between two non-existences? — impossible.
You must be deluded.
You must have projected it, it must be a projection,
a wish-fulfillment.
It is not there; the screen is empty.
The story is within you;
the projector is hidden in your mind
and you go on projecting.
You live in a dream and a dream needs sleep.
That's why I say:
'You are fast asleep; I can hear you snoring.'

When I talk about sleep I mean metaphysical,
not the ordinary sleep that you go into at night.
That is sleep with closed eyes,
and in the day you sleep with open eyes.
Only eyes open and closed;
that is the only difference
between your day and your night.

Have you ever observed the fact that in the night
you completely forget your day life absolutely?
In fact, in the morning you may remember something
of the night dream,
but in the night
you never remember anything of your day life —
nothing at all.

What does it mean?
It means even dreams are a little truer.

You can remember.
When you awake in the morning
you can remember the night dreams for a few seconds.
Their reality goes deeper in you.

But in the night when you fall asleep,
not for even a few seconds do you remember your day life —
who you are —
a president of a country, a prime minister,
a beggar or a nobody.
You don't remember at all.
Even your name is forgotten.
Are you a husband or not? A father or not?
Everything is forgotten.
Rich or poor, everything forgotten.

Chuang Tzu says that once he dreamt
that he had become a butterfly.
Then in the morning he was very much puzzled
because a suspicion arose in his heart
that if Chuang Tzu can become
a butterfly in the night, in a dream,
the vice versa is also possible:
the butterfly may be dreaming
that now she has become Chuang Tzu.
If Chuang Tzu can become a butterfly in a dream,
why can't a butterfly
become a Chuang Tzu in her dream?

All dreams,
whether Chuang Tzu dreams
that he has become a butterfly,
or a butterfly dreams
that she has become Chuang Tzu —
all are dreams.

All becoming is dreaming;
becoming as such is dreaming.

The True Sage

When you awake, you come to being; becoming disappears.
Then you don't become anything.
Neither Chuang Tzu becomes a butterfly
nor the butterfly becomes Chuang Tzu.
When you come to being you suddenly realize
that there is no Chuang Tzu and no butterfly.
Only one God exists and He is neither. He is beyond.

Then he walked up and down
beside the man for a long time.
'Will you be my servant?' he finally asked.

'I should like to,' the man replied,
'but what would be my duties?'

'To remind me,' said Rabbi Naftali.

It will be difficult for you to find a man
who can constantly remind you.
But the story is simply symbolic, it is a parable.
You can make your mind the servant to remind you.
The mind can become the watchman.

Just the other day there was a question:
'Can the mind be used in any way for the spiritual awakening?'
Yes. It *has* to be used.
It can be used and it has to be used.
The mind has to be made a servant to remind you.

Ordinarily, the mind has become the master
and you have become the servant.
If the mind has become the master
and you have become the servant,
this is the state of sleep.

If the mind becomes the servant
and you become the master,
you are on the way to awakening.
Then the mind reminds you.

What is meditation?
Meditation is an effort
to use the mind to remind yourself.
Meditation is also a function of the mind,
but the relationship is totally different.
You are the master; the mind becomes the servant.
Use the mind as the servant, and mind is beautiful.
Let the mind become the master
and everything goes ugly.

The man of the world lives in an ugly state.
The mind is the master and he himself is the servant.

The sannyasin, the other-worldly man,
just reverses the situation.
Everything is the same but the order is changed.
Now the mind is the servant
and he himself becomes the master.
Then he uses his mind to remind himself.
And a moment comes
when there will be no need to be reminded.
Then awareness has become natural,
a flowing phenomenon.
Then you can relieve the mind,
the mind can be retired.

So three states: mind, the master —
ninety-nine percent of people are in that state;
then, mind the servant —
very rarely, few people, the seekers,
those who are on the path;
and then, the mind with no function now, retired,
because awakening has become natural —
the state of a Buddha.

Use your mind as the servant
and continuously remember
that the mind has to be retired one day.

The True Sage

When the mind is retired completely,
the world disappears.
Then there is no coming back to the world.
That's what Hindus call:
'the stopping of the cycle of birth and death'.
When one is absolutely awakened,
that awareness has no birth and no death.
It is eternity.

Use the mind.
Step on the mind, let it be a stepping-stone.
Just the order has to be changed.

I will tell you one story.
It happened that a man was in search
and he came upon a man on the path who said:
'There is a well-hidden in the caves.
Go there and ask a question.
If you sincerely ask, the well replies.
It is a miracle only known to great adepts.'

The man searched.
It was difficult to reach to the well,
but somehow he reached.
Leaning down in the well, he asked: 'What is life?'

No reply came. The well only echoed.
He repeated his question,
and the well repeated: 'What is life?'
But the man was really sincere, so he continued.
It is said for three days, day and night,
he asked again and again: 'What is life?' —
and the well only resounded his own voice.
But he was not tired — he continued.

If you work with the mind for many many days, years,
the mind will not give you the key;
it will simply resound you.

But a sincere seeker goes on and on and on;
he is not tired.

After three days
it is said the well realized that the man was sincere
and that he was not going to go.
So the well said: 'Okay, I will tell you what life is.
Go to the town nearby.
Visit the first three shops and come back and report.'

The man was puzzled
because what type of answer was this?
But, 'Okay, if the well says it has to be done. . . .'
He went to the town and visited the first three shops,
but he was even more puzzled and bewildered.
There was nothing.

In the first shop there were a few people
working with some metal pieces.
He went into the next shop;
a few other people were there,
and they were preparing some strings.
Into the third shop he went;
it was a carpenter's shop,
and people were working with wood.
He said to himself: 'This is life?'

He went back to the well and said:
'What do you mean?
I went there, I visited.
This is my report, but I don't see the point.'

The well said: 'Now, I have shown you the path.
You travel it.
Someday you will see the point.
I have indicated the way, now you go on it.'

The seeker was simply angry and said:
'This has been a deception!

What have I gained by asking this well
for three days continuously?
What have I gained by putting my heart
with such sincerity before the well?
This has been a deception.
I have not gained anything.'
Frustrated, he went away.

After many years of wandering
he came near a garden one day.
It was a moon night, a full moon night,
and somebody was playing a sitar.
He was enchanted.
The magic worked.
As if pulled by a magnet, he came into the garden.
He didn't ask permission.
He went up to the player
and the man was deep in his meditation,
playing on the sitar.
He sat there, he listened.
In the moonlight he looked at the man, the instrument.
He had never seen that instrument before.

Suddenly, he realized that those carpenters
were working on things like this.
They were preparing sitars.
And the people who were working on metal —
those pieces were also on the sitar.
And the strings.

Suddenly, as if the clouds disappeared
and there was a breakthrough,
he started dancing.
The musician became aware; he stopped the music.
But now nobody can stop the dance of the seeker.

The musician asked: 'What is the matter?
What has happened to you?'

The man said : 'I have understood.
Life has everything. Just a new combination is needed.
I looked into three shops.
Everything was there, but there was no sitar.
Everything was separate.
An order was needed; everything was in chaos.
Everything as there; whatsoever was needed was there.
Just a synthesis, just a unity was needed —
and such beautiful music comes out of it.
Life has everything — now I have understood.
Just a new order is needed.'

You have everything that you need.
God never sends anybody as a beggar into the world.
Everybody is born an emperor but lives like a beggar,
not knowing how to arrange things.

Mind should be the servant,
consciousness should be the master —
and then the instrument is ready,
and then a great music is possible.

And there comes a moment
when the instrument is not needed at all.
It is said that whenever a musician becomes perfect
he throws the sitar because then it is useless,
because then the inner music has come in.
The outer sitar just helped to move withinwards.
Whenever an archer is perfect, he throws the bow.
Then there is no need for it.
Whenever there is perfection, it becomes unconditional.

First make the sitar of your life
and then be able to retire the mind completely.
Then you have gone beyond the circle of birth and death.
And that's what God is.

That's what this beautiful story is saying :

'To remind me' —
so that I don't fall again and again a victim
of the old pattern:
mind, the master; and myself, the servant.
'To remind me' —
that I am the master.

14th October 1975

Questions and answers

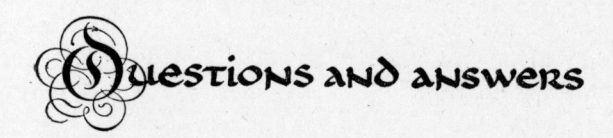

*Why does all that you say seem completely familiar?
I have heard it all before in various contexts,
but at the same time,
it sounds full of wonderful revelations.*

   That's the quality of truth:
it is neither old nor new — or, it is both.
Truth is eternal.

In a way you have heard it millions of times,
in many contexts.
You may not have understood it but you have heard it.
You carry the memory.
It is not that you are here
for the first time on this earth.
In the time of Buddha,
in the time of Jesus,
in the time of Krishna,
certainly you were there.
You have heard it but you have not understood it.
That's why you are again here.

The True Sage

The day you understand, you disappear.
Understanding is a great death,
death from this world of fantasy, dream, illusion.

You are right.
Your feeling is right that you have heard it before.
It sounds familiar and yet it reveals much.
It sounds familiar because it is familiar.
Still, it reveals new dimensions,
because a new understanding is dawning on you.

Truth is neither old nor new
because it doesn't belong to time.
Anything that belongs to time
is bound to be new or old.
That which is new today will be old tomorrow.
That which is old today was new yesterday.
New and old are two aspects of time.
Truth is timeless, truth is timelessness.
It is always there —
as old as existence, and as new as this moment.

If you understand,
the familiarity carries deep mysteries
hidden behind it.
So don't be deceived by the familiarity.
You may have heard the words;
you have not understood the truth.
Otherwise you are transformed.
Transformation is a function of truth.
Says Jesus: 'Truth liberates.'
The moment you understand, you are liberated.
There is nothing else to do afterwards.
The very understanding is enough, is liberation.

Listen, but don't compare.
Listen, but don't bring your memory in.

Otherwise your memory
and your feeling that it is familiar
will be a distraction.

The moment your mind says it is familiar,
the mind is saying there is nothing new to understand.
There is much!
There is an infinite amount to be understood.

Don't look through the memory and don't compare.
Look direct. Look immediate. Look without memory.
Let there be a clarity of perception.
Don't compare with anything that you have heard before.

I tell you, you may have heard it before,
but you have not understood it.
So what is the point of hearing it before?
And if you are too much in this idea of familiarity,
you will miss it again.
And again, whenever you will hear it,
the idea will be there that it sounds familiar.

Comparison is a disease.
It obstructs; it doesn't help.
So even when you feel it is familiar
you also feel, side by side,
new flowers of understanding blooming.
They bloom in spite of your comparison.

If the comparison is completely dropped,
you are liberated.
If you can rightly listen to me,
there is nothing else to do.
One moment of total listening will be enough.
You will be awake.
And one moment is enough
because that becomes the door for eternity.

THE TRUE SAGE

*The words 'introvert' and 'introspection'
have morbid connotations.
How do they differ
from healthy self-awareness and turning within?*

In self-awareness, there is no within and no without.
You don't turn within.
In self-awareness,
the within and the without have disappeared.
There exists only one.
Within and without is the division of the mind,
is the division of the analytical mind.
What it within? And what is without? How do you demark?

So when people say: 'turn withinwards,'
they are just using your language to help you
because if they say: 'turn beyond within and without,'
it will be almost impossible
for you to understand what they mean.
But that is exactly what they mean.

Self-awareness is a total unity of within and without,
the higher and the lower, the valley and the peak.
All dualities meet and merge into it.

Yes, 'introvert' has a morbid connotation;
it is a morbidity.
A person who is an introvert
is a person who is incapable to move without.
He is confined, closed,
a flower which cannot open,
a song which cannot burst,
a river which cannot flow to the open sea.
The introvert is morbid. He cannot relate, he cannot love,
he cannot move in the world,
he cannot spread, he has no expansion.
Confined. Closed. Like a seed — he is not like a tree.

But remember, the extrovert is also morbid.
In Western psychology the introvert is morbid,
but the extrovert is thought to be healthy.
That simply shows
that this type of psychological thinking
has been developed by extroverts — nothing else.
They think they are healthy
and that the opposite is unhealthy.

There is an opposite school also in the East.
The Eastern psychology thinks the introvert healthy
and the extrovert unhealthy.
But to me, both are unhealthy,
because both are confined to a certain direction
and are incapable to move to the opposite.

To me, health means:
the capacity to move in all directions.
To be healthy is to be whole.
The word 'health'
comes from the same root as the word 'whole'.
To be healthy is to be whole,
to be whole is to be all together.
So to be healthy means: where opposites meet
and are no more opposites
but are transformed into complementaries.

A healthy person is one
who when he wants to move in, he moves.
There is no hindrance.
He has no compulsion to be an extrovert.
And vice versa.
If you are compulsively an introvert —
whenever you start moving without,
there are inner hindrances.
You have to fight, you cannot flow, you have to force.
Then you are ill.

A healthy person, a healthy being, a healthy energy,
is always ready to move anywhere.
There is no compulsion to be somewhere in particular.
A healthy energy is a flowing energy.
When you go to the market, you move out.
Nobody inside condemns:
'To move out is worldly, materialistic.'
Nobody condemns.
When you go to the temple you move withinwards.
Nobody condemns: 'To go within is morbid.
This is for foolish people, unworldly, simpletons.
This way you will lose all,
because all the riches are outside.
Where are you going by closing your eyes
and watching your navel?
You are becoming a fool.'

In the West, when they want to condemn the East,
they call them 'navel-watchers' or 'lotus-eaters'.
One cannot be alive by just eating lotuses.
They must be mad people.

And when in the East, people want to condemn the West,
they call them 'money-oriented' 'materialistic' 'worldly'.

But both these types of psychologies
are ill and morbid.
A true psychology is still to be born —
a psychology of the whole person,
a psychology of flow, of no compulsion, no obsession.

A man should be as capable of coming in and going out
as you are capable of going into
and coming out of your house.
When the climate is beautiful, you go out.
You sit in the garden under the tree.
Then the sun rises and it is too hot —
you seek shelter, you come in.

In the day you go out, in the night you come in.
A deep balance is needed.

And for a deep balance,
opposites should not be taken as opposites —
and they are not; they are complementaries,
yin and yang, man and woman, day and night,
summer and winter, *sansar* and *nirvana*.

Remember — my whole emphasis is
for the meeting of the opposites.
Then you are not confined,
then you have no limitation,
then you are unlimited, then no boundary exists.
And this is the emphasis of Hassidism also.

A Hassidic sage is as worldly as anybody,
and a Hassidic sage is as unworldly as anybody.
He lives *in* the world, but he is not *of* the world.
He moves in the world, but remains untouched by it.
He is beyond.
This is true religion.

The religion that you call religion
is not true religion.
It is just in opposition to the world.
It is a choice.
That's why if you choose that type of religion,
you may change,
but fundamentally you will remain the same.
The change will be just on the surface.
The change will be just as if
one goes from one imprisonment to another.

One imprisonment is on this side of the road,
another is on that side of the road.
You live in one prison and you think of the other,
as if *there* is freedom.

It is opposite.
Things *are* different there,
but again it is a confinement.

Between these two imprisonments
there is the open road —
the way of the white clouds.
Just exactly in the middle, between two opposites,
is the way.

To me, an extrovert is morbid;
an introvert is also morbid.
When you are neither, you are healthy.

Remember the word 'flowing'.
The more energy flows, the more healthy it is.
You can reach to the highest peak
and you can come down to the lowest world —
and there is no problem.
You can meditate and you can love.

Meditation is going withinwards,
love is going without.
Meditation is reaching to one's own being.
Love is an effort to reach to the other's being.

There are religions which say
that if you meditate, you cannot love.
There are religions which say
that if you love, how can you meditate?

Christianity is an extrovert religion.
The emphasis is on serving people, love, compassion.
The emphasis is not on meditation —
because if you meditate, that looks selfish.
When the world is in such a misery,
people are hungry, ill, dying,
and you are meditating —
the whole thing looks to be too cruel.

Somebody is dying on the road, a beggar,
and you are sitting in your temple and meditating.
It looks selfish.
'Throw this meditation away,' says the extrovert religion.
'Go and help people —
that is the only way to reach God.'

One of the greatest Indian poets, Rabindranath,
was much impressed by Christianity.
He has written a poem in which he says:
'Don't seek me in the temple. I am not there.
If you really want to seek me, come to the road
where the stone-cutter is cutting the stones
or where the farmer is tilling the ground.
I am not in the temples.
Come to the world where the labourer is working
and the beggar is begging.
There I am.'
This is an extrovert religion —
a reaction against too much introversion.

In India, introvert religions have existed.
They say that this world is *maya,* illusion.
Beggars have always been dying
and they will always die
and you cannot change anything.
Move withinwards, close your eyes.
In your deepest core of being is God.
Outside, it is just a dream world.
Don't waste your time there. The real is within.

To me, both are morbid.
A part is always morbid — only the whole is healthy.

So I tell you: God is everywhere.
In the temple when you close your eyes, there is God.
And on the road also, where the stone-cutter is,
working hard in the hot sun —
there also is God.

The True Sage

Only God is. God is the whole.
But mind always tries to choose a part.

I have heard:
You must have known
a very famous movie dog, Rin Tin Tin.
His trainer was asked to describe Rin Tin Tin.
He tried to describe,
but the dog had such marvellous qualities,
such indefinable qualities,
that he was at a loss to describe
and define the qualities.
So at last he stumbled upon a definition.
He said: 'Rin Tin Tin is God in the form of a dog.'

'God' and 'dog' — both words have the same balance.
God may be the introversion of energy.
Dog may be the extroversion of the energy.
But the energy is the same,
because only one energy exists.
The world is a unity.
The mind creates opposites.

One very great Zen monk, Rinzai, was asked once. . . .
The questioner must have been a very sceptical mind.
He asked: 'You go on emphasizing
that everything is God and everything is Buddha.
Do you mean to say that even a dog is a Buddha?'
Rinzai laughed. Didn't answer.
On the contrary, he jumped, and started barking.
That's exactly the right answer:
a Buddha barking like a dog.
He showed the fact rather than talked about it.

You are morbid if you are confined to anything —
whatsoever the name.
You are healthy
if you are flowing in all directions together.

Questions And Answers

If opposites meet in you, you become perfect.
That's why a perfect man can never be consistent;
he has to be contradictory,
because opposites will be meeting in him.
Only ordinary people can be consistent.
The true sage is never consistent — cannot be —
because he will have to move
in all the directions together.

Walt Whitman says:
'I'm vast. I contain contradictions.'
Then what to say about God? — vast!
He contains all contradictions.
He is in the lowest and He is in the highest.
In the lowest He exists as the lowest.
In the highest He exists as the highest.
He is in sex and He is in samadhi.
He is in this world as matter
and He is in that world as non-matter.
He is the sinner and He is the sage.
The true sage is always contradictory.
That's the difficulty in understanding him.

It is very easy to understand your mediocre saints;
they are plain.
No contradictions exist in them;
they are always the same.
You can rely, you can predict.
They are like a simple line, no complexity.
They are simple and, in a way, simpletons.
They don't have the beauty of complexity.

The true sage is very complex;
he contains contradictions.
And that's why it has always been very difficult
to recognize him.
He eludes.
You catch hold of him from one direction,
and he is moving in another.

The True Sage

You cannot see because your eyes are morbid.
You can see only a part.
You can see a man as a sinner,
you can see a man as a saint,
but it is difficult to understand a man like Gurdjieff
who is both.

In him, the sinner and the sage meet.
In him, even the sin is transformed.
In him, even the sage is transformed
and becomes a worldly being.
To understand Gurdjieff
you will have to drop all your categories,
all your labels of sinners and saints,
and this and that.
The true sage is godly.
God is contradictory.

That's what Krishna says in the Gita.
He says: 'Don't be worried,
because I am the killer and the killed.
Don't be worried, because I am in both.
The one who is killed, I am —
and the one who is going to kill also is me.
My two hands, right and left,
in a game of hide and seek.'

All your conceptions of God are very poor.
Theologians go on trying to explain
but they can never explain
because the contradiction creates the trouble.

If you say: 'God is just,'
then you cannot say: 'God is compassion.'
That's the trouble for the theologian.
If God is just, then compassion cannot exist.
If God is compassion, then He cannot be just.
Both are not possible together.

For thousands of years
theologians have been thinking how to manage.
God seems to be unmanageable, chaotic.

God is both.
He is compassionate in His justice
and He is just in His compassion.
But then it is absurd,
because how can a judge be both?
If the judge has compassion,
then he would like to forgive.
If he is just, then the criminal has to be punished —
punished according to the law, with no compassion.
Then he has to remain indifferent.
Justice has to be neutral.
Compassion is love; it cannot be neutral.

God is both.
Let me tell you:
God is bondage, God is freedom — both.
That's why I say: 'Don't be in a hurry.'
Even in the market He exists.
Even in this world, so ungodly, He exists —
because otherwise is not possible.

Once you can see it,
such deep silence descends in your being.
Because when you can see the contradictions
meeting in God,
then the contradictions within you
immediately meet and dissolve.
Then freedom becomes your nature.
Then you move freely, then you become freedom.
Then there is no goal.

The only goal is to delight here-now.
Nothing is to be achieved,
because all achievement is always against something.

The True Sage

You have to leave this and attain that.
You have to drop this and do that.
All achievements, ambitions, goals,
are choosing something against something else.
And God is both.
That's why Krishnamurti goes on insisting
that the only way to attain to truth
is to be choiceless.
Choose — and you have become morbid.
Don't choose, float choicelessly.
Don't be the chooser.
Just watch and flow — and you are freedom.
This is what *moksha* is — absolute freedom.

Why am I afraid of other people?

If you are afraid of yourself,
only then are you afraid of other people.
If you love yourself, you love others.
If you hate yourself, you hate others.
Because in relationship with others,
it is only you mirrored.
The other is nothing but a mirror.

So whatsoever happens in relationship, always know
it must have happened before, within you —
because the relationship can only magnify.
It cannot create; it can only show and manifest.

If you love yourself, you love others.
If you are afraid of yourself,
you are afraid of others.
Because, in coming in contact with others
you will start manifesting your being.

You have been conditioned —
in the East, in the West, everywhere.

Christian, Hindu, Mohammedan, Jain —
you all have been conditioned to hate yourself.
It has been taught to you continuously
that to love oneself is bad.
'Love others. Hate yourself.'

This is asking for absurdities, impossibilities.
If you don't love yourself,
who is nearest to yourself,
how can you love anybody else?
Nobody loves himself —
yet he is trying to love others.
Then your love is nothing but hatred —
masked, hidden.

I tell you to love yourself first,
because if love happens within you,
only then it can spread to others.
It is just like throwing a stone into a silent lake.
The stone falls, ripples arise,
and then they go on moving,
moving to the farthest bank.
They will go on and on and on,
but the stone must have fallen within you first.

Love must have happened to you. You must love yourself;
that is a basic requirement —
which is missing all over the world.
That's why the world is in such a misery.
Everybody trying to love but it is impossible to love
because the basis is not there —
the foundation lacking.
Love yourself. And then suddenly
you will find yourself reflected everywhere.

You are a human being
and all other human beings are just like you.
Just forms differ, names differ,
but the reality is the same.

Go on moving farther and farther —
then animals are also like you.
The form differs a little more. But the being?
Then the trees are also like you.
Go farther and farther; the ripples spread —
then even rocks, because they also exist like you.
Existence is the same, similar.

This is the only way to love God:
start by loving yourself and let the love spread.
Then don't let there be any boundaries.
Go on and on — to the very infinity.
This is what prayer is, this is what devotion is.

But if you miss the first point,
if the stone has not been thrown,
and then you go on waiting and watching,
and the ripples never arise. . . .

It cannot start anywhere else;
It can only start in your heart.
Because love is a ripple in the heart,
a vibration in the heart, a throbbing,
a sharing of whatsoever you are,
a deep, intense urge to go and reach the other,
to share your being and your delight and your song.

But your heart is almost dead-frozen,
and you have been taught to condemn yourself —
that you are ugly, that you are bad, that this is sin.
'Don't do this. You are guilty.'
You cannot accept yourself.
How can you accept anybody else?

A deep acceptance is needed.
Whatsoever and whosoever you are,
a deep acceptance is needed.
Not only acceptance — but a delight that 'I am.'

'I', 'Here', 'Now' —
all the three points, the triangle of being,
should be filled with delight.
You should not ask anything else.
There should not be any 'ought'.
Drop all 'shoulds'
and the whole world becomes different.
Right now, you continuously think :
'I should be this and that.
Then I can love and be loved.'
Your God is nothing but the greatest condemnor
looking at you from the skies, saying : 'Behave well.'
This gives you a bad feeling about yourself.

By and by, you become afraid
because you are suppressing yourself.
If you relate with somebody,
the suppression may break,
everything may bubble up, surface.
Then what ?
So you are afraid,
afraid to come in contact with anything —
so you remain hidden within yourself.

Nobody knows how ugly you are.
Nobody knows how angry you are.
Nobody knows how full with hatred you are.
Nobody knows your jealousy, possessiveness, envy.
Nobody knows.
You create an armour around yourself,
you live within yourself.
You never make any contact —
so that you can manage your image.
If you come deep in contact,
the image is bound to break.
The reality, the real encounter will shatter it —
that is the fear.

The True Sage

You ask : *Why am I afraid of other people?*

You are afraid because you are afraid of yourself.
Drop that fear, drop the guilt
that has been created in you.

Your politicians, priests, parents,
they all are guilt-creators,
because that is the only way
that you can be controlled and manipulated.
A very simple, but very cunning trick
to manipulate you.
They have condemned you,
because if you are accepted, not condemned —
loved, appreciated,
and if it is relayed to you from everywhere
that you are okay —
then it will be difficult to control you.
How to control a person who is absolutely okay?
The very problem doesn't arise.

So they go on saying —
the priests, the politicians, the parents —
that you are not okay.
Once they create the feeling that you are not okay,
now they become the dictators;
now they have to dictate the discipline.
'Now this is the way you should behave. . . . '
First they create the feeling that you are wrong;
then they give you guidelines of how to be right.

Here you are with me,
involved in a totally different experiment.
I have no condemnation,
I don't create any guilt feeling in you.
I don't say: 'This is sin.'
I don't say that I will love you
only when you fulfill certain conditions.

I love you as you are,
because that's the only way a person can be loved.
And I accept you as you are,
because I know that is the only way you can be.
That's how the whole has willed you to be.
That is what the whole has destined it to be.

Relax, and accept, and delight —
and there is transformation.
It comes not by efforts;
it comes by accepting yourself
with such deep love and ecstasy,
that there is no condition,
conscious, unconscious, known, unknown.

Unconditional acceptance —
and suddenly you see you are not afraid of people.
Rather, you enjoy people.
People are beautiful. They are all incarnations of God.
Maybe Rin Tin Tin . . .
but still . . .
incarnations of God.
You love them.
And if you love them,
you bring their God to the surface.

Whenever you love a person
his godliness comes to the top.
It happens — because when somebody loves you,
how can you show your ugliness?
Simply, your beautiful face comes up.
And, by and by, the ugly face disappears.

Love is alchemical.
If you love yourself the ugly part of you disappears,
is absorbed, is transformed.
The energy is released from that form.
Everything carries energy.

The True Sage

Your anger has much energy involved in it,
your fear also has much energy,
crippled and suffocated in it.
If the fear disappears, the form falls down,
energy is released.
Anger disappears — more energy is released.
Jealousy disappears — still more energy.

Whatsoever are called sins simply disappear.
I don't say that you have to change them;
you have to love your being and they change.
Change is a by-product, a consequence.
So much tremendous energy released —
you start floating higher and higher and higher,
you attain to wings.

Love yourself.
That should be the foundational commandment.
Love yourself.
All else will follow, but this is the foundation.

*I am confused about the difference
between individuality and personality.
What, if anything, is left of the individual
after the exit of the ego?*

Individuality is your essence.
You come with it, you are born with it.
Personality is borrowed.
It is given by the society to you.
It is just like clothes, subtle clothes.

A child is born naked;
then we hide his nakedness — we give him clothes.
A child is born with essence, individuality.

We hide that too,
because naked individuality is rebellious,
non-conformist.

Individuality is exactly what it means.
It is individual.
Personality is not individual; it is social.
Society wants you to have personalities,
not individualities,
because your individualities will create conflict.
The society hides your individuality
and gives a personality.

Personality is a learned thing.
The word 'personality' comes from a Greek root
which means mask — *persona*.
In Greek drama, the actors used to wear masks
to hide their real faces and to show some other face.
From *persona* comes the word personality.
It is a face that you wear;
it is not your original face.

When the personality disappears, don't be afraid.
Then for the first time you become authentic.
For the first time you become real.
For the first time you attain to essence.
That essence in India has been called *atma,* the soul.

The ego is the center of personality,
and God is the center of essence.
That's why so much insistence, from every corner,
that ego has to be dropped.
Because you must know what you are,
not what you are expected to be.

Personality is false; it is the greatest lie.
The whole society depends on personality.

The True Sage

The state, the church,
the organizations, the establishments —
they are all lies.
The Western psychology
goes on thinking too much about the personality.
That's why the whole Western psychology
is a psychology based on a basic lie.

In the East, we think of the essence,
not of the personality.
That which you have brought,
that which is your intrinsic nature, *swabhava*,
that which is your intrinsic essence —
that has to be known.
And that has to be lived.

Personality is that which you are not,
but try to show that you are.
Personality is that which, when you move in society,
you have to use as a convenience.

You are walking, you have gone for a morning walk.
And then somebody passes by. You smile.
The smile can be either from the essence
or from the personality.
The smile can really be a delight in seeing the person,
in seeing the God in that person,
in seeing the heart, the love, the formless,
that has become incarnate in that person.

That's why in India
we never use phrases like 'Good Morning'.
They don't mean much.
We say: 'Ram, Ram . . . '
We welcome each other by the name of God.
It is a symbolic act: 'I see God within you.'
'Ram, Ram' means 'I see Ram within you.
Welcome. I am happy, blessed, that you passed by.'

Questions And Answers

If it comes from the essence,
then the smile spreads all over your being.
You feel a deep content.
You feel blessed that this man passed by.
The man may be gone, but the blessing remains
and lingers around you like a subtle perfume.

But you can simply say : 'Good Morning' —
because the man is a banker, or a political leader,
or can be sometimes mischievous,
or can be dangerous.
It is risky not to say 'Good Morning.'
Then you say it and you smile ;
you bring a smile to your face.
That is *persona,* that is personality.

In each act you have to watch.
It is arduous, but it has to be done.
There is no other way.
In each act you have to watch from where it comes.
From personality or from essence ?

If it comes from essence, the essence will grow,
because you will give an opportunity
for the essence to be manifested, expressed.
If it comes from the personality,
then personality will become harder
and harder and harder,
and it will suffocate the essence completely.

Watch.
Remind yourself again and again :
'From where does it come ?'

If you come home
and you bring ice cream, flowers — to your wife,
is the present from the personality
or from the essence ?

If it is from the personality it is a lie.
You may have talked to somebody else's wife,
and you were charmed.
You felt attracted, a desire arose in you.
And then you started feeling guilty:
'This is not faithfulness. So bring ice cream home.'

Remember — your wife will immediately suspect.
Otherwise, you never bring ice cream.
There must be something in it;
you must be hiding something.
Why are you so good today? —
so suddenly, unexpectedly good?

You cannot deceive women;
they have an instinct, they are lie detectors.
They immediately feel — because they don't think.
Their feeling is immediate and direct.
They function from the center of emotion.

You are feeling guilty;
then you bring some presents to the wife.
It is a gift from the personality. It is very dangerous.

A similar but opposite case can happen.
The situation may be the same.
You were talking to your friend's wife.
You were charmed.
She was graceful and beautiful,
and because of her beauty, because of her grace,
you remembered your wife.
Because when you love a person
every other beautiful person reminds you of the person.
It has to be so.
If the woman was charming,
it immediately reminds you of your beloved.
Something of the beloved was there — a part, a gesture.
Something of your wife was there.

You loved the woman in that moment
because she reminded you of your wife.
Then you are full of the memory.

Then you may bring ice cream or flowers or something . . .
or nothing — just a smile.
Then it is from the essence, then it is totally different.
The situation may be the same,
but you can behave in a totally different way.

Personality is an effort to deceive.
Essence is an effort to reveal your being;
whatsoever it is — it is.
Let it be revealed, and be open, and be vulnerable.

Try to live from the essence
and you will become religious.
Try to live by the personality
and you will be the most irreligious possible.

To me, religion doesn't mean a ritual.
It doesn't mean going to the church or the temple.
It doesn't mean reading the Bible or the Gita every day, no.
Religion means to live from the essence,
to be authentic, to be true.

And remember, howsoever you lie, you cannot lie,
because a lie is a lie.
Deep down you know it is a lie.
You may pretend that you don't know
but your pretension will be there
and that will indicate.
You cannot lie to anybody
because anybody who has any eyes,
who has any awareness, any intelligence,
will penetrate into it.

There was a case.

The True Sage

A woman was suing Mulla Nasrudin.
She claimed that her child was Mulla Nasrudin's child.
And Mulla was denying vehemently in the court.

Finally, the judge asked : 'Say only one thing —
did you sleep with this woman, Nasrudin ?'

Nasrudin said : 'No, your honour — not a wink.'

Your lies are apparent,
because the truth has a way of coming up.
It finds a way. In the end the truth is known,
and you wasted your whole life in lies.

Don't waste a single moment.
All the time that is wasted in lies
is absolutely wasted.
And through lies nobody ever becomes happy ;
it is impossible.
Lies can give only pretensions of happiness ;
they cannot give you true happiness.

True happiness is part of truth.
Hindus have defined God as 'bliss' — *satchitanand.*
Anand, bliss, is the final, the ultimate core.

Be true, and you will be blissful.
Be authentic, and you will be happy.
And that happiness will be uncaused ;
it will be just a part of your being true.

Happiness is a function of truth.
Whenever there is truth, happiness functions.
Whenever there is not truth,
happiness stops functioning and unhappiness functions.

Don't be afraid.

You say :

*I am confused about the difference
between individuality and personality.
What, if anything, is left of the individual
after the exit of the ego?*

In fact, because of the ego,
nothing of the individual is left.
When the ego is gone, the whole individuality arises
in its crystal purity : transparent, intelligent, radiant,
happy, alive, vibrating with an unknown rhythm.
That unknown rhythm is God.
It is a song heard in the deepest core of your being.
It is a dance of the formless.
But one can hear the footsteps.

Everything real arises only when the ego has gone.
Ego is the deceiver, the falsification.
When ego is gone, *you* are there.
When ego is there, you simply think you are,
but you are not.

*I can think of nothing that I wish more clearly
than to come closer to your inner temple.
Is this possible while I am still doing my own thing?
Or is it a prerequisite
to drop all activities and interests
not connected with you and your work?*

If you really are doing your own thing
you have come closer to my inner temple.
There is no other way.
I am here to help you to do your own thing.
I am not here to drag you away from your own thing.
That's what the so-called religions
have been doing all along.

The True Sage

Remember this: I am not to make anything out of you.

If you can be yourself, it is enough —
more than enough.
If I can help you to be yourself
then the right thing has happened.
If, in some way,
I become an opportunity to distract you
from your own being,
then I am an enemy, not a friend.

So never again think it a prerequisite
to drop all activities and interests
not connected with me and my work.
You are my work. *You* are my activity.
Nothing else is more important than you.
You are supreme; there is no higher value than **you**.
So if you are fulfilled, my work is done.
If you are blissful, my activity is fulfilled.
There is no other work.
I have no idea, ideology
that has to be fulfilled through you — no.

I am, at the most, just an opportunity
where you can find yourself.
When you reach to your innermost home,
you have reached to my temple.
And there is no other way.

You have said that the proper relationship
of mind to consciousness
is that of the servant.
How is the servant to be treated?
Is it not to be mistreated?
How am I to know when that is happening?

Remember — if you are really a master
you never mistreat the servant.
That is one of the qualities of the master.

You mistreat the servant only
when you are not certain that you are master.
That mistreatment is a deep insecurity.
You try to mistreat to know
whether you are the master or not.
If you are absolutely certain that you are the master,
you love the servant.
You treat him as a friend, you respect him even.
So only those who are suspicious of their own mastery
treat the servants in a wrong way.

A man who is absolutely certain,
who knows he is the master —
then there is no problem.

It is said of a Hassidic Master, Magid. . . .
He went to see another Master. He was a little late.
The lecture hall was full
and the other Master was speaking,
so he sat just near the door
where people had left their shoes.

Somebody looked at him.
The quality of Magid attracted him.
He told his neighbour that some rare being was there —
'But why is he sitting there?
That is not a place for a Master to sit.
And he is so radiant.'
And it is said that by and by
the whole audience turned towards him.

The Master who was talking, and who was a faker,
was surprised at the phenomenon.

Magid had not uttered a single word;
he was just sitting with closed eyes.
The pseudo-Master, later when they were alone,
asked Magid: 'Tell me the secret. What happened?
I was there, the leader of the congregation,
and I was to talk.
What happened? Why did people turn towards you?'

Magid said: 'Since I became a Master
it almost always happens.
It is not something to be done. It simply happens.'

A Master has a quality.
When you are really the master,
you have become a watcher and become the master.

And it is such a simple thing
that you just say something and it happens.
You just say to the mind: 'Enough —
now you be the servant, because you are the servant.'
And, I say, it is just that simple.

You are afraid: that is why it cannot happen.
You know that it will not happen.
Then you can say something and it will not happen.
But it is not happening
because you knew it would not happen.
Otherwise it will happen.

You have not treated the mind *really* as a servant.
Otherwise, you simply say: 'Sit down,'
or you simply say: 'Listen' — and the mind listens.

Vivekanand was in America.
He talked one morning and he told a story,
and he emphasized the fact
that faith can move mountains.

Questions And Answers

One old woman who was worried by a mountain very much
said: 'This is good! I never tried it.'

Just behind her house there was a big mountain.
And because of the mountain
the sun would not come to her house.
Because of the mountain, air would not reach.
Her house became very stuffy.

So she said: 'This is simple.
Now I will go and I will have faith!'

She went immediately to her house.
She opened the window
and looked at the mountain for the last time —
because now it would disappear.
There would be no chance again to see it.
She closed the window, closed her eyes,
and said: 'I have faith. Now move!'
Thrice she said it,
because she thought maybe once it may not work.

Then she opened the window.
The mountain was still there.
She started laughing and said:
'I already knew it was not going to happen.'
If you know all the way, then it will not happen —
because you have not fulfilled the condition.

I also say that faith can move mountains —
but faith, remember!

And faith need not say it thrice.
It is doubt which says it thrice.
What is the point?
Once you say it, you're finished —
and faith will not open the window and look.
It is finished!

The True Sage

I have heard, in a town it happened:
rains were not coming.
It was already getting very late in the season
so the priest of the town
gathered all the people one morning,
called them all to come to the temple
so that they could pray for it to rain.

The whole town went —
and the whole town laughed at a certain child.
A small child came with an umbrella.
So everybody talked and laughed and said:
'You fool — why are you carrying your umbrella?
You may lose it somewhere. Rains are not coming.'

The child said: 'But I thought that when you would pray,
the rains would come.'

Only one child was carrying an umbrella.
How can rains come?
If that child had prayed, there was a possibility of rains.

Faith can only be total — otherwise not.
And the people who were laughing about that child
were simply stupid.
If you don't have total faith,
then why are you going to pray?
And when prayer will not be fulfilled,
you will say that you knew
it was not going to happen all along.

Faith is a different quality of inner functioning.
If you really say to the mind:
'Be the servant from now onwards' —
it is finished!
Don't open the window again to see.
And this is how it happens,
and this is how it is going to happen to you,

because there is no other way.

When you are a master you treat the servant like a friend.
You feel grateful to the servant.
He serves you. Why mistreat him?

Mistreatment comes only
when you see that the servant is the master.
Then you react, then you are angry, then you mistreat.
Your mistreatment simply shows
that the servant is not the servant
and the master is not the master.

*Listening to your words: 'The sky appears to,
but nowhere does it touch the earth,'
a deep feeling gathered around me
that the sky is touching the earth right through me,
that I am the horizon wherever I am.
The feeling, like a honeycomb, with no substance in it,
just the wide open sky penetrating every pore of it,
has remained ever since as a constant meditation.
It feels light and blissful to be in it.
Please comment.*

   There is no need to comment.
I bless you.
This is what should happen.

*Is everything in one's life,
particularly the degree of spiritual progress,
predestined?
Or is one's life
a series of challenges and possibilities
without anything being known about the outcome?*

The True Sage

   The essence is predestined,
the personality is just an accident.
That which you are is predestined,
that which you appear to be is just an accident.
Your being a Hindu, your being a Christian, is an accident.
Your being a man, your being a woman, is an accident.
Your being a German or an Indian is an accident.
Your being black or white is an accident.
But your *being*, simply your being, is destined.

Try to find that which is destined,
and don't be too concerned
with that which is irrelevant, accidental.

Your nose is a little long or a little short.
Don't be bothered much about it; it is just accidental.
Or your skin has a pigment and you are black.
Or your skin doesn't have that pigment —
not worth more than four annas.
Don't be too worried about it. It is just irrelevant.

Try to find that which is absolutely destined.
That is your nature, that is your essence.

But you are lost in accidents.
You pay too much attention to accidents;
you are too worried about them.
Your whole time and energy is wasted in them.
You become so much occupied with the non-essential
that the essential is forgotten.

This is the state of the man who is asleep:
always focused on the non-essential.
Thinking of money, thinking of power,
thinking of the house, thinking of the car,
thinking of this and that —
but never looking at that
which is your innermost core, which is *you*.
That innermost core is absolutely destined.

Outside, nothing is destined.
Inside, everything is destined.
Pay more attention to it.
That's what sannyas is all about:
a turning towards the essential,
and a turning away from the non-essential.

I am not saying that you don't eat,
that you don't live in a house — no.
That is not the meaning.
Live in a house, but don't be too concerned.
One has to eat to live.
Eat — but don't make eating your whole business.
There are people who continuously think of eating.

Money is needed, but don't make money your God.
Use it when you have it.
When you don't have it,
then use that non-having also,
because that has its own beauties.
When you have money, you can have a place. Have it.
When you don't have the money, become a vagabond
and live under the sky.
That has its own beauty.
When you have money, use it. Don't be used by the money.
When you don't have it, enjoy poverty.
Richness has its own richness,
poverty has its own richness also.
There are many things
which only a poor man can enjoy —
never a rich man.
There are many things only rich people can enjoy —
never a poor man.
So, whatsoever opportunity. . . .
When you are rich,
enjoy that which a rich man can enjoy.
Whenever you are poor,
enjoy that which poor men enjoy.

The True Sage

But what do you do? — you do just the reverse.
When you are rich, you suffer for those things
which only poor men can enjoy.
And when you are poor, you suffer for those things
which only a rich man can enjoy.
You are simply foolish; I don't see intelligence.

I was staying with a friend.
He is a vice-chancellor, an old man, a drunkard —
almost always drunk —
but he is a very good man,
as drunkards are always.
A very sweet, a very polite, a very loving man.

In the night, he had taken too much,
and I was sitting with him.
He became suddenly afraid.
He became so paranoid that he told me:
Please write a letter immediately to the police station —
to send two intelligence officers.'

I wrote the letter, but I committed an error.
I wrote to the police superintendent:
'Please send two *intelligent* officers.'

The old drunkard looked at the letter
and started laughing and said:
'Who has ever heard of intelligent officers?
Write "intelligence officers", not "intelligent officers".'

It is almost impossible
to find an intelligent officer,
because it is almost impossible
to find an intelligent man.
Intelligence is absolutely lacking.

When you have money, enjoy it.
Live like a king when you have it.

But I see people —
they have money and they live like beggars.
They are saving it for the future,
and when it is lost,
then they start thinking about it:
'Why did we waste time? We should have enjoyed.'

Poor persons, poor people,
always thinking about living in palaces,
while they can enjoy the tree where they are.
The singing birds, and the sun, and the air —
the world is more open to a poor man.
A poor man can enjoy a beautiful sleep,
because for a rich man, sleep has become difficult.
He may have better sleeping-rooms,
he may have more comfortable mattresses,
but he will not be able to sleep.
Then he will think about beggars
and will feel envious and jealous
that these poor people are sleeping so well, snoring,
and, 'I cannot sleep.'

When you can sleep well, sleep well.
When you have beautiful mattresses, enjoy them —
and suffer insomnia.
But be intelligent!

*Ancient Jewish mythology
places Lilith as the first person on earth —
not Adam.
Why was this version lost?
Would you tell us about it?*

There is not a secret in it, just male chauvinism.
It was difficult for man to think
that a woman was made first and man followed.

The True Sage

No — it is against the pride.

The original version said
that Lilith was created first —
and it seems natural that woman should come first,
because she carries the womb.
A woman should come first.
That seems natural, biological, true.
But it is difficult for man to entertain the idea.
He changed the story.
He created another myth that Adam was created first.
But then there was trouble —
because then how to produce Eve from Adam?
So a rib was taken, because there was no womb.
Now the whole story is foolish.

With a woman it would remain simple.
With man it was almost impossible.
A rib was taken out and Eve was created.

The first story is true. I agree with the first.
I reject the second.

15th October 1975

When the son
   of the Rabbi of Lentshno was a boy
he saw Rabbi Vitzhak of Vorki,
   praying.
Full of amazement,
   he came running to his father
and asked how it was possible
   for such a zaddick
to pray quietly and simply,
   without giving any sign of ecstasy.

His father answered:—
   'A poor swimmer has to thrash around
in order to stay up in the water.
   The perfect swimmer rests on the tide
and it carries him.'

The perfect swimmer

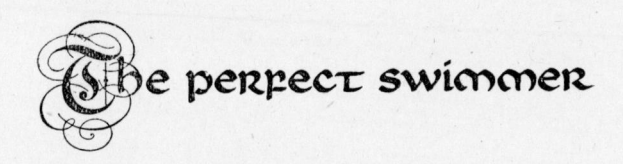

THERE is one very ancient tale.
If you listen well,
you will find yourself also in it.
But if you only hear it,
you will laugh at it and forget it.

Sometimes you simply laugh to forget a thing,
to hide a thing.
Many times I have observed that you laugh
just to hide your tears.
You laugh, because if you don't laugh,
it will be too much, too heavy.
Laughter is a way of avoiding a thing.
So please, listen to it as deeply as you can.

I know hearing is simple,
and listening is very difficult.
You hear it
and you think that you have listened to it.
Hearing is just mechanical.

When you listen with perfect awareness,
then listening becomes possible.

The True Sage

Hearing is just like eating without tasting.
You can fill the belly,
but deep down, the hunger remains.
The body may be satisfied, even overloaded,
but the subtle hunger remains —
because it can be satisfied only
when you become capable of taste.
But to taste a thing is to be aware, alert.

Listen to it —
the story is one of the most wonderful
I have ever come across.
It is a Hassidic story.

It says that there was a very great city.
It appeared great to those who lived in it.
In fact, it was not bigger than a small saucer.
The houses of the city were skyscrapers.
And the people who were the dwellers —
they claimed that their house tops
almost touched the sky.
But to those who were not deluded,
the height of the city
looked not more than that of an onion.

In that city,
people of ten cities were assembled —
millions of people.
But to those who could count,
there were only three fools in that city,
not a single person more.

The first fool was a great thinker;
he was a great system-maker, a metaphysician —
almost an Aristotle.
He could talk about anything.
You could ask him, and he had readymade answers.

The Perfect Swimmer

It was spread in the town, the rumour was in the town
that he was the greatest seer.

Of course, he was absolutely blind.
He could not see the Himalayas
just in front of his eyes,
but he could count the legs of the ants
crawling on the moon.
And he was absolutely blind —
but he was a logic-chopper.

He saw things which nobody had ever seen:
God, angels, heaven and hell.
He was very condemnatory of the mundane world
which could be seen.
He was always appreciating the unseen,
which he only could see and nobody else could see.

The second man used to hear the music of the spheres.
He used to hear the dancing atoms,
the harmony of existence —
but he was stone-deaf.

And the third fool, the third man,
was absolutely naked.
He had nothing.
He was the poorest man who had ever existed —
except that he had a sword
which he always carried on guard.
He was always afraid, he was paranoid —
afraid that somebody was going to rob him someday.
Of course, he had nothing.

They all conferred because there was a rumour
that their city was in a deep crisis.
All the three fools who were thought to be very wise
were asked to go deep into the phenomenon:
Is it true that the city is in danger?

The True Sage

Some crisis is coming? Some future catastrophe?

The blind man looked into the far horizon
and said: 'Yes. I can see thousands of soldiers
of the enemy country coming.
I cannot only see them,
I can count how many there are.
I can see to which race
and to which religion they belong.'

The deaf man listened silently, brooded,
and said: 'Yes. I can hear what they are saying,
and I can also hear what they are not saying
and hiding in their hearts.'

The beggar jumped, the third fool jumped,
took his sword in his hand, and said: 'I am afraid.
They are going to rob us.'

This is your story.
Think about it.
Move around and around and penetrate deeper into it.
This is the story of man.

Man is always pretending that which he is not;
that's a way of hiding oneself.
The ugly man tries to look beautiful.
The man who is in anguish tries to look happy.
The man who does not know anything
tries to prove that he knows all.
This is how it goes on and on.
And unless you become aware
of these three fools within you,
you will never become a sage.
To go beyond the three fools,
one becomes the true sage.

Try to stick to the fact;
don't try to hide it in a fiction.

Fictions are easy, cheap;
one need not do anything, one can simply imagine —
and imagination is a way of auto-hypnosis.
If you go on continuously repeating something,
you will start feeling that you have that thing.

What have you got in this world?
What do you possess?
You don't possess even yourself.
Then why are you so afraid
that somebody is going to rob you?

People come to me and they say:
'We cannot trust because we are afraid.'

I ask them: 'Why are you afraid? What have you got?'

They say: 'If we trust, somebody may deceive us' —
the third fool.

What have you got?
Empty-handed you come. Empty-handed you go.
And just in between, between and betwixt,
the foolishness that you possess something.

That is the meaning of Jesus
when he says that even camels
can pass through the eye of a needle,
but a rich man will not be able to enter
into the kingdom of God.
What does he mean by rich man? —
he means one who has nothing and thinks that he has.

Everybody is poor.
Empty-handed we come. Empty-handed we go.
All ideas of richness are fictions.

By a rich man
Jesus doesn't mean those who have on this earth.
Nobody has anything.

The poor are poor; the rich are also poor —
sometimes even poorer than the poor,
because they are more deluded that they have something.

If *you* have something, Jesus is right:
a camel can pass through the eye of a needle,
but you will not be able to pass
through the kingdom of God.
The doors will be closed.
It is not for fools.

And the very idea that you possess something is foolish.
And once the idea settles in,
then you try to protect it,
then everybody else becomes the enemy —
because everybody else is trying to snatch
that which you have.
In the first place you don't have anything.

The more you protect,
the more others think
that you must be having something.
Otherwise, why are you protecting so much?
They are running after you,
thinking that you must have something.
Seeing that they are running after you,
you think there is danger and that protection is needed.
This is how the vicious circles goes on.

Nobody has anything in this world.
Once you realize this, all fear disappears.
Once you realize this, you have become a sannyasin.
Not that you leave your houses,
and your wife, and children, and the world,
and move to a mountain top — no.
Those who are running to the mountain tops —
they still think
that they are leaving something that they had.
That is the very foolishness.

First you were deluded that you have;
now you are deluded that you have renounced —
but the basic hynosis still exists.
First you continuously counted your money —
how much you have.
Now you will be counting how much you have renounced.
But renunciation is nothing but the other side
of the bank balance,
the other side of the river, of the market.

A man who knows has nothing to renounce,
because a man who knows
and comes to understand his situation,
knows that he has nothing.
How can you renounce? What can you renounce?
Your hands are empty.
And suddenly — you are moving in a different space.
The possession, the renunciation —
both have become irrelevant.

There are persons who come to me.
I can see that I am in front of them
and they cannot see me.
But they say they have visions, spiritual visions.
Beautiful colours float in their minds.
Kundalini arises, the snake-power, the serpent-power.
It rushes towards the last chakra.

I am in front of them and I can see they are blind;
they can't see me.
Their kundalini is arising,
and they have tremendous light in their third eye.
And they have come, so that I can confirm:
'Yes, that's so.'

If I say: 'Yes, that's so,'
they are very happy and fulfilled.
If I say: 'No,' they are very angry.

They become my enemies.
And they cannot see me —
but they can count the legs of the ants
crawling on the moon.
They are stone-blind.
To hide their blindness,
they create many fictions around themselves.

A man came to me.
He said: 'Just as it happened in Mohammed's life,
it is happening in my life.
I receive messages in the night.
God Himself, Allah — He gives me messages.
But the trouble is that in the morning,
I always forget what the message was.'
It happened in Ahmedabad.

I told him: 'Do one thing.
Keep a pad and a pencil just near your bed,
and while you go to sleep,
continuously go on remembering
that whenever God reveals anything,
your sleep will be immediately broken,
and you will be able to write.
And write it, whatsoever it is.

He said: 'These messages are tremendous truths.
They can transform the whole world.
The trouble is — I always forget in the morning.'

So I said: 'You do it —
and whatsoever it is, you bring it.'

Next day he came.
He was very much worried
and sad, and depressed, and frustrated.
I said: 'What happened?'

The Perfect Swimmer

He said: 'I cannot believe what happened.
Whatsoever you have said, I have followed.
I went on remembering while I was falling asleep
that whenever the message is delivered,
I will be able to get up immediately
and write the message down.
And it happened as you said.'

'But then,' I said, 'why are you so sad?'

He said: 'But the message makes me very sad.'

'What was the message?'

He was feeling a little embarrassed.
The message was: 'Live a little hot. Sip a Gold Spot.'
The advertisement board was just in front of his house.
He must have been passing and. . . .

So he said: 'Please don't say this to anybody,
because I am very much frustrated.
How did it happen?
Is it some kind of joke God is playing on me?'

Your dreams are bound to be your dreams:
'Live a little hot. Sip a Gold Spot.'
They cannot go beyond it!
Your visions are your visions;
they cannot be more than you.
Your experiences are your experiences.
They are bound to be below you; they cannot be beyond you.
Your kundalini is going to be your kundalini;
it cannot be a Buddha's kundalini.

Ninety-nine percent is the possibility
that you have been imagining.
Man is so poor, he imagines in millions of ways
to convince himself: 'I am rich.'

If you have not been able to attain
to the worldly things,
then you start attaining to the non-worldly things.
If you don't have a bank balance here on the earth,
then you have a bank balance there in heaven —
but you have a bank balance.

Remember always : your mind is stupid.
Mind as such is stupidity. Mind cannot be intelligence.
Intelligence happens only when the mind has gone.
Intelligence is not the function of the mind ;
it is the function of the whole.
Mind is stupid, repetitive.
It cannot know the unknown,
it can only go on repeating the known —
'Live a little hot. Sip a Gold Spot.'
Continuously looking at the advertisement board,
it has become settled.

If you are born a Hindu, your kundalini will rise.
If you are born a Jain, never —
because Jain scriptures don't advertise for kundalini.
If you are a Christian, you will see Christ and the cross.
But if you are a Hindu,
Christ never bothers to come on your path.
And the cross — never.
You will see Krishna playing on the flute,
because Krishna is advertised
and Christ is not advertised.

All your spiritual experiences are nothing but conditionings
that the society has given to you.
Don't rely too much on them,
because death will force you to realize the fact
that you lived a fictitious life —
the opportunity lost.

The Perfect Swimmer

Become aware that you have nothing.
Once you feel that you have nothing, fear disappears,
because fear is always part of the feeling
that you possess something which can be lost —
hence fear.

When you realize the fact
that you don't know anything,
that you are blind, that you cannot see. . . .

All that you have been seeing is your own projection.
You create it and you see it.
You are the director in the drama
that you call your life.
And you are the storywriter also.
And you are the actor.
And you are all that is happening.
And you are the audience.
There is nobody else.
You are looking at it.
You are creating it.
You are directing it.
You are playing a role in it.

Once this is seen —
and this can be seen in a flash of light,
just by listening to me rightly, it can be seen —
then the whole drama disappears.
This is what Hindus call *maya*,
the world that you have created around yourself,
which is not real, which is not there —
your own creation.

When it drops,
then for the first time, you are not blind;
your eyes open.
Then you see that which is.

The True Sage

Don't go on listening to distant harmonies,
and the music of the spheres,
and the dancing steps of the atoms.
Don't befool yourself.
As it is, you have already befooled yourself too long.
No more. It is enough!
Say: 'It is enough' —
because unless you are freed
from your wrong notions of eyes, and ears, and riches,
the right cannot become available to you.

To be freed from the wrong
is to be available to the right.
To be freed from the false
is to be on the path of that which is real.

And remember this trick of the mind:
that the mind creates the opposite.
If you are angry, you have a polite smile on your face.
The mind creates the opposite.
If you are afraid,
you have fearlessness showing on the face.
If you are full of hatred,
you go on trying so many love affairs.

It is said about Lord Byron
that he fell in love with hundreds of women.
Looks like a great lover, a Don Juan — but he is not.
He must have been too full of hatred.
He could not love anybody.

When you cannot love anybody,
when the love is not flowing,
you go on moving with new partners
just to create an illusion
that you are a great lover —
you love so many people.

One love is enough!
If it is really love, it can satisfy you so deeply,
it can make you so contented,
such infinite tranquility can happen through it,
there is no need for anything else.
But when it is not there,
then you move from one to another.

I was reading a drama.
The drama belongs to the category
that they now call 'Absurd Drama'.
The curtain rises.
The actors are there, sitting in a restaurant.
There are a few people.
The waiters are serving.
And the people are eating, enjoying food, talking —
saying how beautiful it is.
But in fact, nothing is happening.
The waiters are only doing the movements;
they are not bringing food.
And the eaters are only doing the movements of eating,
they are not eating food.

But everybody is afraid:
'If I say that there is no food,
then the whole restaurant, so many people,
will think me mad.'

Everybody is eating,
but on nobody's plate is there any food.
People are putting the food in the mouth,
biting, chewing, eating, *and* enjoying,
and telling about it, how beautiful it is.
You have to follow;
otherwise, you will be the only one
who is mad, who has gone mad, insane.

And everybody is in the same situation :
afraid to say that there is no food,
and that the waiters are bringing only empty plates,
and that the people are eating nothing —
just empty movements of the hands and the mouth.
Not only that —
the people are describing how tasteful it is,
how delicious it is.
You will be mad if you say anything.
It is better not to say.
Save your sanity and go home.

Everybody moves out of the restaurant,
talking about the food.
But everybody is hungry. And everybody seems tired.
When you make empty movements, you are bound to be tired.
Everybody seems wearied of life, almost dead —
but still talking about the food.

This is the situation about love.
You fall in love, you do the movements,
but love is not there, real food is not there.
You simply do the movements
that lovers are expected to do.
And not only that —
then you say : 'How beautiful !'
You know deep down that there is nothing,
nothing is happening.
But if you say that nothing is happening,
you will be found to be wrong.

The whole world lives in dreams.
If you want to live with them, you have to be a part.
You say : 'Yes. So beautiful' —
but then you are wearied and tired.
And the whole life
seems like a long boredom, non-ending.

And again and again, the same routine you follow.
And again and again, you come to the same frustration.

Look! Is not this your life?
The mind will say: 'No, this is not my life;
it may be of others.'
But that is the way of the mind to protect oneself.
'Others may be fools; I'm not.'

The wise man thinks in a different way.
Says Lao Tzu: 'Everybody seems to be very very wise;
I am the only idiot here.'
The wise man looks like an idiot.

Let me tell you a Hassidic tale.
It happened: from Poland, a group of Jews
were migrating to America.
In old Jewish communities, it has always been so:
there was always a village sage,
and there was always a village idiot —
to balance things.

And Jews are very balancing.
It has to be balanced that way.
If the village has a sage, the village needs an idiot also.
Otherwise, who will balance?
The sage may create too much wisdom;
it may become indigestable.
He may become too heavy with his advice,
he may create too much seriousness around.
An idiot is needed — to bring balance to things.

Rarely, but sometimes it also happened
that it was the same man — the sage and the idiot.
Then the sage flowers perfectly,
because then the village is not balanced;
the man *himself* is balanced.
And it was such a case in this story.

The True Sage

The village idiot,
or you can call him the village sage —
his name was Yosel.
He was also migrating with the whole community.

After the third day, there was a great storm.
Life was in danger.
The ship would be sinking any moment.
It was chaos —
the captain shouting orders,
the sailors lowering the lifeboats,
children crying, women screaming,
and all the passengers milling around the deck
in deep confusion, afraid.
It was great pandemonium.
Only Yosel was amused.
He was watching everybody, smiling.
He was entertained by the whole situation.

An old man of the village scolded Yosel:
'This is too much. The ship is sinking!
What are you doing? Amusing yourself?'

Yosel said: 'Why are you getting so excited, Uncle?
Does the ship belong to you?'
This can be the statement of an idiot,
this can be the statement of a sage.
It can be both. It *is* both.

There is a point
where the sage and the idiot meet,
where the sage looks like the idiot,
where the idiot looks like the sage —
because opposites merge
and a single synthesis is attained.

A sage has nothing to defend;
he can afford to be an idiot.
You cannot afford to be an idiot

The Perfect Swimmer

because you know you *are* an idiot,
and you have to defend it by your so-called wisdom.

What I am saying is:
you always create the opposite.
You are not one, you are a multitude, a crowd.
Whatsoever you feel inside,
you try to pretend just the opposite
so that no one comes to know your inner poverty,
your inner stupidity.
If you are stupid, you study scriptures.
You can find many stupid people
studying the Torah, the Bible, the Gita, the Koran —
hiding their stupidity.

It happened: one day, a man knocked at Naftali's house.
Naftali opened the door and, as was his custom,
he asked: 'Why have you come?'

The man said: 'I have come to study with you.'

Naftali closed the door and he said:
'Go somewhere else. I am not a teacher.
You can find somebody else who can teach you scriptures.'

'Why?' Naftali's wife asked.
'Why have you denied that man?
He looked like a sincere seeker.'

Naftali said:
'People who are interested in studying scriptures
are almost always stupid.
They want to hide.'

Another day, another man knocked.
Naftali opened the door and he asked:
'Why are you here? What do you want from me?'

The man said: 'I have come to be near you,
to learn how to serve humanity.'

Naftali said: 'Go away.
You have knocked on the wrong door.'

The wife was very much puzzled.
She said: 'He was not asking to study scriptures.
He seems to be a great social reformer
or something like that.
He wanted to serve humanity.
Such a pure, pious mind — why have you refused him?'

Naftali said: 'Those who don't know themselves —
they cannot serve anybody else.
All their service finally becomes a mischief.'

Social reformers are mischievous people
unless they know themselves.
How can you serve anybody?
And how can you serve humanity?
You have not served that small being
that is within you.
Light it first —
then try to light others' lives.
If you are dark within,
and you go and start helping others,
you will not help, you will harm —
because who is there to help?

Another day, another man knocked.
Naftali opened the door and asked:
'Why have you come here?'

The man said: 'I am very stupid.
Can you help me a little to get rid of it?'

Naftali kissed the man and said:
'Welcome. I am waiting for you.'

This is the first step towards wisdom:

The Perfect Swimmer

to realize that you are not wise,
to realize that no trick of hiding it
is going to help.

One who realizes that he is ignorant
is already on the path.
One who realizes that he is poor
is already on the path
of the Kingdom of God, the real treasure.
One who realizes that he is blind —
his eyes are already opening.
One who realizes that he is deaf
will sooner or later become capable of listening.
And then he will know the music,
the music of existence.

Don't try to create the opposite.
Rather, know the innermost quality of your being.
Don't hide it; open it to the sky.

If you hide it, you help it —
because in darkness it grows,
and becomes bigger and bigger,
and takes infinite proportions.
Open it to the light and the sky and the air
and it dies — because it cannot live in light.

Ignorance is like the roots of a tree:
if you bring them out, they die.
In the light they cannot survive.
They are the dwellers of darkness;
in the pure air they cannot survive.
But if you hide, then you help them grow.

Remember this:
whatsoever you feel inside, don't try to hide it,
because it can be hidden only by the opposite.

And then you will always be divided,
and you will never become one,
and you will never be a harmony.
And only the innermost harmony
can know the outermost harmony.
That's the meaning: only the soul can know God.
Soul means: inner harmony attained.
God means: you have become available to God
and God has became available to you.

Now, this small anecdote — very significant.

The Perfect Swimmer

*When the son
of the rabbi of Lentshno was a boy,
he saw Rabbi Vitzhak of Vorki,
praying.
Full of amazement,
he came running to his father
and asked how it was possible
for such a zaddik
to pray so quietly and simply,
without giving any sign of ecstasy.*

One of the most delicate
and significant points to be remembered:
agony becomes ecstasy.
If you are in deep agony,
then the same energy which was agony
will become ecstasy when you meditate.
You will dance with ecstasy,
but that is not the last point —
because even in your dance,
something of your agony will be present.
The ultimate dance happens only
when even dancing stops.

The Perfect Swimmer

You have seen Mira dancing, Chaitanya dancing;
nobody has seen Buddha dancing, Mahavir dancing.
Mira and Chaitanya have reached almost to the goal,
but one step more is needed.
They were unhappy; now they are happy.
They have transcended unhappiness.
Now they are in happiness —
but that too has to be transcended.
Because if you continue to be in happiness,
unhappiness will follow like a shadow.

Dualities go together.
If you are dancing,
sooner or later, you will fall in agony again —
because the energy is the same.
It was anguish within.
You were hiding it; it was like a wound.
Now you have expressed it —
the same energy released, and you are dancing.
But you have not gone beyond.

Dancing is good, but it is allowed only
up to the steps of the temple, not inside.
Nobody reaches God without dancing;
nobody reaches God with dancing.
One has to dance, so that the agony is transformed,
but agony transformed is still agony.
It has become beautiful, it has lost its poison,
but still, it is of the same category.

For example, I tell you a joke.
You laugh,
but your laughter has something
of your sadness in it;
it is bound to be so.
You are sad for twenty-four hours.
You laugh out of your sadness.

In fact, you laugh because of the sadness,
because it becomes too much.
One has to release.
It becomes such a tension, a built-up tension —
you have to release.
You laugh loudly —
good, therapeutic, but nothing spiritual.
Good, medicinal, but medicine has to be dropped
when you are really healthy.

If you have to keep your medicine
continuously with you,
then something of the illness is still lingering on.
When the disease has completely gone,
you throw the medicine also.
When the pain has gone,
what is the point of carrying pleasure?
When the suffering is no more,
what is the point of celebrating?
Then your whole being is a celebration,
then you don't celebrate.
Then your whole being is a laughter,
then you don't laugh.

The perfection of laughter
is almost like no laughter.
And the perfection of happiness
has nothing of happiness in it,
because if something of happiness is still there,
you can watch —
just by the corner, unhappiness is waiting for you.
Any moment it can jump, and possess you.

A happy person can become unhappy.
You cannot make a Buddha unhappy
because he is no more happy;
he is beyond the clutches of duality.

The Perfect Swimmer

The child was worried,
because the zaddik, a Master, meditating —
and not in any ecstasy?

Hassidic disciples are very escatatic people;
they dance, they sing, they enjoy.
Delight is their prayer, and it should be so,
because there is no other way
to express your thankfulness,
your gratefulness to God.
Delight, dance, tears of joy;
that is the only prayer possible.

*When the son
of the rabbi of Lentshno was a boy,
he saw Rabbi Vitzhak of Vorki,
praying.*

The boy must have seen many Hassidic disciples,
dancing, full of tears of joy,
weeping, crying, embracing each other,
in deep gratitude, in deep remembrance of God.
The boy must have seen
that when people meditate, they celebrate.

*Full of amazement,
he came running to his father
and asked how it was possible
for such a zaddik, such a great Master
to pray quietly and simply,
without giving any sign of ecstasy.*

He does not seem to be happy,
he does not seem to be celebrating —
not a single expression around him of ecstasy.
How is it possible?
And he is such a great Master.

The True Sage

The child must have heard
many things about the zaddik —
that he has attained.
He is asking: 'What is he doing?
In his silence, ecstasy is not happening.
Something is lacking.'
This is the childish attitude.

If you bring a child to Buddha,
he will think something is lacking.
But if you bring the child to Chaitanya,
he will know that everything is there,
that nothing is lacking.
Chaitanya is dancing, drums are beating.
He is ecstatic, intoxicated —
he is not of this world.
He is lost somewhere into the unknown.
Any child will be able to recognize
that something has happened.

To be with a Buddha is to be mature.
Chaitanya can be followed even by children.
That is what is happening to Hare Krishna people —
childish, immature.
But they think that this is how one attains.
Nothing is wrong in dancing — remember.
But one should remember:
dancing, ecstasy, is just outside the temple.
Inside, everything has to become silent;
your very being has to dissolve.
Who will dance there? You are no more.

His father answered:
'A poor swimmer has to thrash around
in order to stay up in the water.
The perfect swimmer rests on the tide
and it carries him.'

The Perfect Swimmer

Mira dancing, Chaitanya dancing —
something still imperfect, not perfect swimmers yet.
Learning, reaching, reaching nearer every day —
but if you are still swimming,
you are afraid of the river, you have not accepted it.
If you are still swimming,
your swing has moved to the other extreme,
but has not attained to the middle point
where everything stops.

Mind moves from one polarity to another.
You are angry; then you feel compassion.
You are full of hate; then you feel love.
Watch it!
Whenever you are hateful, suddenly, in the wake,
a very loving, caring attitude follows.

All lovers know it:
whenever they fight, are angry,
and there has been a conflict,
a clash of personalities,
in the wake, a very deep love follows.
The greatest peaks that lovers attain
are all always after the fight,
because when you are fighting,
you are moving in one direction —
just like the pendulum of an old clock.
It moves to the left, goes to the very extreme.
Apparently it is going to the left,
but deep down it is earning momentum,
gaining momentum to go to the right.
Then from that same energy it will go to the right.
When it goes to the right,
you will see it is going to the right,
but it is again gaining momentum to go to the left.

When you are angry, you are gaining momentum to love.

The True Sage

When you are in love,
you are gaining momentum to be angry.
This is how the pendulum of the mind goes on.

So Mira has moved from the world.
The agony of the world has gone —
the ecstasy of God has happened.
But this is also movement.

Buddha is just standing in the middle.
The clock has stopped, the time has stopped,
the movement has stopped,
the pendulum moves no more.
There is no tick, tock — absolute silence.

You will be impressed more by Mira and Chaitanya
and you will not be impressed so much by a Buddha,
because Buddha will be too beyond you.

You can understand Mira.
She may be opposite, but the language is the same.
You are in agony; she is in ecstasy —
but the language is the same.
What is ecstasy? — not agony.
What is agony? — not ecstasy.
The language is the same. You can understand.

And you can be greedy about it,
and you can cherish an idea, a hope
that someday you will also be able
to dance like Mira.
What beauty, what happiness, what ecstasy —
but the language is the same!
And remember, you can understand only that
for which you have a language, a common language.

It happened: a religious man,
a very simple, sincere, authentic man
was invited to a town.

The Perfect Swimmer

The man who was arranging
for his lectures in the town was a politician.
He had always been arranging tours
of politicians, presidents, prime ministers,
ministers, chief ministers, this and that.
He was the best convener in the town,
so people persuaded him: 'You do this also.'

The religious man was absolutely unknown
to the politician, the convener.
He had heard his name, he knew about him,
but still, he had never been in contact
with any religious man.

Politics has nothing to do with religion,
and if it has to do something with religion,
it is itself politics, it is not religion.
They are diametrically opposite goals.
A politician cannot be religious;
a religious man cannot be political.
Because a religious man cannot be ambitious.

The religious man was to come
and he was also apprehensive,
because the town was new and the man was unknown.
So he telegrammed before he came:
'Arrange a room in the circuit house —
silent, vegetarian food, cow's milk,
etcetera, etcetera, etcetera.'

He arrived. Everything was arranged.
Everything was as he had wanted. He was happy.
Then he went into the bathroom to wash his face
because he was tired from the journey.
But immediately he came back very puzzled,
because in the bathroom he saw three beautiful women —
but still, they were ugly; they looked like prostitutes.
He came back and he asked the politician:
'What is the matter? Who are these three women?'

The True Sage

The politician said: 'Who are these three women? —
the three etceteras!
Etcetera, etcetera, etcetera.'

The religious man was aghast, he couldn't believe it.
'What do you mean?
I have never come to understand
that etcetera means a woman.'

The politician said:
'You don't know the language of the politicians.
I have always been arranging for them,
and this is a code word: etcetera.
If they write one etcetera, one woman;
if they write two, two;
if they write three, three.'

You understand a particular language.
You can understand Chaitanya and Mira —
however far away they may be,
because your agony
can understand the language of ecstasy.
In fact, agony is seeking ecstasy constantly.

The child could not understand.
A great zaddik, praying quietly and simply,
without giving any sign of ecstasy —
not dancing, not swaying, tears not flowing.
By his face, you cannot say what he is doing.

In fact, when you are really in prayer,
you are not doing anything at all.
Prayer has nothing to do with doing,
it is simply being.
Being in the presence of God is prayer.
Feeling the presence of God is prayer.
Dissolving yourself in Him is prayer.
Agony will take you away.

Ecstasy will also keep you away.
Remember this.

Ecstasy is better than agony,
but both exist around the subtle ego.
When you are lost, who can be ecstatic? —
you are no more there,

The child could not understand.
A child can never understand,
because a child can understand tears, happiness —
the language of immaturity.

Many times, Hare Krishna people come to me,
and I see such immature minds.
But they think this is all: jumping on the streets,
singing 'Hare Krishna, Hare Ram . . . '
Of course, it gives a sort of excitement,
and a sort of intoxication.
It is alchoholic, but it is not the goal.
The goal is absolute silence.
Such tranquility, that there is nothing else in it.
Pure tranquility.

The child could not understand.
And the child within you
will also be unable to understand.

His father answered:
'A poor swimmer has to thrash around
in order to stay up in the water.'

So don't think that is swimming.
It is just a poor swimmer, just a beginner.
He thrashes around, throws his hands.
Don't think that is swimming; that is just learning.

When a swimmer has become really perfect, attuned,
he knows that now there is no need to swim.
He can trust the river.

The True Sage

He can leave all thrashing,
because that thrashing is still a fight,
a sort of struggle — trying to conquer the river.

*'A perfect swimmer rests on the tide
and it carries him.'*

A perfect meditator rests on the tide of God,
and it carries him.
He does not do anything,
because with doing, the ego remains.
With non-doing, it disappears.
He is not in agony, he is not in ecstasy.
All that we can understand, the ordinary language,
has become useless.

That's why, when you ask a Buddha :
'What have you attained?' —
he keeps quiet, he does not answer.
Because whatsoever he will say will be misunderstood —
'etcetera, etcetera, etcetera.'
You have your language, a code language.
Whatsoever he says will be misunderstood.
If he says : 'I am ecstatic,' what will you understand ?
You will understand that he is not in agony.
If he says : 'I am happy,' you will say :
'Right. So he is no more unhappy.
That's what I need to be.
That's my greed also, my hope also.'
Your desire will be provoked.
And the happiness of a Buddha
comes only when you become desireless.
Whatsoever a Buddha says
is bound to be misunderstood.

Lao Tzu says : 'When people don't understand me,
I know well, I have said something true.

When they understand, then I know well
that something has gone wrong.'

'Etcetera, etcetera, etcetera . . . . '
You have your own language.
Buddhahood has its own language.
It is neither of agony nor of ecstasy;
it is of a deep let-go.
Let-go is the language of a Buddha.

*'A perfect swimmer rests on the tide
and it carries him.'*

I was reading the life of Rabbi Leib.
Somebody asked him: 'You lived with your Master,
your zaddik, for twelve years.
What were you studying there? What were you observing?
Twelve years is a long time — almost a whole life.
Have you been studying the scriptures?'

Rabbi Leib said: 'No.
I was not there with my zaddik to study the Torah.
I was there to watch my zaddik, my Master.
To watch him — how he unlaces his felt shoes,
how he laces them again.
It took twelve years to watch simple movements,
because each of his movements was meditation:
the way he breathes,
the way he stands up,
the way he sits down,
the way he sleeps. . . .
It is such a mystery that it took me twelve years —
first to forget my own language which was a barrier,
to clean my mind completely of all that I know.
And then, by and by, glimpses started coming to me.
Then, by and by, clouds separated
and I could see my Master.'

If you can see your Master,
you have seen meditation incarnate.
It is not a question of doing;
the being has to be watched.

The rabbi of Lentshno was right,
the child's father was right,
because he had attained to maturity.
Drop the child within you — become mature, alert.
Watch —
that your language should not distort what I say.
Always look to what I mean.
You will be the only barrier in it.

If you listen through your mind,
you hear me, but you don't listen to me.
If you put aside your mind, and look at me,
you listen to me.
Right listening is the door.
Through right listening,
right seeing will become possible.
Through right seeing,
the right world of riches becomes available.

Those three fools are within your minds.
By and by, drop them.
Don't protect your mind
because your mind is the enemy.
And that's what you have been doing continuously:
you go on protecting it.
Surrender it. There is no need to thrash around.

'A poor swimmer has to thrash around
in order to stay up in the water.'

Here you are with me, with a tide.
Relax. Let go — and allow the tide to carry you.

The Perfect Swimmer

This is what sannyas is:
a deep let-go with someone who has arrived.

Don't be a poor swimmer.
You have thrashed around too much already.
You are so tired — and the tide is available.

Trust the river,
and the river will take you to the ocean —
and there is no other way to reach to the ocean.
Fight, and you will lose.
Surrender, and in your surrender is the victory.

16th October 1975

Questions and answers

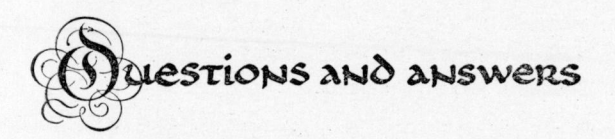

I don't have eyes to see. I don't have ears to hear.
And I am absolutely stupid.
You promise us liberation some day.
How is that possible
with such a helpless case as I am?
And on the other hand,
sometimes I am filled with grace
which no words can describe.
What happens? And where am I in all this?

A good beginning.
If you can feel that you don't have eyes to see,
sooner or later, you will have eyes.
To feel that you are ignorant,
you have taken the first step towards knowledge.
To feel that you are lost is to attain to the path.
That is why sometimes you are filled with grace.
The very understanding that you are ignorant
suddenly illuminates your being.

The problem is with those people who think they know.
They are in real trouble.
They know not and they think they know.

So there is no possibility for their growth.
And they insist and they defend their knowledge.
In defending their knowledge,
they are defending their ignorance.

If you are ill, you seek a physician.
But if you pretend that you are not ill,
and you are ill,
you avoid the physician.
Even if the physician comes to your home,
you will say : 'Why have you come here ?'

Gurdjieff, working with his disciples one day,
told a group :
'Unless you know your chief characteristic
and become aware of it,
you will not be able to enter into your essence
and you will remain stuck to your personality.'

Somebody asked : 'Please give us concrete examples.'

Gurdjieff said : 'Look at the man
who is sitting in front of me.
His chief characteristic is that he is never at home.'
Everybody could see the absent-mindedness
on the man's face.

But the man shrugged his shoulders and said :
'What did you say sir ?' —
because that is the chief characteristic :
he is not at home.
He is always somewhere else, and he wants to grow.
Impossible — because you have to be at home to grow.

Then Gurdjieff turned to another and said :
'Look at this man.
His chief characteristic is that he is always arguing
with everybody and everything.'

The man became very heated and said:
'Sir, there you are wrong! I never argue!'

Find out what you are defending.
That may be the clue to enter within.

Just last night,
a sannyasin said that from her very childhood,
she has been feeling that she is stupid.
And she is afraid, so she goes on defending.
She tries not to do anything which is stupid.
Now she is in a mess, because what can you do?
You can avoid, but *who* will avoid? —
the stupid mind will avoid.
In avoiding, you will do the same stupidity again.

A stupid person ...
and all persons are stupid
unless they bceome aware and alert.
All persons are stupid.
So when I say stupid, I don't mean any condemnation —
I simply indicate a state of unawareness.
Everybody is born stupid.
Fortunate are the few who don't die stupid.

Stupidity is the sleep you live in.
How can you avoid it?
How can a man who is fast asleep avoid dreaming?
If he tries, he will create another dream.
In the very avoidance, he will do something stupid.

Don't avoid it. Accept it!
Because avoidance is trying to defend it.
You don't want anybody to know that you are stupid,
but that is not going to help.
And the trouble is, that by avoiding continuously,
you may yourself forget that you are stupid.

Then you are settled in it. Then there is no way out.
That's how you have created your troubles.
You have been avoiding them.
Then you deceive others and by and by
you are deceived yourself.

People come to me with problems,
but those are not the real problems.
Rarely a person comes with an authentic problem.
Otherwise they don't know exactly
what their problem is.
They have a false problem,
so they can be engaged in solving it.

They will never be able to solve it —
because a real disease can disappear;
an unreal disease cannot disappear.
In the first place, it is not there.
How to make it disappear?
And by fighting with the wrong disease,
they are defending the right disease.
They are engaged in fighting
with something which is absolutely pseudo.
So they are giving time
for the real disease to grow and spread,
and become a cancerous phenomenon in their being.

To look at the right problem is difficult
because from the very beginning
you have been taught to avoid.

In the Poona newspapers, every day I see somebody dies,
a husband dies, a wife dies,
and in the memory a picture is printed:
'My wife left for the heavenly abode,
this very day, one year ago.'

You don't say 'death'.

That word is too real and hits too hard.
'Left for heavenly abode. . . . '
Who are you deceiving? —
not the wife who has already left.
You are deceiving yourself.
You are afraid of death.
You are hiding death in a beautiful terminology:
'heavenly abode'.
Now there is no fear;
in fact, even a little desire to go yourself.

The basic problem is death.
You have made a code and you may forget completely.
And this is how you are working with life.
You feel angry, but you don't say that you are angry.
You say: 'I feel restless.'
Restlessness is not a condemnatory thing.

I was reading about a Quaker, a very religious Quaker.
One night, a thief entered. The Quaker got his gun.
He wanted to say: 'You son of a bitch,'
but he couldn't say that.
A quaker, a religious person, how can he say that?
So he said: 'Dear sir, you are standing in the place
where I am going to shoot.
Please don't move!
And I don't intend to kill you;
this is just accidental.
You are standing in the place where I am going to shoot.'
How can a Quaker kill?

You go on deceiving.
Your language, your philosophy, your religion —
everything.

Once it happened:

The True Sage

I was talking and I used the word 'pissing'.
Ananda Prem wrote a long letter to me immediately,
saying: 'Please don't use this word;
"urination" has to be used'.

'Urination' is clinical.
Nobody urinates. It is a texbook thing.
'Pissing' is alive. The very sound of it gives you the idea.
But reality has to be hidden.
And that day I understood why Ananda Prem is so upright —
she has been urinating!
You have to be uptight then.

Be real, authentic, true, true to life.
But even words. . . .
I will tell you one story.

A woman came to listen to a so-called saint
with her small child, a young boy.
Just in the middle of the discourse
the boy started fidgeting
and then he said loudly: 'I wanna go to piss.'

The saint was of course very angry —
such a mundane thing in such a sacred atmosphere.
He said: 'You have to teach manners to him.
Otherwise, don't bring him here.
This is not only unmannerly, it is insulting.'

The woman said: 'You tell me how to teach him.'

So he said: 'You can make a code word.
He can say: "I wanna sing." Then you will understand.'
So the woman taught the boy.

After one year it happened:
the saint came to visit the woman's house;
he stayed there.

Questions And Answers

One night, the woman had to go to another town;
her mother was ill,
so the saint was left with the child.
Just in the middle of the night, two o'clock,
the child awoke the saint and said: 'I wanna sing.'
But by that time, the saint had forgotten the code.
One year had passed and. . . .

So he said: 'Wanna sing? This is no time to sing!'

The child said: 'But I sing every day. Even twice.'

'But you are a very stupid child,' he said.
'In the day you can sing, but not in the night.
And don't disturb me! Keep quiet and go to sleep.'

After a few minutes, again the child said:
'But I cannot go to sleep.
And if you don't allow me,
it will come out by itself, I tell you!'

The saint said: 'What type of singing?
Even the neighbours will be disturbed.
You go to sleep!'

The boy said: 'I cannot sleep.
First I will have to sing.'

So the saint said: 'Okay.
You come near my ear and sing slowly.'

So the boy sang!
Then the saint understood the code.

Never hide in codes. Be true.
And life is simple,
but because of your pretensions
you complicate the whole thing.
Don't complicate it.

The True Sage

Ninety-nine percent of your illnesses
are your own working.
Be alert and watch.
If you are stupid, you are stupid.
This is the first ray of intelligence
that has happened to you:
that you feel that you are stupid —
perfectly beautiful.

To understand that one is stupid
is to already be intelligent.
To understand that one is blind and cannot see light,
one is already on the way.
Now something is possible.

But a blind man goes on imagining
that he knows what light is.
He dreams about light, he dreams about the eyes.
And if somebody says that he is wrong
he is ready to protect himself,
defend, rationalize, argue.

Look at the bare fact.
Whatsoever it is, to accept it is good.
You are blind — everybody is born blind.
Nobody comes with eyes.
If you have eyes, there is no need to come.
You come only to learn how to be able to see.
And from the very beginning,
you start thinking that you have eyes.

You come here to be enlightened.
Life is a process of enlightenment.
If you live it truly, Buddhahood is bound to happen.
It is not some accident; you carry the seed within you.
Just give the right soil and the seed will sprout,
and a Buddha will flower in you.

Questions And Answers

Buddhahood is not accidental,
is not only for the chosen few —
it is everybody's destiny.
Delay you can, but when you attain,
there is nothing to brag about.
I will repeat: Delay you can,
but when you attain it,
there is nothing to brag about.
It is very ordinary. It has to be so.
It is your intrinsic being. It is your essence.
Only the personality has to be dropped.
Personality is the falsification.

Watch. And always be true.
Whatsoever you say about yourself, be true,
and you will never be a loser.

In the beginning
it will seem that if you say that you are stupid,
everybody will know —
but stupidity is not such a thing
that you can hide it.
Everybody already knows *except* you.
Everybody already knows. Only you are deceived.
Drop all deceptions, because finally, eventually,
you will discover that nobody else was deceived,
only yourself.
And nobody is a loser for it. You lose.

Drop all codes. Drop all falsifications.
And when I say 'drop,'
I don't mean that any effort is needed.
Just see, and they drop. Seeing is dropping.
That's why if you feel: 'I don't have eyes to see,'
eyes start opening.
If you feel: 'I don't have ears to hear you,'
you have already heard me!

The True Sage

If you say : 'I am absolutely stupid,'
intelligence has arrived —
the first ray has penetrated your being.

You promise us liberation . . .

I don't promise you anything.
It is already promised by destiny.
You are here for it.

How can I promise something? Who am I to promise?
I can promise only because I know —
it is already there.
I know — whether you know it or not —
that it is already there.
I can see the flame inside you.
You may have forgotten it,
but I can penetrate and see.
I promise because I know it is already there.
Right now, it is the facticity of your being.
Nothing is to be done.
One just has to become a little more alert,
a little truer, a little more in the essence.

Don't cling to the personality
that you have created around you.
Go to the center.

You feel : *How is that possible
with such a helpless case as I am?*

Anybody who moves on the path feels helpless.
Only those who never move on the path
feel themselves very strong.
Anybody who moves on the path feels helpless,
because on the path one becomes flexible,
on the path one becomes aware — how things are.
One becomes aware how small one is.

One becomes aware of the tininess
of his own existence,
and the vastness of the reality around.
One is just a small drop in an infinite ocean.
Of course, one feels helpless.

But once you feel helpless,
the ego has been dropped.
And for the first time,
from every nook and corner of existence
help rushes towards you.
The whole ocean rushes towards you.
In your helplessness, the drop drops.
You become the ocean.

And that's why you say:
*On the other hand,
sometimes I am filled with grace.*

Yes, it happens.
It is part of the whole process.
If you feel helplessness,
you will feel grace reaching to you.

If you feel that you are already strong,
the door is closed.
You don't need grace.

There is a very ancient story.
Krishna is sitting down.
His wife, Rukhamani, has brought food for him,
and he was just going to take the first bite.
He dropped it and rushed towards the door.
Then he stopped at the door for a single moment,
came back, and started eating.

Rukhamani was puzzled.
She said: 'What is the matter?

The True Sage

You rushed towards the door
as if there is some great emergency,
as if the house is on fire or something,
or somebody is going to die.
And then you stopped, and then you came back.
I'm puzzled. Tell me, what is the secret?'

Krishna said: 'One of my devotees, a lover,
was passing through a big city.
He is almost mad in love with me.
People were throwing stones at him.
They thought he was crazy.
And when the stones hit him and the blood flowed,
he just said: 'Krishna, Krishna,' and danced.
He was so helpless, I was needed. So I rushed.'

Rukhmani asked: 'Then what happened?
Why did you come back from the door?'

Krishna said: 'By the time I reached the door,
he had taken one stone in his hand.
He was throwing stones himself.
Now I am not needed.
He has taken the whole situation in his own hands.
I am not needed.'

God comes to you when you are helpless.
When you are strong, God is not needed.
The divine reaches to you when you are empty.
When you are too full of yourself, there is no need.

Helplessness is the capacity to call, to invite grace.
Grace is always available; you only have to be helpless.

But in your ego, you feel you are strong.
You feel you are the master.
You feel nothing can harm you.
You feel everybody else dies, not you.

You feel very superior,
and nothing is there in that superiority;
it is just a bubble, a soap bubble —
inside, nothing but emptiness.
And you know it,
because anybody can touch the bubble
and it is no more there; it explodes.

Feel helpless and you will never be helpless again.
Feel empty and you will be full with the divine.
That's the secret.

*And on the other hand
sometimes I am filled with grace
which no words can describe.*

Yes, the grace cannot be described,
because when it comes,
the mind is not there which can describe.
When it comes, the mind ceases to exist.
Who can give and bring a report?
The reporter is not present.
It comes only when the mind is not,
and mind could have described.

*What happens?
And where am I in all this?*

You are nowhere in this.
The moment you come,
the grace has disappeared.
When you are not, God is.
When you are, God is not.
Your presence is His absence.
Your absence is His presence.
Crucify your ego and you will resurrect
into a greater infinite life.

Does a Buddha also need something as a complementary?
Who is complementary to a Buddha?

Buddha or Buddhahood is not any polarity.
It is not opposite to anything.
It is beyond the duality.
Night is against day.
Life is against death.
Love is against hate.
Buddhahood is not against anything.
It is to transcend the duality.

When you are neither day nor night,
you are a Buddha.
When you are neither life nor death,
you are a Buddha.
When you are neither this nor that, *neti neti*,
you are a Buddha.

Buddhahood simply means transcendence of duality.
So Buddhahood is all and nothing.
There is nothing as polar opposite to it,
and there is no complementary to it.
Remember this:
you would like to become a Buddha
because you would like to be happy.
But then you misunderstand.

Buddhahood is beyond happiness and unhappiness.
That was the insistence in yesterday's talk:
it is beyond agony, and beyond ecstasy also.
So the man who has really attained to ecstasy,
you will not see any ecstasy in him.
Agony has disappeared, ecstasy also.
The world has disappeared, and the nirvana also.
The body has disappeared, and the soul also —
because those are all opposites.
They are meaningful only when the other is present.

Have you observed?
If you ask the scientists: 'What is matter?'
they say: 'Not mind.'
'And what is mind?' — they say: 'Not matter.'
Now look at the foolishness.
When you want to define matter,
you have to bring mind in.
Mind itself is undefined yet.
To define one thing,
you bring another undefined thing.
How can you define something
by another undefined thing?
'What is matter?' — you say: 'Not mind.'
And when it is asked: 'What is mind?'
you bring matter in — that it is not matter.

Dualities depend on each other.
You cannot define love without bringing hate in.
What type of love is this
which needs hate to be defined?
You cannot define life without bringing death in.
This life cannot be much of a life.
What type of life is this
which needs death to define it?

There is a life beyond life and death,
and there is a love beyond love and hate.
That love, that life, is Buddhahood —
transcending all the opposites.

So don't choose!
If you choose, you will be in the quagmire.
Don't choose!
A choiceless awareness is the goal.
Just remain aloof; don't choose.
The moment you choose,
you have fallen into the trap of the world,
or into the trap of the mind.

The True Sage

It is reported that Rinzai, a great Zen Master,
was asked by a disciple:
'I have left the whole world, renounced all.
Now why am I still to wait for nirvana?
Why isn't the enlightenment happening?'

Rinzai said: 'You have left the world,
now leave enlightenment also.
Otherwise, it will not happen.
Because whatsoever you call enlightenment
is nothing but the opposite polarity of your world.
In your idea of enlightenment, your world still exists.
Maybe it exists as negated, but one still exists.
Drop enlightenment also.'

It is said the disciple understood. He laughed.
And the Master said: 'Finished. You attained.'

In a single moment it is possible.
But if you cling to the duality,
then for lives together you can go on and on and on.
Try to see the point.
It is only a question of vision and clarity.
Try to see the point that you cannot choose one
without choosing the opposite.
If you choose love, you have already chosen hate.
Love is a love-hate relationship.
If you choose love, you have already chosen hate.
It will lurk just behind your love,
and many times it will come up.
And you will have to relax,
because nobody can love for twenty-four hours.

Where will you relax?
You will relax in hate; it is lurking just by the side.
You will fight.
After a fight, again you are ready to love.
Now you are fed-up with hate. Again you fall in love.

This way you go on moving:
happy, unhappy; sad, ecstatic; in anguish, in bliss.
But these opposites are two aspects of the same coin.
When the head is up, the tail is hidden.
When the tail is up, the head is hidden.
Just close by, like a shadow, the opposite follows.

To understand this is to become a Buddha.
Then you don't desire,
because every desire will be a choice.
Then you don't say: 'I would like love,
and I don't want hate.'
If you want love you have already wanted hate,
you have already fallen into the trap.
Once you understand the duality and the trap of it,
you simply laugh, you don't choose.
You say: 'Enough. I understand now. I don't choose.
In that choicelessness
a pillar of awareness arises in you, a flame.
You are transformed.

Choicelessness is the alchemy of transformation,
of inner mutation.
A new being is born
who has nothing to do with the past,
who is absolutely discontinuous with the past.
He has no desire.
And when there is no desire,
for the first time you live.

Desire doesn't allow you to live.
It goes on forcing you towards the future.
It doesn't allow you to be here-now.
It doesn't allow you to let go.
It doesn't allow you to flow.
It doesn't allow you to move with the tide.
The desire creates fight.
The desire says: 'Fight for the goal.
You have to reach somewhere.'

The True Sage

Life is not reaching anywhere.
It is sheer delight! It is just here-now!
The desiring mind is always somewhere else.

What Gurdjieff said about that man
is true about many —
you are never at home.
You have made your abode in desires.
Life is always here,
and you are always somewhere else.
Except here, you may be anywhere.
But you are never here.
A choiceless consciousness is here-now.
It lives. Only *it* lives. Only *it* can live.
You only hope. You never live.
You think to live; you plan — but you never live.
Your whole life goes in planning —
thinking of the morrow,
thinking how to enjoy tomorrow, and missing today.
And there is no tomorrow.

I get bored in the discourse.
Then I fear and feel guilty.

This is from Swami Vishnu Chaitanya.
Boredom is your chief characteristic,
so don't avoid it.
Be bored. Know it. Watch it. Be aware of it.
There are many people
whose chief characteristic is boredom,
who are always bored in everything.

Maybe in the beginning . . . .
you fall in love with a woman and you are not bored,
but the next day, or the next hour, or the next minute,
you are bored — the same face, the same eyes,

and the topography is known, and the geography travelled.
Now there is nothing.
Finished. You are bored.

Every day the same sun rises,
and every day the same moon,
and every day things move in a circle and a routine,
and you are bored.
And every second the breathing comes in and goes out.
Nothing seems to be new.

You are excited sometimes when you see something new,
but soon it will be old.
Once it is old, excitement is gone.
Then you are again searching for something new.

I have heard:
Henry Ford was celebrating
his fiftieth wedding ceremony — golden jubilee.
He was a very happy man.
Rarely, after fifty years of marriage,
is one so happy with a wife as he was.

Somebody asked: 'This seems unbelievable,
and particularly in America.
It seems unbelievable
that you are still happy with a woman
that you have been married to for fifty years.
Fifty years looks almost like fifty centuries.
It looks like it is almost from the very beginning.
Fifty years, the whole life —
and you still feel happy? And you still look in love?
What is the secret?'

Henry Ford said: 'The same rule that I follow
in manufacturing cars — I stuck to the same model.
I have never tried to change the model of my cars,
and I have not tried to change the model of my wife.

But she is new every day.
She has never been old and I'm not bored.'

So boredom is because you don't know
how to find the newness every moment.
In a way it is true
that the same sun rises every day,
but it is not the same.
If you have the eyes to see,
it has never been the same.
The sky is different.
The poetry is different.
The colour is different.
It is never the same.
The climate is changing every moment.
Nothing has ever been the same.
In existence nothing repeats,
but it feels repetitive
because you are not intensely alert.

If you are intensely alert, everything is new.
If you are absolutely alert, everything is absolutely new.
Never does any dust of oldness settle on it.

In a way,
I go on saying the same thing every day.
In another way,
I have never uttered any single thing twice.
It depends on you.
If you listen while you are fast asleep, snoring,
you will be bored.
But don't blame me; it is your characteristic.

I am not bored with your faces.
Nor am I bored with your problems.
Every evening, excitedly, I wait for you.
Every morning, excitedly, I wait for you.

Questions And Answers

You are bored — so something must be wrong with you.

Just think of me — your problems and your faces,
and all sorts of stupidities that you bring.
I am always happy listening to them,
because to me, every individual is so unique
that you cannot bring anybody else's problem;
you always bring *your* problem.

You are changing every moment. You are a river.
Today you come in a different mood and climate.
Tomorrow you will come in a different mood and climate.
I have never seen the same face twice.
It changes. It is continuously changing.
But one needs penetrating eyes to see.
Otherwise, dust settles and everything becomes old,
and everything seems to be repetitive.
That is the attitude that decides.

Listen more consciously. Make yourself alert.
Whenever you feel that you are getting bored,
give a good jerk to the body.
Not others' bodies, your own body — you give a jerk.
Open your eyes. Make yourself alert. Listen again.

Boredom is one of the greatest problems of human life.
No animal is ever bored. Have you seen any animal bored?
No animal, no bird, no tree is ever bored;
only human beings are bored.
Why? — they have missed the natural flow of life.
They have moved away from life.
The more you move away from your essence
and your inner life,
the more things will be dead, and you will be bored.

Come back home.
Be part of the existence:

of the trees and the rocks and the rivers,
of the sky and the sun and the moon
and the birds and the animals.
Come back home.

And look at everything as a child looks : fresh, young.
Jesus says : 'Nobody will be able to enter
into my kingdom of God unless he is like a child.'
What does he mean?
What is the quality of a child?—
a child is fresh and never bored.

Have you observed?
Tell a story to a child. He listens, he gets excited.
And he says : 'Uncle, tell it again.'
The same story! He is saying : 'Tell it again.'
Now he is even more excited.
You tell him and he says : 'Now, once more.'
You cannot understand
what is happening to this child,
because it is the same story.
But for a child, it is never the same story.
Every night he listens to the same lullaby,
but it is never the same.
His consciousness is so fresh
that dust never settles on it.

Your consciousness is so dusty already
that you are not in a state to mirror reality.
Even when I am saying something,
you are understanding something else.
Your dust distorts!
I say something ; you understand something else.
And you understand that which you already know.
Of course, you become repetitive. You are bored.

I am not saying the same thing.

In a very very deep sense
I am saying the same thing,
but that same thing is absolutely fresh,
and it is always fresh.
Freshness is its intrinsic quality.
Truth is never old. It is eternal.
It is not part of time
where things are new and become old.

So if you are bored,
catch this characteristic of boredom
and make yourself more alive, more aware,
and you will feel less bored.
Bring your awareness to a deeper clarity, transparency,
and boredom will disappear.
You have to do something with your being.

And it is not only a question while listening to me;
it is a characteristic.
Everywhere you will find it.
Wherever you will go,
you will carry your boredom around you.
Everything will bore you.

Nothing can give you
the sheer excitement of a child —
running after a butterfly,
or gathering coloured stones on the sea beach.
You think: 'What nonsense. These stones are valueless.'
But for a child, these stones are not commodities
to be purchased or sold.
These stones have nothing to do with money.
Each stone is unique, a *kohinoor*.
The value is intrinsic.
It is not to be decided in any market;
it is not a commodity.

The True Sage

And you can say whatsoever,
the child goes on collecting.
Every morning he goes and collects stones.

But sooner or later
you will destroy his consciousness;
his essence will be lost.
A crust of personality will arise,
and he will also think: 'These stones are useless.
But, diamonds? No. They are not useless.'
They are also stones, but they are not useless.
Why? — because they have a market value.

Now life itself is not valuable.
The value has to be decided
by the fools who run the market.
They are the valuators. They will decide it.
Now you will always be bored.
If you want to attain
to a fresh stream of consciousness,
drop personality, and the values attached to it.
Become a child again!

That's what meditation is all about:
to become a child again, and to look with fresh eyes.
Look again with a new consciousness,
and trees will be greener, and flowers will be redder,
and the sun will be new every morning, and the stars —
then they become infinitely valuable things.
But the value is not of the market; it is of the heart.
Then you listen to me. Then I am not talking to you.
Then these are not mere words
that I am telling to you.

I will tell you one story.

It happened:

A great Hassidic Master had a big book
always by his side,
and he would never allow anybody to look into it.

When there would be nobody around,
he would close the windows and doors.
And people thought: 'Now he is reading.'
Whenever there was somebody,
he would put the book aside.
And it was prohibited — nobody should touch it.
Of course, it became a great curiosity.

When he died, the first thing the disciples did. . . .
They forgot about the old Master.
He was lying dead; now nobody was to prohibit them.
They jumped on the book.
It must carry something tremendously meaningful.

But they were very much disappointed.
Only one page was written —
and the rest of the book was empty.
And on that page also, there was not much,
only one sentence.
And the sentence was: 'When you can make a distinction
between the container and the content,
you have become wise.'

If you listen to the container, the words,
you will get bored.
But if you listen to the content,
you will be exhilarated, you will be in deep ecstasy.

I am not speaking for speaking's sake.
I have no message that can be delivered through words —
but there is no other way to indicate it.

I am not trying to say something;
I am trying to show something.

The True Sage

These are not words.
These words carry my silence.
These words are only containers.
Don't bother about the containers;
look at the content.

These words are alive.
They have the throb of my heart.
I bring them to you as a gift.
They are not doctrines.
At the most, you can call them poetries.
At the most, you can call me a good storyteller,
that's all.

I am not a philosopher,
not a theoretician, not a theologian.
I have something within me
and I would like to share it with you.
Because you cannot understand silence,
I am forced to use words.
Once you are ready to understand my silence,
I will drop words.
Then I will look into you.

But right now you are not at home!
If I look into you, there is nobody,
so I have to knock hard.
My words are nothing but knockers on your door,
so that you can come home.

Accept my gift.

How can I be authentic?
How can I speak and act the truth
when the society and the world
on which I have to depend for my worldly needs
are based upon lies and untruth?

Then be untrue.
Then don't create any misery for yourself.
But the life for which you are going to be untrue
will be taken away from you sooner or later.
Death is certain.

So if you want to live in an untrue society,
comfortably — then live comfortably.
But that comfort
is not leading you anywhere except death.

Whatsoever you call a comfortable and convenient life,
I call only a comfortable way to die.
It is slow suicide.

But the choice is yours.
I am not forcing any goal, any structure on you.
I am simply stating bare facts:
that if you want to be comfortably, conveniently dying,
compromise with the lies that surround you.
But you will never feel comfortable deep down.
An unease will remain inside your heart.

And I know well
that if you become authentic and true,
it is going to be arduous.
Otherwise, why should so many people be liars?
Why should so many people live a life of lies?
It is arduous. It is *tapascharya*. It is austerity.

When you start becoming authentic,
you will be in conflict.
But that conflict is worth it.
It is the price one has to pay
to attain to inner life.
One has to pay it. You cannot avoid it.

If you want a life of infinite bliss,
a life which is beyond death, a life which is eternal,

then you have to pass through the austerity —
and the austerity is only in the beginning.
It is in the beginning only —
because you become a stranger
to a life where everybody is a liar,
and where everybody is a hypocrite,
and where everybody is trying to show
the way he is not.

If you become true, you don't fit —
but that is only in the beginning.
You don't fit with the society,
but immediately you fit with God.
And one who fits with God does not bother
whether he fits with the society or not.
He has entered into a greater harmony.

Only in the beginning,
while you are not in the greater harmony
and you have lost contact with this tiny society
and it's so-called harmony,
in the transitory period, in this gap
there will be a little uneasiness.
You will feel a stranger, an alien — alienated.
But that is only for a small period of time —
and it is worth it.

Once you enter into the greater harmony of God,
the cosmic harmony —
with the trees and the rivers
and the rocks and the sands —
who bothers about your stupid society
and the establishment and the government?
Who bothers? They have nothing to give.
The whole structure is false.
They only pretend. They only promise.
They give you hope, but nothing comes out of it.

Once you know the greater harmony,
you are not bothered.
You accept the fact
that you will be in a little rebellious conflict
with the society.
That's why every religious man is rebellious.
If a religious man is not rebellious, know well,
he is simply pseudo-religious, he is not religious.

A Christ is religious, but not the Vatican Pope.
The Pope is pseudo, false. He fits with the society.
Christ is rebellious. Christianity is against Christ.
All religions are pseudo-religious.
Buddhists are against Buddha,
and Jains are against Mahavir,
and Christians are against Jesus,
and Jews are against Moses and Baal Shem.
They live in a different harmony;
the harmony is of the total.

Your society is a tiny thing.
Just think of the earth — what it is:
a tiny lump in the vast universe.
Nothing much to brag about.
And then on the earth, there is human society —
even a smaller part.
And then in that human society,
even smaller and smaller patterns:
Christians, Protestants — even smaller.
And it goes on and on.
You make smaller wholes against the bigger whole,
and then you are suffocated.
Then you don't have any freedom to move,
you don't have any space around you.

Why not look at the sky
and have the whole space which is available?

The True Sage

But you say: 'No, I am a Hindu;
I cannot move into the whole sky of humanity.
I am a man;
I cannot move in the whole space of all beings.
I am a soul;
I cannot move into the whole space of existence.'

Why do you confine yourself?
It gives a little comfort, I know.
It feels good that you are an Indian;
you have somewhere to belong to.
It feels good that this country is yours;
it gives you a certain solidity,
something to stand up on.
But then it becomes the imprisonment also.

To be left in the open sky one feels afraid, alone —
but freedom is always in aloneness.
Aloneness is tremendously beautiful,
but in the beginning it looks tremendously terrible,
because you have never known aloneness.
You have always lived in the family,
in the society, in the establishment, this and that.
You have never been alone.
Religion is: the art to be alone.
Religion is: what you do with your aloneness.
It has nothing to do with the crowd.
It is to come to the original source of one's being,
to the very center.

So, the choice is yours.
I am not forcing anything on you.
If you want to live comfortably —
of course a hypocrite's life,
false, untrue, tasteless, boring —
then live in the prison.
It is very comfortable and convenient.

But if you want freedom
then you have to be a little courageous,
because freedom is only for those
who are adventurous.

If you want to move
into the infinite sky of God, the cosmos,
you have to leave the small wholes
that you call the society, the religion, the church.
You have to come out of them — out of the caves
that your mind, in fear, has created.

Remember always,
rebelliousness is the very substance of religion.
And there is no other beauty in the world,
no greater ecstasy than to be a rebel.
You have to understand the word.
I don't mean that by being a rebel
you have to be a revolutionary, no.

A revolutionary is again in the same trap.
He is trying to change the society.
He is concerned with the society and the state.
A revolutionary may be against this society,
but he is not against society as such.
A revolutionary is against this society
and wants to create another society
of his own imagination — his own utopia —
but he is not against society.

A rebel is a dropout.
He does not bother about this society
or any other society.
He knows all societies will be imprisonments.
At the most, they can be tolerated — that's all.

There is no possibility of any society
which will be really free.

The society cannot be free.
No revolution is going to succeed;
all revolutions have failed.
And those who know —
they know that revolution as such is not possible.

To change the crowd is not possible
because the crowd doesn't have any heart.
To change the structure is not possible
because people cling to structure.
They can change it
if you give them another structure.
They can change this structure for another.

A capitalist society can become a socialist society.
A socialist society can become a communist society.
A communist society can become a fascist society.
They can change structure,
they can change their presence,
they can change their slavery.
But they cannot be free. A crowd is afraid to be free.
It clings. It wants to belong.

The inner emptiness forces everybody
to belong to somebody, to something —
to some dogma, to some party, to some nation,
to some philosophy, to some church.
Then one feels: 'I am not alone.'

Freedom is the capacity to be alone.
And when you are infinitely alone,
a purity, an innocence is achieved.
That purity is religiousness.

A rebel is one
who has dropped all hope of social revolution.
A rebel is one
who knows that society will always remain the same.

Questions And Answers

Revolution will change the outer form
but deep down it will remain the same.

Only the individual can change,
only the individual can become a Buddha.
The society can never become enlightened.
All societies will remain barbarous, crude, primitive.
Only individuals can reach to that height —
the peakest peak — of being totally alone,
totally silent, totally one with existence.

Be rebellious.
And don't mistake revolution for rebellion.
Revolution is the game of society.
Rebellion is the insight
that the society is going to follow
its own rotten, beaten path.

You drop out —
I am not saying that you escape from it.
That dropping out is an inward phenomenon.
You remain in it, but you are no more of it.
You don't belong to it.
On the surface you go on.

You go to the market,
you go to the office, to the factory.
You fulfill things,
but deep down, you are no more part of it.
You become a lotus flower;
the water of the society does not touch you.
This is what I mean by a dropout.

I don't mean a hippie,
because the hippie will come back sooner or later.
He will have to come back.
That's why there are not old hippies —
only young people.

By the time they reach thirty,
they are going back to the establishment;
then they become afraid.
By the time they reach thirty,
they get married, they have children.
Now, what to do?
They move back to the establishment.
Now their children will become hippies,
but they themselves become squares.

Even when hippies or others drop out of the society,
they create their own society.
Then they start belonging to *that* society.

If you are a hippie and you don't have long hair,
you will be a stranger among hippies.
If you are a hippie and you are not dirty,
and you wash your face,
and you take a shower every day,
you will not fit.

They have their own rules;
they have their own alternate society.
It is small, but they have their own rules,
forms, manners, language, ways of relating,
and they are as traditional as anybody else.
They have their own tradition.
Maybe it is a tradition against tradition,
but it is a tradition.
They have their own conformity.

A real dropout is one
who has dropped out from within.
On the surface he goes on moving,
lives in the society
because there is nowhere else to go —
but deep down he has moved.
He closes his eyes
and he is no more a part of the society.

When he comes home, he forgets the factory,
the market, the office — everything.
The society remains an outer thing;
he doesn't allow it to enter inwards.
That's what I mean when I say a dropout.

A dropout is a drop-in!
Drop in, and you will be a real dropout.

*When do we come to know love?
For me, the more inside I go,
the less love I seem to have.
I seem to have lost the need
to express myself lovingly to others,
especially those I've loved in the past,
such as a girlfriend, mother, old friends and others.*

When do we come to know love?
It is really a very very difficult thing to understand,
because it has nothing to do with understanding.

George Gurdjieff never talked about love
in his whole life.
He never wrote a single line about love.
Once, his disciples pressed him very much
and they said: 'Say at least a few words.
You have never said anything about love.
Why don't you talk about love?'

Gurdjieff said: 'As you are, love is impossible.
Unless *you* know love,
whatsoever I say, you will not understand.'
He condensed his whole feeling about love
in one sentence.
He said: 'If you can love, you can be;
if you can be, you can do;
if you can do, you are.'

And he said: 'Don't force me any more.
I won't say much.'

Love is not possible ordinarily.
Love is a fallacy.
Where you are, love is a fallacy.
It is not possible. You cannot love! —
because in the first place, you are not;
you simply think that you are.

You are not one; you are a crowd.
How can you love?
One mind falls in love;
another mind doesn't know anything about it.
One mind says that it loves;
another mind, at the same time,
is thinking how to hate,
another mind is already moving towards hatred.

You are a crowd inside;
you are not a crystallized whole, you are not one —
and only one can love who is one.

Love is not a relationship; love is a state of being.
So whatsoever you call love is not love.
That's why it is happening: the more inside you go,
the less love you seem to have —
because whatsoever you have called love was not love;
it was a counterfeit, it was not real.
It belonged to the personality,
to the world of lies, falsifications.

When you move inwards,
you go away from the personality.
You go away from the love
that your personality was thinking to be love.

Don't be afraid.

Questions And Answers

It is good to drop the false,
because only when the false disappears, the real arises.
Soon a different quality of love will happen
when you have settled within.
But then it will not be a need.
Then it will not be a desire.
Then it will not be a relationship.
You will be simply loving;
it will be just a quality of your being.
And then it has a totally different flavour.
Then it never creates a bondage.
Then you share unconditionally.
Then your love is just the way you are.
Then you sit lovingly. Then you stand lovingly.
Then you move lovingly. Then you look lovingly.
Then whatsoever you do has the quality of love.

It happened:
A Hassidic mystic was travelling with his disciples.
They came to a *saraya*. They rested the whole night.
In the morning,
the keeper of the *saraya* served tea and breakfast.
While they were drinking their tea,
suddenly, the keeper fell at the Master's feet,
ecstatic — crying and laughing together.

The disciples were puzzled.
How could he know that this man was the Master? —
because this was a secret thing,
and the disciples were told
that nobody should be told who the Master is.
The Master was travelling in a hidden way.
Who had told this *saraya*-keeper?
The disciples were worried.
They inquired, but nobody had told;
nobody had even talked to that man.

The True Sage

The Master said: 'Don't be puzzled.
Ask this man himself — how he recognized me.
Nobody has told him; he has recognized.'

So they asked: 'We cannot recognize.
Even we are suspicious
about whether he is truly enlightened or not,
and we have lived with him for many years.
Still, a suspicion somewhere goes on lurking.
How have you recognized?'

The man said: 'I have been serving tea and breakfast
and food to thousands of people.
I have been watching thousands of people,
and I have never come across a man
who has looked with such deep love at the teacup.
I could not help but recognize.
I know all sorts of people passing from here —
millions of people —
but I have never seen anybody
looking at the teacup with such love,
as if somebody is looking at one's beloved.'

This man must have something
of a totally different quality, a being full of love.
Otherwise, who looks at a teacup with such love?

A teacup is a teacup.
You have to use it. It is a utility.
You don't look with love.
In fact you don't look at your own wife with love.
She is also a utility —
a teacup to be used and thrown away.
You don't look at your husband with love.
The husband is a means.

Love is possible only
when everything becomes the end.
Then even a teacup has the quality of the beloved.

QUESTIONS AND ANSWERS

Love is not a relationship;
love is a fragrance that arises in you
when you have reached home.
Before that, you can talk about love,
you can fantasize about love,
you can write beautiful poetries about it,
but you will not know what it is.

Try to enter within yourself.
There will be much difficulty,
because your love will start disappearing.
It has never been there,
so it is good that a false thing disappears.
In fact, it is not disappearing;
you are only becoming aware that it is false.

It has never been there.
You have been deluding yourself.
When it has disappeared completely,
when your essence is separate from your personality,
when that which you have brought into the world
is separated from all that the society
has given to you,
when you are naked in your being
and all clothes have been dropped,
a new love arises.
That is the love Jesus calls 'God'.

Jesus says: 'Love is God.'
Your love has been nothing but a hell.
It has never been God. It has not even been a heaven.
It may have promised a heaven,
but it always proved to be a hell.
And Jesus says: 'Love is God.'
That love only arises when you have arrived
to your innermost core.

You will have to lose the false to gain the true.

You will have to lose darkness to attain to light.
You will have to lose death
to become really, authentically alive.
That is the price one has to pay!
But you are so egoistic that you cling.
You feel: 'If this love disappears
then I will be empty.'
And your ego creates a problem:
'Maybe it is false. Let it be false.
Something is there. The ego can feed on it.'

It happened once: A king felt thirsty.
He said to his courtiers: 'My throat feels dry.'
He could have simply said: 'I am thirsty' —
but a king is a king; they have their own way.
It is too common to say: 'I am thirsty.'
So he said: 'My throat feels dry.'

His lackeys ran to the market immediately.
They thought and pondered over what to do
when the throat is dry.
Of course, they couldn't think
of bringing common water,
because that won't suit for a king.
So they brought lubricating oil.

The king drank it. His throat was no more dry,
but he was in more difficulty than before
because his whole mouth was tasting awful
and he was feeling nausea.

He said: 'What have you done?
Of course, the throat is no more dry,
but I am in more of a mess than before.'

So the greatest doctor of the capital was called.
He came and suggested pickles and vinegar.

Questions And Answers

So it was taken.
It helped a little, but it gave a stomachache.

More medicines were given.
Somehow the stomachache disappeared,
but again the throat was dry.
So somebody brought scented syrups,
wine and other things.
He drank the wines, the syrups.
and everything else that was given.
He felt a little relieved,
but his digestion was disturbed.

An old man, a wise man
who was watching this whole nonsense said:
'I think, your Highness, you need water,
common water.
You are thirsty.'

Of course the king was very angry,
and he said: 'This is an insult —
to suggest common water to a great king.
This is for common people —
to feel thirsty and be quenched by common water.
I am not a common man.
You have been insulting me.
And moreover, it is illogical.
Look at the illness; it is so complicated.
So many medicines have been given and nothing helps.
You are a simpleton to think that by common water
it can be helped.
The greatest doctor has come
and even he was not of much help.
So what do you think about yourself?
Are you a physician?'

The man said: 'No, I am not a physician.

The True Sage

I am just a common man, but whenever it happens . . .
but I don't know about kings. . . .
Sorry. Excuse me.
I don't know about kings. I am not a king.
But whenever it happens to me, common water helps,
but that may be because I am a common man.'

The king said: 'You are not only a common man,
you are an idiot.'

Amidst idiots, wise people prove to be idiots.

Your disease is very ordinary. Common water will do,
but that doesn't suit the ego of the king.

People come to me
and they bring their complex illnesses.
I say: 'Don't be worried. Just meditation will do.'
They look suspicious.
They say: 'But why do you go on suggesting
and prescribing meditation to everybody,
each and everybody?
And my problem is different.
Maybe it helps others, but it won't help me.
Tell me something specific, something special.
What should I do?
I cannot love. I cannot feel.'

Or somebody says: 'I am very angry,
and the anger continues like an undercurrent.
What should I do?'

Or somebody says: 'I am too sexual,
and the fantasy continues in my mind.
What should I do?'

Or somebody is greedy, miserly,
with millions of diseases — very complicated.

And they have been to psychoanalysts,
and they have failed.
And they have been to this saint and that,
and everybody has failed.
In fact, they feel very good
that everybody has failed
because they are not ordinary people;
their disease is very complex, complicated.
If I just suggest common water,
if I just suggest that meditation will do,
they look suspicious.
And I tell you — meditation will do.

Your ego has to be put aside.
It creates all sorts of problems.
Only meditation will do.

And what is meditation? —
it is just putting the mind aside.
Being without mind for a few moments is meditation.

And once you know for a few moments,
you have the key.
Then whenever you need, you can move withinwards.
It is just like the ingoing and the outgoing breath.
You go out in the world, it is the outgoing breath.
You come into yourself, it is the ingoing breath.
Meditation is the ingoing breath.

Forget about love, anger, greed —
a thousand and one problems.
Problems may be a thousand and one,
but the medicine is only one.
And you may be surprised: the word 'meditation'
comes from the same root from where 'medicine' comes.
'Medicine' and 'meditation' come from the same root.
Meditation is a medicine; it is *the* only medicine.

So forget about your problems;
just move into meditation.
And the deeper you move,
the more false things will disappear.

First there will be emptiness, nothingness.
You will feel afraid, but don't be afraid.
That's how it happens to everybody.
I have been in that same state of fear.
I know it happens. I can understand.
But be courageous and move on.

If you can move on and on,
any day, any moment, suddenly it happens —
just a click, something clicks.
The old has disappeared, and the new has appeared.
You are resurrected.

17th October 1975

On a certain Passover
   before the seder celebration,
Rabbi Yisakhar Baer called his guest,
   the rabbi of Mogielnica,
a grandson of the maggid of Koznitz,
   to the window~
and pointed to something outside.
'Do you see, Rav of Mogielnica?'
he said. 'Do you see?'

   After the feast was over,
the rabbi of Mogielnica
   danced around the table
and sang in a low voice:~
'The holy old man, our brother,
has shown me a light.
   Great is the light he has shown me.
But who knows?~
   who knows
how many years must pass,
   how long we still must sleep
before it comes to us,
   before it comes to us?'

The light behind the window

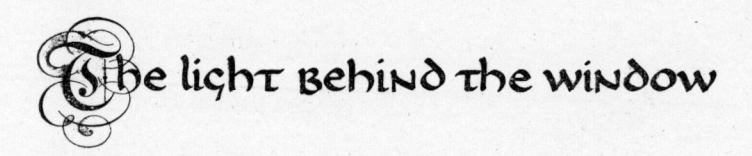

A king heard that one part of his kingdom
was almost in a chaos.
People were fighting with each other.
They were hurting each other in every way possible.
He was worried.

He sent a special messenger to this part
with a magic glass.
The magic glass had the quality
that if you looked through it,
you would see things as they are —
not as you imagine,
not as you think,
not as you interpret.
The magic glass would negate your mind
and you would see things directly, immediately.
Once you looked at things as they are,
the experience became transforming.
Then you could not be the old one.

The messenger left the magic glass with the people
and went back to the capital,
knowing well what was going to happen,
because he had been on such trips before.

The True Sage

The magic glass was placed on a crossroad,
so that everyone could look through it
and be transformed,
so that it was available to everybody.

But this is how people reacted:
a great majority gave a name to the glass
and worshipped it as if it was a superhuman being.
But they neved looked through it.
They worshipped, but they never looked through it.
In fact, their worship was a way
of avoiding the magic glass.

Another part of the people
were sceptical from the very beginning.
They said: 'This is simply foolish.
How can a glass help to see things as they are?
It is superstitious.'
They never experimented;
they never even gave the glass a try.
They were the sceptical people —
and the sceptical are superstitious.

Deep down, both groups were the same
because they both avoided —
one by worshipping;
one by saying that this was superstitious and useless.
That's what has happened to the whole world.

Theists and atheists —
both have been avoiding meditation.
One by saying that there is no God;
one by saying that there is God
and only worship is needed.
Deep down they are not different.

Then there was a third part of the people —
practical, pragmatic, empirical.

They said: 'The magic glass is interesting,
but we cannot imagine how it is going to help us
in the practical things of the world.
It is impractical.'
They also never looked through it.
They were the scientists, the empirical minds.

Then there was a fourth part of the people.
They said: 'Not only is the glass useless,
it is dangerous —
because whosoever looks through it becomes distorted.'
They were against it,
and they were planning to destroy it
whenever the opportunity arose.
They also had not looked through it.

Then there was another group who avoided it.
They stopped walking through those streets
near where the glass was.
They never passed through those crossroads.
They said: 'We are happy as we are.'
They were not happy. But they thought:
'It may disturb our usual pattern of life.'

But a few people were there who were simple, innocent.
They looked through it and they were transformed.
They became totally new beings.

But then the rumour spread all around
that they had been hypnotized by that stupid glass,
that they were fools.
Otherwise how could a glass transform a human being?
They were thought to be mad.

Forget about the story —
because this is the situation of the whole world.

Religion is a magic glass.

The True Sage

The secret quality of it is to transform you.
But it cannot force transformation.
You have to allow it to happen;
you have to be in a receptive mood.
Worship won't help. That is very cunning and tricky.
Logic won't help
because it is a question of experience,
not of logical syllogism.
Scepticism is not of much use,
because just by doubting
you cannot come to know anything.
One has to pass through the experience.
Only the experience can be the criterion
of truth or untruth;
thinking is not enough.

Avoiding, escaping from seeing life as it is,
you remain a coward
and you miss the whole point of it,
the whole adventure of it.

Only those who are innocent, childlike,
who are ready to look through it,
who are ready to be transformed, changed, mutated —
only they will be helped by religion.
So only very few people have been helped by religion.
Christians are millions; Hindus, millions;
Buddhists, millions; Mohammedans, millions;
but religious people — very few.
You can count them on your fingers.

To belong to an organization is not to be religious.
To take the jump in deep trust and innocence
is to be religious.

To be a Hassid is to be ready to see,
to see life as it is.

This has to be understood because you also see,
but you don't see things as they are.
Before they enter your being,
you have transformed their colour,
you have given new shapes, forms,
you have already interpreted.

Your mind goes on falsifying things.
And your mind goes on creating illusions around you.
And you feel that you see things as they are —
but you never see.
Because once you see things as they are,
things disappear — only God remains.
Once you can see things as they are, only one remains.
Millions of forms disappear into one : the formless.

Then the tree is no more there.
Then the rock is no more there.
Then the river is no more there.
One existence is there,
throbbing everywhere in a thousand and one ways.

Until you see the one, you have not seen at all.
If you see the many, you are blind.
If you hear the many, you are deaf.
If you have heard the one sound —
the soundless sound —
then for the first time you have heard.
If you love many, your love is false.
It comes from the mind ; it is not of the heart.
If you love the one in the many,
then for the first time you are in love.

Remember : one is the criterion.
Many is the world ; one is God.
A Hassid is one who has attained to the vision of the one.

Now, look at this beautiful story.

The True Sage

*On a certain Passover
before the sedar celebration,
Rabbi Yisakhar Baer called his guest,
the rabbi of Mogielnica,
a grandson of the Maggid of Koznitz,
to the window —
and pointed to something outside.*

An old man called a young man to the window
and pointed to something outside.
'Do you see,' he said. 'Do you see?'

What was he showing?
You must be wondering what was outside the window.
You must be wondering why it has not been named —
that which was shown.

There was nothing special outside the window.
The window was as ordinary as all windows are.
Outside was the ordinary world as it is everywhere.
That's why what he was showing has not been named.
In fact the whole emphasis
is not on the object of seeing;
the whole emphasis is on: 'Do you see?'
It is not a question of what you see;
it is a question of whether you see.
This emphasis has to be understood,
because the whole thing is focused there.
The whole secret key is there: 'Do you see?'

People come to me and they ask: 'We hear you.
We would *also* like to see God. Where is He?'
They are asking for the object
and God is not an object.
If you can see, He is there.
If you can't see, He is not there.
It is not a question of what you see;
it is a question: 'Do you see?'

The Light Behind The Window

The emphasis is on the capacity to see,
to perceive, to receive.
The emphasis is on the eye, the capacity to see.

'Do you see,'
said the old man to the Rav of Mogielnica.
'Do you see?'

There was nothing outside the window;
it was just as ordinary a window as any.
Nothing was pointed at.
On the contrary, the capacity to see was pointed at.

In India, we have called philosophy, 'darshan'.
It means the capacity to see.
We don't call it a love of thinking,
as the word 'philosophy' means.
We call it: the capacity to see.
Philosophy is not a right translation of darshan.
The right translation of darshan would be *philosia* —
'a love to see'.
Philosophy means love of thinking.
Sophia means thinking and *philo* means love.

The Indian philosophy is not philosophy;
it is *philosia*.
Sia means to see.
The whole emphasis is not on the object;
the emphasis is on the subject.
Subjectivity is religion. Objectivity is science.
To pay attention to the object is to be scientific.
To pay attention to the subject is to be religious.

You look at a flower.
If you pay attention to the flower,
then it is scientific.
If you pay attention to the witness of the flower,
it becomes religious.

A scientist and a religious man
may be standing side by side,
looking at the same flower —
but they are not looking in the same way.
The scientist is looking at the flower
and has forgotten himself completely.
The religious man is witnessing the flower,
and remembering himself.
It is a change of gestalt.
Try it sometimes. Look at a flower —
then suddenly change the gestalt.
Now look at the seer of the flower.

You are listening to me right now.
You can pay attention to what I am saying —
then it is a scientific listening.
Or you can be aware
of the one who is listening to me within you —
then it becomes religious.
The difference is very delicate and subtle.

Try it right now.
Listen to me. Forget yourself.
Then it is scientific.

A scientist while working is absolutely concentrated.
Science is concentration. Religion is meditation.
And that is the difference
between concentration and meditation.

Concentration is not meditation.
Meditation is not concentration.
Concentration is focusing your eyes on the object;
meditation is focusing yourself on your self.
Meditation has no object in it;
it is pure subjectivity.

Listen to me. Concentrate.
Then you forget yourself.

Then you don't know who you are.
You are simply a listener.
Then change the focus.
It is a knack. It cannot be taught how to change it.
You simply change it.
You just become aware that you are listening.
Awareness becomes more important
then what you are listening to.
Immediately, a deep change has happened in your being.
In that moment you become religious.

If you go on paying too much attention to the object
you may come to know many secrets of nature,
but you will never come across God
on any of the paths that you will travel.
It will never be a pilgrimage, a *teerthyatra*.
You will wander and wander
into the wilderness of the world and matter.
That's why science cannot think that God is —
it is impossible.

God is not an object.
Your very approach is such
that God is excluded from it.
God is not an object! God is your withinness.
It is not in the object of concentration.
It is in the subjectivity of meditation.
He is you.

I have heard one beautiful story.
There was a man, a great devotee of Buddha.
He had a beautiful statue of Buddha,
a wooden statue, a piece of art —
an antique, very valuable.
He carried it like a great treasure.

One night it happened :
he was staying in a cold hut.

The True Sage

And the winter was really ice-cold
and he was shivering.
It seemed that he was going to die.
There was no wood for his fire.

At midnight, when he was shivering,
it is said that Buddha appeared and said:
'Why don't you burn me?'
The wooden statue was there.
The man became afraid. This must be a devil.
He said: 'What are you saying?
Burn the statue of Buddha? — never!'

Buddha laughed and said:
'If you see me in the statue you will miss me.
I am in you, not in the statue.
I am not in the worshipped, the object;
I am in the worshipper.
And I am shivering within you!
Burn this statue!'

God is your subjectivity. He is there within.
When you focus outside, there are objects.
When you become unfocused
and look within, without any focus,
He is there — absolutely alive, throbbing, ticking.

'Do you see, Rav of Mogielnica?' he said.
'Do you see?'

Remember the emphasis.
He is saying: 'Do you see?'
He is saying: 'Have you got eyes to see?'

After the feast was over,
the rabbi of Mogielnica
danced around the table

*and sang in a low voice:
'The holy old man, our brother,
has shown me a light.
Great is the light he has shown me.
But who knows? —
who knows
how many years must pass,
how long we still must sleep
before it comes to us,
before it comes to us?'*

Each word has to be understood.
*After the feast was over,
the rabbi of Mogielnica
danced around the table
and sang in a low voice...*

Something has transpired, something has happened —
something from the unknown,
something not of this world.
The moment the old man said:
'Do you see? Do you see?' — something had happened.
What had happened?

For the first time
this young rabbi became aware of his witnessing self.
He had been seeing many things in his life,
but for the first time
he has had a glimpse of the seer itself.

When you are near a person who has become a true sage,
who has attained,
it is very easy to ride on his tide.
Near a Buddha, there are moments
when you can look through his eyes.
That is the meaning of finding a Master, a zaddik.
Teachers are many; zaddiks, rare.

The True Sage

If you find a teacher,
he will explain to you many many things,
but he cannot give you his eyes.
He has none. He is as blind as you are.
The blind leading the blind.
He may be more experienced than you,
he may have been groping in the dark longer than you,
but he is still blind.
He can give you many explanations,
but he cannot give you any experience.
He himself has none.
You can share only that which you have.
You cannot share that which you don't have.

A zaddik is a man who has known,
who has become centered.
Now the search is over —
and he is overflowing with the attainment.
You can ride on his tide.
Of course, that cannot become your experience,
but it can be a glimpse.
And a glimpse can be very very important.

A glimpse can transform your whole life.
It will be only a taste;
your hunger will not be satisfied by it.
In fact, just the contrary will be the case —
for the first time you will become hungry.

Up to now,
you have been avoiding the fact that you are hungry.
When there is nothing to eat
it is better to forget that you are hungry,
it is better to pretend that you are not hungry.
When you are thirsty and no water is available,
it is better to forget the thirst.
Otherwise it will be a deep anguish.

The Light Behind The Window

When you come to a man who has known,
who is no more hungry,
his very presence
becomes a deep stirring in your being.
For the first time you feel the hunger
that you have been hiding for centuries, for lives.
You were avoiding facing it.
You have been thirsty;
you have never known satiety.
But it was so difficult to live with the thirst
that you had suppressed it,
suppressed it into the unconscious.
You had thrown it deep inside your being
so that you wouldn't come across it
in your day-to-day world.
It was there already.

When you come to a man who is in deep satiety,
whose whole being is flowering,
in whom there is no thirst, no hunger,
who has attained,
suddenly your thirst arises.
From the depth of your unconscious
it surfaces to the conscious.
You become really thirsty and hungry
for the first time.

If a man has attained,
he can allow you a glimpse from *his* window.
That is the meaning of the story.
He can call you: 'Come near me.
Look from this window. Do you see?'
So the window is not the ordinary window of a house;
it is the window of the heart.

And when the old man said: *'Do you see? Do you see?'*
he was saying: 'Are you getting the point?

Are you receiving my eyes and my vision?'
Of course, it can be borrowed only for a single moment,
and then it is gone.

Enlightenment cannot be borrowed.
It can, at the most,
become a lightning in a dark night.
It cannot become a permanent light.
But in a dark night, when you are groping,
and there is sudden lightning,
for a single moment everything becomes clear.
Then the lightning goes.
But the lightning has changed everything.

Now you know the path exists.
Maybe you are not on the path yet.
A thousand and one barriers may be there,
but you know the path exists.
Just to know that the path exists
is a great achievement,
because uncertainty dissolves, doubt disappears,
hesitation is no more there.
Faith arises. Trust arises.

The path exists:
this becomes a deep-rooted phenomenon within you.
Now you don't believe in others; you yourself know.

Maybe it has become just a memory now,
but the memory will lead you, guide you.
Now you will be groping in the right direction;
the groping will no longer be blind.
You have seen where the path is.
North, south, east —
you will be groping in the right direction,
knowing well that it is there.
It is only a question of time.

You will reach it.

When the old man says: *'Do you see? Do you see?'*
he must have become a lightning to this young man.
That lightning is the window.
He must have flashed;
for a single moment he must have burned
for this young man,
so he could have a taste, so he could have a look.
It is a small glimpse,
but then he will never be the same again.

Gurdjieff used to say
that there are seven types of men.
Let me explain those seven types to you.

The first three types are very ordinary.
You will find them everywhere, within and without.

The first, man number one, Gurdjieff calls 'body-oriented'.
He lives in the body.
He is ninety-nine percent body.
His whole life is body-oriented.
He eats not to live; he lives to eat.

The second type of man, number two, is emotional —
the feeling type, sentimental.

Number three is the intellectual.

These are the three common types.
They are almost on the same level.

These three, in India, we have known long before.
The body-oriented we have called the *sudra*.
The feeling-oriented, the emotional
we have called the *kshatriya*, the warrior.
And the intellect-oriented we have called the *brahmin*,
the intellectual, the intelligentsia.

The True Sage

The fourth, the *vaisya*, the businessman,
is in fact not a type —
but an amalgamation of all the three.
Something of the *sudra* exists in him,
something of the intellectual also exists in him.
He is not a pure type; he is a mixture.
And, in fact, he is the majority,
because to find a pure type is very difficult.
To find a really perfect *sudra* is rare.
To find a perfect *brahmin* is also rare.
To find a pure warrior, a samurai, is also rare.
The world consists of the fourth, which is a mixture,
which is not really a type, just a crowd.

These are the three types.
Unless you go beyond the three
you will not be able to see.
They are *all* blind.

One is blinded by the body.
Another is blinded by feelings, emotions.
Another is blinded by the intellect, thinking.
But they are all blind.

Number four Gurdjieff calls: one who has become aware.
Up to number three they are all unaware,
unconscious, fast asleep.
They don't know where they are.
They don't know who they are.
They don't know from where they come.
They don't know where they are going.
Number four is the one who has become a little alert,
who can see.

When this old man
called the young rabbi to the window,
he must have felt the possibility
of the fourth man, number four.

The Light Behind The Window

Only number four can be called to the window.
Only with number four can the Master share his experience.

With the first it is almost impossible to talk.
To the first you can give prasad.
The first one you can invite for a feast.
Religion is nothing for him but a feast.
Whenever a religious day comes,
he eats better, he dresses well, he enjoys it.

To the second you can give emotional food:
prayer, tears flowing down, sentimentality.

To the third you can talk much.
He will appear to understand but will never understand.
He is the intelligentsia, the intellectual.

Only with the fourth is a sharing possible —
only with one who is a little alert,
or is just on the brink of being alert.
He is asleep, but turning in his sleep,
and you know, now he is going to wake up;
now any moment he is going to wake up.
In this moment only, can a Master share his vision.
When he sees that you are just on the brink
of waking up, or are already awake
and just lying down with closed eyes,
or if just a little shaking is needed
and you will open your eyes . . .
it must have been such a moment in this story.
The young rabbi must have been of the fourth type
or just close to it.

'Do you see? Do you see?' said the old man.

This saying, 'Do you see?'
is a shaking to help him to become alert —
even for a single moment; that will do.

The True Sage

Once you have tasted awareness, you will long for it.
That will become your goal, the very end.
Then you cannot be satisfied
with this ordinary world
and all that it offers.
Then there will arise a strange discontent
which cannot be satisfied with *this* world.

Rabbi Leib has said: 'I have such a discontent
that it cannot be satisfied with this world.
That's why I know there must be a God.
Otherwise, who will satisfy my discontent?
There must be another world,
there must be another way of being.'

The very discontent shows another way of being
because it cannot be satisfied here.
Nothing can satisfy here.
A thirst which cannot be quenched here
is an indication
that there must be some other type of water,
some other type of quenching agent, some other world.

Rabbi Leib says: 'I don't know that God is,
but I know that in me there is a discontent
which indicates that there must be some place,
some space of being,
where this discontent will disappear.'

God is the possibility only for those who can see:
the fourth, number four.
With number four, religion enters into the world.

Up to number three the world is materialistic.
Number three may be found in prayer houses,
churches, temples, gurudwaras —
but that makes no difference.
With number four, religion becomes alive —
throbs, beats, breathes.

The Light Behind The Window

This young man must have been number four.

I'm here only for those who belong to number four.
Make haste to become number four,
because if you are a little alert,
I can lend my being.
You can have a vision through it.
I can bring you to my window
and can ask you: 'Do you see?'
But this is possible only with number four.

Then there is number five,
whose awareness has become settled.
Now for number five there is no need of lightning;
he has his own inner light burning.

Then there is number six,
all of whose discontent has disappeared,
who is absolutely content.
Nothing is there for him to achieve any more.

Then you will be surprised —
then why does number seven exist?
For number six everything is attained, fulfilled;
there is nothing to attain.
There is no higher than number six;
number six is the highest.
Then why number seven?

With number seven even contentment disappears.
With the sixth, there is the feeling of fulfillment,
a deep content, and arrival.
With number seven, even that disappears.
No content, no discontent; no emptiness, no fullness.
Number seven has become God Himself.
Number seven we have called the *avatara*:
a Buddha, a Mahavir, a Krishna, a Christ.
They are number seven.

This young man must have been of number four.

And you should remember this :
that I can go on talking to you —
that talking is just preparing a ground
so that one day I can wake you up
and bring you to my window.

So the whole effort should be : how to see.
The whole effort should be :
how to increase the quantity
and the quality of seeing,
how to become eyes with your whole being.

God is not to be searched.
Vision has to be created.

*After the feast was over,
the rabbi danced around the table
and sang in a low voice . . .*

Something has happened,
something tremendously significant.
Only by singing can you be grateful.
And that, also, in a very low voice —
because to be too loud would be vulgar.
Something from the unknown has penetrated ;
something from the beyond has come to the vision
You can only sing in a very low voice.
The very thing is so significant, so sacred,
that one walks cautiously, as in a winter stream,
or as if afraid of enemies. One hesitates.
That is the meaning of *sang in a low voice.*

'The holy old man, our brother . . .'

The holiest — a Buddha, a Christ —
but still, our brother.
That is the beauty.

The Light Behind The Window

A Buddha may have gone beyond,
may have become a god,
but he remains a brother to us,
because he was once a part.
He travelled on the same path;
he groped in the same darkness.
He is of our family.
He has become the holiest —
the holy old man, our brother.

God is so far away.
He is the holiest of the holy —
but to call God 'our brother' won't look right.
That's why something unbridgeable,
an abyss, exists between you and God.
The bridge is no more there.

Only a Buddha or a Jesus becomes a bridge,
because the bridge is joined
both to this shore and that shore.

Jesus is called 'son of God' and 'son of man'.
He is both.
Son of man, our brother; son of God, the holy old man.
The bridge has two sides.
One belongs to our shore;
the other belongs to the other shore.
That's why a Master
is even more significant than God.

Just a few days ago I was talking about
a woman mystic, Sahajo.
She says: 'I can leave God
but I cannot leave my Master,
because God has only given me this world, the bondage.
My Master has given me freedom,
has given me God himself.

I can leave God, but I cannot leave my Master.
I can renounce God, but I cannot renounce my Master.'
A very significant assertion. A great statement of love.
And understanding!

God is so far away. Jesus is both : near and far.
God can be the goal,
but Jesus is both : the path and the goal.
How can you reach to the goal without the path?
It will hang in emptiness.
There will be no bridge to reach it.
Jesus is both the end and the means :
son of man and son of God.

Beautiful is this assertion :
'The holy old man, our brother,
has shown me the light . . .'

What is that light he has shown? —
the light that comes with the clarity of eyes,
the light that comes with the awakening of the seer,
the light that happens when you become a witness.
Not that he has shown something!
He has simply shown you the capacity of your vision,
that even God is possible with the right eyes.

'Do you see?'
If you see, everything is possible.
If you don't see, nothing is possible.
The possibility opens with your opening eyes.

'The holy old man, our brother,
has shown me the light.
Great is the light he has shown me.'

But he never forgets for a single moment
that this light is something *he* has shown.
'I have not seen it. It is not *my* attainment yet.
He has lent his vision to me.

The Light Behind The Window

He has been compassionate, he has been loving.
He has shared.
He called me to his eyes, to his windows;
I looked through them.
He has shown me the light.
Great is the light! A great lightning it is!
He has shown me, but it is his.
I am thankful, I am grateful
that he has been so loving and kind.'

'But who knows? —
who knows
how many years must pass,
how long we still must sleep
before it comes to us,
before it comes to us?'

He is aware that in the lightning
he has seen something.
But who knows when the morn will come?
When the morning will come, who knows?
In fact, now a thirst arises.
That thirst is in the song. A hunger arises.

'He has shown me the light.
Great is the light he has shown me.'

No, for the first time, a discontent:
'The light exists and I have to attain it.'

'But who knows? —
who knows
how many years must pass . . . '

to attain it, to earn it, to make it one's own?
Maybe a long journey will be needed.
But now the trust has arisen.
Howsoever long it is, one can go on singing.
It is there — that much is certain.

The True Sage

Then time is not much of a problem.
One can go on singing.
Once you know it is there,
then you can wait infinitely.

The reason you cannot wait is because deep down
you are not yet certain that it is there.
The patience is difficult
because you think maybe it is not there.
Maybe it is just wasting life.
Maybe it is just wasting time and energy.
Your impatience is nothing but your doubt.
Trust is patient; doubt, very impatient.

Many times you think it is your trust
which is impatient; you are wrong.
Many times you think you are impatient
because you are such a great lover; you are wrong.
Many times you think: 'My impatience simply shows
my strong desire and longing.'
You are wrong.

Impatience simply shows
that you are not ready to waste time
because deep down you are afraid, suspicious:
'Maybe the whole thing is just foolish.
God doesn't exist.
The truth?— who knows whether it exists or not?
Life eternal may be just a wish-fulfillment.
Something beyond death? —
it may be just a trick of human mind.
To tolerate death?
To accept death?
To live with death?
It may be just a trick of the mind.'
Then you are impatient.

But once you have seen the light . . .

even the light of somebody else,
which cannot light your path,
but can give you a trust.
From the Masters, one doesn't learn the truth;
one only learns trust.

Truth has to come to you.
Whenever you are ready, it will come.
Nobody else can give you the truth.

But trust? —
a man who has attained — in his aroma, in his climate
trust is infectious; you can catch it.

If you are near me — not only physically close,
but really close, open, vulnerable to me —
sooner or later, only one thing is possible:
and that will be trust.
But trust is enough.
I don't say that trust is the goal.
But without trust there is no goal.
Trust is the beginning, the seed.
When the seed is in your hand,
the tree is not far away.
It is already on the way.

'*Great is the light he has shown me.
But who knows? —*'
A strong longing has arisen.
'*But who knows? —
who knows
how many years must pass . . .*'

But they can be passed singing, dancing;
They can be passed in faith and trust;
they can be passed in waiting.
And I tell you, it will not be waiting for Godot!
Because the trust has arisen.

The True Sage

Now it is not that you don't know
for whom you are waiting.
You know exactly for whom you are waiting!
You know absolutely for whom you are waiting!
You are no more waiting for Godot;
you are waiting for God.
And that's the difference between Godot and God.

Godot is just something promised by your mind;
God is something glimpsed
through someone who has known.
God is trust; Godot is belief.
Godot is through scriptures and teachers;
God is through Masters.

'Who knows how many years must pass . . . '

But then one can wait.
And, in fact, waiting becomes a deep delight.
When you know that something is going to happen
and shower on you,
you wait with such tranquil excitement.
Let me use the paradoxical term, 'tranquil excitement'.
Excitement is there every moment, but absolutely calm;
a deep reservoir of longing, with no ripples
because even ripples will disturb and divert.

One waits relaxed and tense.
It is difficult to explain it.
Relaxed and tense, both.
Tense, because something is going to happen.
Relaxed, because it can happen only
when you are relaxed.

One German thinker, Herrigel,
was learning archery in Japan with a great Master.
For three years he worked hard and failed —

because to understand the Eastern mind
is very difficult for the Western mind;
they function on totally different levels.

The Western mind is logical;
the Eastern mind is alogical.
It may not be illogical, but alogical.

Herrigel learned the whole art of archery.
He was hitting his targets one hundred percent.
But the Master was not satisfied.
The Master would say:
'You are still not in the right posture.'

And what is the right posture?
The right posture is
that when you pull your arrow back
your muscles should be relaxed.
But this is absurd.
Because when you pull the bow
the muscles are bound to become tense.
But the muscles should be relaxed.
Herrigel went many times
and touched the Master's muscles
when he was pulling the bow — and they were relaxed.
So you cannot say that relaxation cannot happen.
They were as relaxed as a child's hand and arm —
no tension.

The Master said: 'The arrow moves by itself
when you are relaxed.
Then God moves it; you are not the mover.
You simply create the situation and then it happens.
You are not the doer.'
This is what tense relaxation is.
You are pulling the arrow tense,
and yet you are totally relaxed.

The True Sage

To long for God is to be tense.
But to allow God to happen
one needs to be absolutely relaxed.
A tranquil excitement, a tense relaxation —
waiting, as if it is going to happen right now,
and the readiness to wait for eternity.
Let me repeat:
waiting as if it is going to happen right now,
this very moment,
and yet ready to wait for eternity.

Whenever it happens it is never late;
whenever it happens it is always early.
The happening is so great
that you cannot claim it for yourself.
You cannot say: 'I have earned it.'
The happening is so great
that it is always through grace and not through effort.
It happens through effortlessness.
Whenever it happens, you know well
that it is through compassion, grace,
that it has happened.
It has nothing to do with you or your earning.

*'The holy old man, our brother,
has shown me the light.
Great is the light he has shown me.
But who knows? —
who knows
how many years must pass,
how long we still must sleep
before it comes to us,
before it comes to us?'*

This is the last thing to be understood
about this anecdote:
when you look through an enlightened man's vision,

The Light Behind The Window

God doesn't come to you; you go to God.
When you yourself become alert
and your sleep has gone,
you don't go to God; God comes to you.
That's the difference.

You can look at the Himalayas from a window,
far away in their majesty —
the sun shining on the white snow.
And even from thousands of miles away
you can feel the coolness, you can feel the glory,
the silence, the height, the sheer majesty, the magic.

But it is your eyes that are travelling far away,
it is not the Himalayas.
It is you going to the Himalayas on a visionary trip.
Your eyes are moving; the Himalayas are not moving.
This happens when you look
through somebody else's window.
This happened to this young rabbi
when he looked through the old man's window.
Far away he travelled.

But when *you* have become capable,
when your own eyes open,
it is just the other way around.
It is not that you go on a faraway journey;
the faraway comes closer.
God comes to you.
Whenever you are absolutely ready to receive,
He rushes.
The rush is natural,
just as when it rains in the Himalayas
the peaks cannot hold the water.
The water rushes down. It rushes to the valley.
Wherever it can find a low ground, a lake, it rushes.

Whenever you are awake, you become a space.

Because whenever you are awake
you are not filled with the ego.
You are an empty space, a valley, a low ground.
It rushes. It fills you.

I have heard:
A very rich man asked a Hassidic Master
to come to his palace.
The palace was tremendously valuable. It was unique.
It was full of valuable things:
paintings, carpets, antiques,
furniture of every kind and of every age.

The rich man took the Hassidic Master
from one room to another.
They moved around for hours and hours;
the palace was vast.
The rich man was bragging very much.
He was feeling very deeply contented in his ego.

When the whole palace was shown
to the Hassidic Master,
the rich man said:
'Now tell me, what is your impression?'

The Hassid said:
'The fact that the earth is strong enough
to carry the burden of such a massive palace,
plus *you* —
this has impressed me tremendously.'
Plus you!

Everybody has made a palace of the ego.
Everybody is too full of it.
Once you become awake, ego disappears;
ego is the sleep.
To feel 'I am' is to be sleepy.

The Light Behind The Window

Suddenly to be without any feeling of 'I am'
is to be awake.
To be without any 'I am' is an opening.

To feel 'I am' is a closed monad-like phenomenon;
it has no windows, no openings.
You live in a cocoon, dead inside.

Once you are awake, you become empty.
You become a nothingness, a nobody.
God rushes to you from all directions;
He comes and fills you.

When the devotee is ready,
the devotee does not travel at all.
When the meditator is ready, he does not go anywhere.
God comes. It is always God who comes.

When we go to God, it is only a vision.
For a moment clouds disperse and the sun is seen.
Again the clouds are there,
and the sun, and the light —
and the experience becomes just a memory.
It haunts you, but it doesn't transform you.

'The holy man, our brother,
has shown me the light.
Great is the light he has shown me.
But who knows? —
who knows
how many years must pass,
how long we still must sleep
before it comes to us,
before it comes to us?'

18th October 1975

Questions and answers

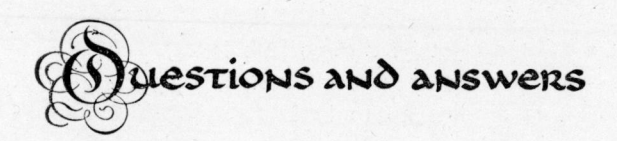

I seem to be neither totally in the world,
nor the watcher on the hill.
How to be some place?
I feel like I am in between everything I do.

Then that is exactly the place you should be.
You go on creating problems.
Wherever you are, be there.
There is no need to be a watcher on the hills.

There should be no 'should'.
Once the 'should' enters life
you are already poisoned.
There should be no goal.
There should be no right and wrong.
This is the only sin: to think in terms of division,
values, condemnation, appreciation.

Wherever you are . . .
nothing is wrong in between the watcher on the hills
and a man in the world.
That's *exactly* where you should be.

And I say: wherever you are, if you can accept it,
immediately then and there
you have become the watcher on the hills.
Even in hell, if you accept it, the hell disappears,
because the hell can remain
only through your rejection.
The hell disappears and heaven appears.
Whatsoever you accept becomes heavenly,
and whatsoever you reject becomes the hell.

It is said that a saint cannot be thrown into hell
because he knows the alchemy to transform it.
You have heard that sinners go to hell
and saints to heaven —
but you have heard the wrong thing.
The case is just the other way around:
wherever sinners go, they create hell
and wherever saints go, there is heaven.
Saints are not sent to heaven.
There is nobody to send and manage all this —
there is nobody.
But wherever they go, this is the way they are:
they create their heaven.
They carry their heaven with them, within them.
And sinners? —
you can send them to heaven; they will create hell.
They cannot do otherwise.

So what is the definition of a saint or a sinner?
My definition is: a saint is one
who has come to know the alchemical secret
of transforming everything into heaven.
And a sinner is one who does not know the secret
of transforming things into beautiful existences.
Rather, on the contrary, he goes on making things ugly.

Whatsoever you are will be reflected around you.

So don't try to be anything else.
And don't try to be some other place.
That is the disease called man:
always to become somebody, to be some other place,
always rejecting that which is,
and always hankering for that which is not.
This is the disease called man.

Be alert! Do you see it?!
It is a simple fact to be seen.
I am not theorizing about it; I am not a theoretician.
I am simply indicating a bare, naked fact —
that if you can live in this moment wherever you are
and forget about the future, goals,
the idea of becoming something else,
immediately, the whole world around you is transformed;
you have become a transforming force.

Acceptance . . .
a deep, total acceptance
is what religion is all about.

A wants to become B; B wants to become C.
Then the fever of becoming is created.

You are not a becoming; you are a being.
You are already that which you can be,
which you ever can be —
you are already that.
Nothing more can be done about you;
you are a finished product.

This is the meaning I give to the story
that God created the world:
when the perfect creates, the creation is perfect.
When God creates, how can you improve upon it?
Just think of the whole absurdity;
the whole idea is absurd.

You are trying to improve upon God; you cannot improve.
You can be miserable, that's all.
And you can suffer unnecessarily.
And you will suffer diseases
which are just in your imagination and nowhere else.
God creating means: out of perfection comes perfection.

You are perfect! Nothing else is needed.
Look right now, this very moment, within yourself.
Have a direct insight. What is needed?
Everything is simply perfect and beautiful.
Not even a cloud I can see.
Just look within yourself —
not even a cloud in your inner space.
Everything is full of light.

But the mind will say, sooner or later,
to be something else, to be somewhere else, to become.
The mind doesn't allow you to be.
The mind is becoming, and your soul is being.
That's why Buddhas go on saying:
'Unless you drop all desiring you will not attain!'

Desiring means becoming.
Desiring means to be something else.
Desiring means not to accept the case as you are,
not to be in a total 'yes' mood —
no matter what the situation.

To say 'yes' to life is to be religious;
to say 'no' to life is to be irreligious.
And whenever you desire something you are saying 'no'.
You are saying that something better is possible.

The trees are happy
and the birds are happy
and the clouds are happy —
because they have no becoming.
They are simply whatsoever they are.

The rosebush is not trying to become a lotus, no.
The rosebush is absolutely happy to be a rosebush.
You cannot persuade the rosebush.
Howsoever you advertise the lotus,
you will not be able
to corrupt the mind of the rosebush to become a lotus.
The rosebush will simply laugh —
because a rosebush is a rosebush is a rosebush.
It is simply settled and centered in its being.
That's why the whole nature is without any fever:
calm and quiet and tranquil.
And settled!

Only human mind is in a chaos,
because everybody is hankering to be somebody else.
This is what you have been doing
for a thousand and one lives.
And if you don't awaken now,
when are you thinking to awaken?
You are already ripe for awakening.

Just start from this very moment
to live and enjoy and delight.
Drop desiring!
Whatsoever you are, enjoy it. Delight in your being.

And then suddenly time disappears,
because time exists only with desiring.
Future exists because you desire.

Then you will be like birds; listen to them.
Then you will be like trees; look —
the freshness, the greenery, the flowers.

Please be where you are.
I am not to create a new desire in you;
I am simply here to make you aware
of the whole absurdity of desiring.
Desiring is *sansar*.

The True Sage

Understanding the futility of desire
is to become enlightened.
One who has found out that he is already that
which he always wanted to be
is a Buddha.

And you are all Buddhas,
howsoever fast asleep and snoring.
That makes no difference.

Let me be your alarm. Open your eyes.
You have slept long enough. It is time to awaken.
The morning is knocking at the door.

When I encounter you,
you are always total compassion and loving warmth.
Why do we never encounter you in total anger
like Gurdjieff or the Zen Masters?
After all, the way we carry on here,
we surely deserve it sometimes.

Of course! You deserve it.
But that is not my way of working;
that is not the way I am.
I don't function according to you;
I function according to me.
I don't do a single thing because of you.
Because then it will be unnatural,
then it will be a pretension,
and then I will be going out of my self-nature.

You deserve it, I know, but nothing can be done.
I am helpless.
You may deserve anger,
but I will go on giving my love.
This much I know:

that the only way to make you alert and aware
is to remain in my self-nature,
so that it becomes a constant remembrance to you
to fall into *your* self-nature.

I would like you to be centered in yourself
so that nothing disturbs, nothing distracts.
Whatsoever happens around you remains like a dream
and you remain rooted in your being.
This can be done in only one way:
I should remain absolutely rooted in myself;
I should not be distracted by you.
Whatsoever you do should not be a consideration.
Whatsoever my self-nature can do spontaneously
is the only consideration.

And this much I know:
that if my love cannot transform you,
my anger will not be able to.
Because love is a greater force than any anger.
If my compassion cannot help you, nothing can help.
The more you become alert,
the more you will feel this.
You can bear my anger easily;
you are already conditioned for it.
But you cannot bear compassion;
it hits you hard and deep.

So maybe Gurdjieff worked in his own way;
it may have been spontaneous to him.
People are different and unique.
Or he may have been working in conditions
which were very strange.
He was working with western minds
in a western climate,
and he was the first
to bring eastern methods to them.

The True Sage

It was difficult;
it had to be translated to their understanding.

Zen Masters hit and beat their students.
They throw them out of their windows and houses;
they jump on them sometimes.
But one thing you should remember: they are not angry;
that too is part of their compassion.
They are not angry at all, because if they are angry
then the whole point is lost.
Then how can you transform the other?
Then you are also in the same boat.
Then you have come down.
No, that will not be helpful.

Anger is also compassion —
but it is possible only in Japan.
In no other country is it possible,
because a certain tradition is needed.
For almost one thousand years
this has been a tradition.
So when a Zen Master jumps and beats his disciple,
the disciple understands the language.
If I beat you, you will not understand it;
you will be simply angry,
and you will go away and report to the police.
And that is not going to help anybody.
No, you won't understand it.

In Japan it is understood.
When a Zen Master beats the disciple,
the disciple accepts it in deep gratitude.
In fact, you may be surprised —
that once a Zen Master beats his disciple,
that disciple becomes the chief disciple.
He has attained to something.
That's why the Master was so loving
and compassionate towards him;

that's why the Master blessed him with a beating.

Zen disciples hanker deep down for the day
when the Master will beat them.
They wait. They pray for it.
They compete with each other.
But that is possible only
because a long tradition exists.
A strange tradition —
but when it becomes deep-rooted
in the unconscious of a race, a country,
it functions.

But that's not my way.
I know that there is no other medicine than love.
Other medicines cannot be so deep-reaching.
If love fails, then nothing can succeed.

So I know that you deserve anger.
Please don't deserve it.

Even while repeating your jokes to others,
we ourselves burst into loud laughter.
But you tell us the funniest of stories
and while the audience roars,
not even a faint smile crosses your face.
What is the secret?

The secret is simple:
I know how to tell a joke and you don't.

The closer I feel to you,
the more you seem to disappear.
It is like coming near a river:
the river is there and yet it is not there.
Where are you Bhagwan?

The True Sage

The closer I feel to you,
the more you seem to disappear.

That's exactly how it will happen.
Because my whole effort is to help you to disappear
The closer you come to me,
the more you will find that I am disappearing.
That's just a hint, a guide
that you should follow me in disappearing.

So if you want to disappear,
only then come closer to me.
That's why there are many who are clever;
they don't come very close.
That is dangerous; that is coming close to a fire.
That is coming close to death!

In the old Indian scriptures
the Master is called death.
The Master is a death — and also a resurrection.
But first he is a death, and then a resurrection.
You have to die in him, and then you are reborn.
But the death is the beginning.

So when you come close to me,
you are bound to feel that I am disappearing.
Take the hint and follow me in disappearing.
Because you can meet me only
when neither I am nor you are.
When both are not there — the meeting, the union

The closer I feel to you,
the more you seem to disappear.

You are on the right path.
Don't be afraid. Come closer.

When Rama Priya comes to see me, she sits far away.
And I have to tell her: 'Come closer.'
Two inches she moves.

Then I say: 'Come still closer.'
Two inches again.
And I say: 'Come still closer.'
She is certainly aware that to come close is to die.
She does come close, but she hesitates; it is natural.
She comes close laughing, enjoying,
but also afraid and hesitating.

I am calling you to come close,
and I will not leave you until you disappear.
I will go on haunting you,
in your days, in your nights,
in your thoughts, in your dreams.
Wherever you are,
once you have been in contact with me —
only once —
then I will haunt you.
Then you will never be peaceful until you die.

It is like coming near a river;
the river is there and yet it is not there.
Yes, I am there and yet I am not there.
If you are far away from me, I am there.
If you come close, I am not there.
If you come deep within me,
you will not find anybody there —
just a nobody-ness, a nothingness, a deep emptiness.

And you ask: *Where are you Bhagwan?*

Nowhere.
The where has disappeared. The when has disappeared.
The time and space are no more relevant.

And remember, if you want to be all,
you cannot afford to be somebody.
If you want to be everywhere, you have to be nowhere.
If you want to become the eternity,
then you cannot be in any point of time.

The True Sage

If you want to be a god, you have to lose all.
That is the greatest gamble ever;
one loses one's self, stakes one's totality.
But one is never at a loss.
One loses one's self, but the whole is attained.

Jesus says to his disciples:
'If you cling to yourself, you will lose yourself.
If you lose, you will attain.
Whosoever clings to life will die.
And whosoever is ready to die
goes beyond death, becomes deathless.'

I am nowhere.
And I am calling you from my no-where-ness
to come and become a no-where-ness yourself.
I am no-when,
and I am calling you from my no-when-ness,
my timelessness,
so that you can also drop.

It is tremendously beautiful to disappear.
It is tremendously ecstatic!
It is the greatest bliss ever — not to be.

Shakespeare says: 'To be or not to be. . . . . '
That's what mind always says.
I would like to change it:
to be *and* not to be — not *or*.
To be *and* not to be, together —
that's how I am right now.

If you look at me from far away,
it is a form: *to be*.
If you come closer the form becomes unclear.
You are entering *not to be*.
To be is only my outside and not to be is my inside.
To be is only my body; not to be is my soul.

That's why Buddha says
that the soul is a no-soul, *anatta*.
It is a not-self. You cannot say it is.
It is better to say that it is not.

To be and not to be, together, is to be the true sage.
Don't choose between to be *or* not to be.
Both are available together;
take them both without any choice.

Then you will be in the world
and you will not be in the world.
Then you will be in the mind
and you will not be in the mind.
Then you will be in the body
and you will not be in the body.
Then you will be in time and space
and yet you will not be in any time, in any space.
And that's the only way to be free.

To be and not to be, together,
is to attain to total freedom —
nirvana, *moksha* —
or whatsoever name you want to give it.

If a being is enlightened, how can he die?

He never dies because he is already dead.

You die because you cling to life.
Then life has to be taken away,
then you have to die.

An enlightened being never dies
because he does not cling to life.
He has voluntarily given it up; he is already dead.
But it appears to you that he also dies like you.

The True Sage

That is only appearance —
don't be deceived by the appearance.

A Buddha dies, of course. A Mahavir dies.
Baal Shem will die, Moses will die —
everybody will die.
And they die just like you on the surface,
but that is only the surface.

Watch an ordinary man dying.
He makes every effort not to die,
he clings to life to the very last,
he cries and weeps tears of anguish
and fear and trembling.
A horror surrounds him; he is terror-struck.
And then watch an enlightened man dying;
it is one of the rarest experiences
to watch an enlightened person dying.
He dies as if he is the bridegroom
going to meet his bride.
He dies as if he is going
on a faraway, beautiful journey
for which he has always been waiting and planning.
He dies as if the training period
in this world is finished.
He is accepted. He has become mature.
Now he is going home from school.
He dies — but death is not there; God is there.
The face of death for an enlightened man
is the face of God.

The face of God for an unenlightened man
is the face of death.

When you know what life is,
God waits for you near the door you call death.

When you don't know what life is,
you are simply afraid —

so much afraid that before the door actually opens,
you are almost unconscious — you miss.
You have missed it many many times.
You have been dying many times and missing it.

There is only one way not to miss it,
and that is: die before death!
That's what I call meditation:
to voluntarily die before death
so that you know the flavour of it.

And it is so beautiful, so blissful
that you will dance when death comes.
You will sing when death comes.
You will wait in deep silence and gratitude and trust.
You will open your heart to it.
You will not be taken away; you will ride on the wave —
not as a defeated man, but as victorious.

The enlightened being never dies.
He has died already and known that there is no death.

Death is a lie.
It exists because you cling to life.

Feel the difference.
When a miserly man gives even one paise to a beggar,
the miserly man clings to it.
He thinks a thousand and one times
whether to give or not.
He argues not to give.
He rationalizes that these beggars are just cheats,
he rationalizes that to give anything to a beggar
is to help begging grow.
A thousand and one arguments are there *not* to give.
And even if he has to give, he gives reluctantly.
That's how an ordinary man dies —
reluctantly, clinging,
trying to find any excuse to linger a little longer.

The True Sage

A man who loves and brings a gift to give
is totally different.
The physical part looks the same.
The gift may not be of any value;
it may be just a flower plucked by the side of the road —
an ordinary flower, a grass flower —
but he comes and presents it.
Or it may be a *kohinoor*; it makes no difference.
When he gives, he gives with totality.
And he is happy that his gift has been accepted.
He feels grateful that his gift has not been rejected.
He thanks the receiver.
He had been dreaming, fantasizing
about the moment when he would give it.

The fact of the two men giving is the same —
the physical fact.
They are both using their hands;
something is to be transferred.
If you ask a scientist,
he will not be able to make any distinction,
he will not be able to feel any difference.
Whether you give reluctantly or you give lovingly
are both physical facts and similar.
But deep down you know they are absolutely different;
not a bit of similarity exists between them.

When you give reluctantly, you really don't give.
When you give lovingly, only then you give.
When you give reluctantly,
it has been taken away from you, snatched away;
you feel robbed.
When you give it lovingly, something flowers within you.
Somebody accepted your sharing, accepted your gift.
You have been blessed.

Death for an unenlightened man is a struggle.

He surrenders —
but only after fighting in every way possible.
That's why he feels defeated.

For an enlightened being, it is a let-go.
He is waiting and waiting —
waiting for the ship to come,
and then he will be going.
He learned whatsoever this life had to give;
now he is ready.
He does not look backwards even once.
No — not even once.
When the ship has arrived, he simply enters
and forgets everything about the world he is leaving,
because he is going to a greater world,
a greater being-hood — to God Himself.

Looking at myself and others here,
is it possible there have been others like us —
such as Buddha's disciples?
Were they amazed
and did they find themselves laughing
at how greedy, cunning, inept, they appeared
and how absolutely unlike
what they thought a sannyasin to be —
or do we take the cake?

Man has always been the same.
Buddha's disciples or Mahavir's disciples —
man has always been the same.
The same misery, the same ecstasy;
the same greed, the same renunciation;
the same clinging to material things,
and the same freedom of the sky, of the open space.

Man has always been the same.

The True Sage

Only outer things change.
Houses are different, roads are different,
transportation is different.
Bullock carts disappearing;
spaceships, buses appearing.
Everything on the outside is different.
But on the inside
the essential man is always the same.
The disease is the same; the health is the same.

I'm reminded of one *haddith,* one saying of Mohammed.
A man came to Mohammed and asked:
'Who was the first to be created in the world?'

Mohammed said: 'Adam.'

The man said: 'And before Adam?'

Mohammed again said: 'Adam.'

The man said: 'And before that?'

Mohammed said: 'If you ask me to the very end of time,
I will go on repeating Adam, Adam, Adam . . .
so please stop.'

The man was puzzled,
and Mohammed was not willing to explain more.

This has remained a mystery.
Why had Mohammed insisted: 'Adam, Adam, Adam . . . . '?
This is the explanation that I am telling you.
Man has always been there.
From the very beginning you have been there —
and there was never a time when you were not.

Man is one of the most
essential existences in existence.
That's why Mohammed says
that there is no 'before' to it.

Man has always been there.

It will be difficult for you to understand it
because the whole modern mind has been taught
to believe in evolution.
Yes, evolution has been there,
but not in the deeper core of man.

There is something in man
which has remained the same.
The outside has been changing
and changing and changing.
Man is like a wheel of a bullock cart :
the wheel moves and goes on changing,
but the wheel moves on an axle which remains static,
which doesn't change.
And the wheel can move only
because something in-moving supports it.
Everything has been changing —
the society, the culture, the civilization.
But something deep in man remains the same.
That depth is what Mohammed calls 'Adam'.

Man, essential man, is the same.
And remember always, he is the same in both ways.
If you go back
and look deeply into the disciples of Buddha,
you will see the same problems.
You can go and look in Buddhist scriptures —
the same problem.
The same greed, the same anger, the same hatred,
the same possessiveness, the same competition —
how to overtake the other —
the same ambition, the same ego.

Why do I say this ? —
because if you look at the discipline
that Buddha gave to his disciples,
then you immediately know.

The True Sage

He says : 'Don't be angry,
don't be greedy, don't be violent.'
If the disciples were already non-violent,
then Buddha looks like a fool.
'Why are you teaching not to be violent ?'
The disciples must have been violent.
Buddha says : 'Don't be possessive.'
The disciples must have been possessive.
Buddha says : 'Don't be greedy.'
The disciples must have been greedy.

There doesn't exist a single scripture in the world
which does not teach the same thing.
The same ten commandents are everywhere.
That shows man has remained the same,
because the same discipline is needed for you —
and the same discipline will be needed always.

Man can exist in two ways only ; there is no evolution.
Either you exist as an ignorant man, unaware, in deep sleep —
then greed, anger, ambition, ego, will follow you —
or you become awake.

Awakening is a jump !
Then the second category of man arises.
Then love, compassion, follows you.
Then there is no greed, no anger.

The ignorant man has the same characteristic today
as he has had always.
And the enlightened man
has the same characteristic as he has had always.

And these are the only two ways of being :
either be sleepy,
and miss the opportunity that is available ;
or be awake, and delight in it and celebrate.

So never think that in past ages, in golden ages,
people were different from you.
They were not different,
even though your priests go on saying they were.
That's why they call it 'the golden age'.
There has never been any golden age;
there will never be any golden age.
There have been golden people,
but there has never been a golden age.

Buddha was respected tremendously.
That shows that other people were fast asleep,
because only people who are asleep respect a Buddha.
If everybody was a Buddha, who would have bothered?
Buddha has been remembered for twenty-five centuries.
That shows that Buddhahood was rare
in those days also.
Otherwise, who bothers?
If Buddha was available in every village,
in every town, in every time, in every nook and corner,
then who would have bothered
to remember Gautam Siddharth?
He would have been forgotten by now.
But he was such a rare flower
that centuries passed and no Buddha was happening.
That's why we carry on and on, in deep reverence —
the name, the respect, the gratitude we feel.

Man has always been the same.
The greatest scriptures of the world
always talk about the lowest characteristics of man;
they have to.

I was reading. . . .
There is a Chinese book thought to be the oldest,
the ancient-most — almost ten thousand years old.

The True Sage

The book is a very small book;
only a few pages of it are left.
And those few pages are written on human skin.
But the teaching is the same:
don't be greedy; don't steal; don't be violent.
Ten thousand years have passed
and the teaching remains relevant,
because man remains the same.

In Babylon
a stone has been discovered with a script on it.
It took almost fifty years to decode it.
But if you read it, you will not be able to say
that it can be seven thousand years old.
It looks as if it is this morning's editorial
in some newspaper.

It says: 'In the golden old days
everything was beautiful.'
Seven thousand years ago, it says:
'In the good olden days, everything was beautiful;
now everything has become chaotic.
And the new generation is completely immoral.'
Seven thousand years ago —
and the new generation is immoral.
'Nobody respects his elders.
The father is no more respected;
the mother, no more respected.
The family is being destroyed.
The very foundation of society is shaking.'
Can you think that this is seven thousand years ago?
This looks just like the editorial
of this morning's *Poona Herald*.

Man is the same. There is no evolution.
Man can pass through a transmutation,
but there is no evolution.

Either you are asleep or you are awake:
this is the only transformation.
But there is no evolution.

A sleepy man has always been the same.
And those who are awakened have always been the same.

So don't condemn yourself.
Don't say this age is in a deep crisis;
it has always been so.
And don't say that in the past
everything was beautiful.
This has always been the idea of people:
that in the past. . . .
That past never existed.

And don't think that in the future
everything will be good.
That too has always been an idea.

If anything is possible, it is here-now!
And the jump is individual.
Society remains the same.
The jump is absolutely individual.
If you want to take the jump, become awake.

Take the jump; don't wait for a golden age to come.
There has never been a golden age.
Of course, a few golden people have existed;
they still exist now.

Many people are in silence now. Do you recommend this?
What is the purpose? Can it be helpful?

I don't recommend, but they understand.
I don't recommend anything in particular —
except understanding.

The True Sage

But if you understand, you would love silence.

I don't say: 'Be silent,'
because then it would become suppressive.
If you understand me, if you look towards me,
you will see silence before yourself.
And you will have a deep desire
arising in you to be silent.
Because in deep silence
all that is beautiful and true becomes available.

But you are in a constant chattering;
the inner talk continues.
Either you are talking with other people
or you are talking with yourself.
You are talking the whole day;
even in the night, in dreams, you are talking.
This continuous talking functions as a barrier,
you cannot see through it;
it is like a fog that densely surrounds you.
Your intelligence is destroyed because of this constant talk.

I don't recommend anything,
because then it becomes a discipline.
Then because *I* say you have to be silent
you force silence.
A forced silence is ugly.
A forced silence will not give you
the right taste of silence.

No. Just understand.
Try to understand me, feel me.
And then you would like to be silent.
And when *you* would like to be silent,
only then can it be beautiful.

When silence arises from your own heart
with a deep understanding,

by and by you become silent.
In fact, then you don't become silent;
you by and by drop the talk —
the inner talk, the outer occupation.
Then silence is not the thing;
you just understand that the whole talking is nonsense.
Why go on talking? For what?
There is nothing to say, but you go on talking.

In the Chinese language there is an idiogram
which means two things together.
The Chinese language
is really something totally different
from any other language —
because only pictures exist, no alphabet.
And each picture means many things.

One idiogram 'pi' means two things.
One is: to explain; one meaning is to explain.
The other meaning is: in vain.
To explain is to explain in vain. Isn't it marvellous?
There is nothing to explain. Nothing to say, really.

Just watch!
What do you go on talking about the whole day?
Ninety-nine percent would have been avoided easily.
I don't say a hundred percent
because I know, a few things —
just day-to-day things —
one has to talk about.
But then things will become telegraphic;
you need not go on round about, round about.
Many times a 'yes' or a 'no' will do.
And many times even that is not needed,
just a nodding of the head will do.
And many times even that is not needed
because the other is not worried what you think;
he is simply unloading himself.

The True Sage

You can just watch; there is no need to listen.

If you become aware,
the outer talk, the inner talk, by and by disappears.
Not that you start practicing silence — no.
It is just that the outer and inner talk
becomes absolutely absurd, futile.
You just drop it. And silence is reclaimed.
When the words disappear, silence arises.
It is not directly to be achieved;
it is an indirect result of understanding.

Yes, many people understand.
I hope you will also understand;
I wish that you will understand.
But, with me, remember always
I don't recommend anything —
because too many things
have been recommended to you.
And they have become ugly.
I don't give you a discipline,
I don't give you an outer mode of life;
I only give you an inner light.
In that inner light you have to find your discipline.

I make you aware about certain things.
Then take the hint
and don't wait for direct recommendations —
because then you will be a loser.
I am not going to give you anything direct,
because direct discipline
is needed only by very stupid minds.
I hope that you behave more intelligently,
more responsively.
Become more responsible.

Do you see the difference?
If I say: 'Be silent!' you will have to follow it.

It will be forced —
as if a flower has been forced and opened.
It has not opened by itself.

A flower opens by itself.
Let your silence become a flower
opening by itself on its own accord.

*I feel the need for effort to stay in the present.
And this effort makes it hard to relax completely.
Letting go often seems to bring back the past or future.
Could you explain about being alert without tension?*

   The idea to be in the present
will not allow you to relax.
In fact, if you relax, you will be in the present.
In the beginning, if you relax,
the past will rush towards you.
Many things that you have suppressed,
many things that you have never allowed
to come up before your consciousness,
many things that you have been avoiding —
they will rush.

When you relax, the doors are open.
These things always wanted
to come before your consciousness
but you never allowed them.
Now that you are not forcing them, *they* will rush.
But this is going to be temporary.

Many dreams about the future
that you have also been suppressing will come.
There will be a chaos for a time being;
you have to relax and watch the chaos.
There should be no anxiety about it —
it is natural.

The True Sage

It is as if a room has been closed for many days;
then you open it and bad smells escape.
But if you keep it open, fresh air will be flowing
and the bad smells will be gone.

Your unconsciousness has accumulated a very bad smell.
It is like a closed house,
and it has become a junkyard.
Whatsoever you think is wrong
or people and priests and politicians say is wrong
you go on throwing into the junkyard.
You are sitting on a volcano.
When you relax, everything will bubble up;
it will surface.
Allow it. It has to be.
And don't be worried.

So don't try to be in the present.
Rather, relax,
so that the past and the future are both there —
and they will go by themselves.
You need not be worried; simply watch.
Don't do a single thing,
because if you do something you will again repress.
Don't do a single thing.
Just watch, as if the birds are flying in the sky
and you are watching — lying down on the grass.
The birds flying in the sky,
the clouds moving, slowly, lazily.
Thoughts are also like clouds; desires are also like birds.
Be a watcher.

The problem arises because you become a doer.
You say: 'This idea should not be there.
Who are you to say that this cloud
should not be there?
Who are you? Why are you trying to manipulate?

The clouds are moving in the outer sky;
thoughts are moving in the inner sky.
Let them be. Just relax.
Doze away. Let them be.
Whenever you want to see, see.
If you don't want to see, then doze.
But don't do anything.
Soon, the sky becomes clear.
If you don't do anything, many things start happening.
And the first thing is:
all repressions that are released flow away from you.
Soon the day comes when the sky is absolutely clear.
Then you will be in the present.

So, you are trying from the wrong side.
Don't try to be in the present; rather, just be in a let-go.
And when you are in a let-go
don't make any conditions what should happen
and what should not happen.
Otherwise you cannot be in a let-go.
A let-go can only be unconditional.
You simply relax; now whatsoever happens, happens.
And if nothing happens, that too is good.

A let-go is a let-go!
Now you don't have any idea what should happen.
If the past rushes in, it rushes in.
If the future comes in, it comes in.
You are not even worried about being in the present,
because that will not allow you to be in a let-go.
You simply relax.

But relaxation has become almost impossible
because you have so many conditions:
this should not be, this should be;
this thought is bad, that thought is good;
this is from the devil, this is from God.

The True Sage

And you are continuously choosing and manipulating
and fighting and arranging.
You cannot be in a let-go.

Drop all morality. Drop all evaluation.
Nothing is good. Nothing is bad.
Everything is whatsoever it is.
Relax.
Suddenly, one day,
the present arises in its deep radiance.
Then there are no clouds
and no thoughts and no desires.

And to be in the present
is to enter the door of existence.

I keep feeling myself authentic.
Yet, within the hour,
I see the way I was as inauthentic.
And then, within the hour,
that fresh authenticity again looks false.
When I laugh about this whole ridiculous situation,
that really feels to be really authentic — that laugh.
But sooner or later I'm doubting that too.
Is the whole concept of authenticity absurd?

No, the concept of authenticity is not absurd.
But it is not a concept.
And the problem is not arising by authenticity;
it is arising by comparison.

In this moment you feel authentic.
After an hour you think about it;
then comparison arises.
After an hour,
the authenticity is no more an authenticity;
it is just a memory.

The memory looks faint,
the memory is already cloudy, hazy.
And you compare this memory with the present moment.
Of course it will look inauthentic,
and the present moment will look authentic.
Then again, after an hour,
that present moment is no more a present moment.
Again you compare.
The problem is arising because of comparison.

Each moment is unique and incomparable;
you cannot compare it.
Forget about it!
Authentic or inauthentic — it is gone.
Forget about it.
There is no need to carry it and to compare.

The morning was beautiful
but the afternoon is not the morning.
You carry the morning
and then you become suspicious
whether it was so beautiful or not.
Because now it is afternoon
and the reality of the morning has disappeared.
Now it is only a faint memory,
a remembrance of something which was.
Was it really there? Now how can you decide?
It is no longer real.
And then you compare the morning with this afternoon.
The afternoon is real.
By the evening the afternoon is gone
but then you compare the afternoon with the evening.
Now beautiful stars are arising and you think:
'Was it real or did I just imagine it?'

The present is always real; the past is always a memory.
Don't compare the present with the past,
otherwise the past will look inauthentic.

The problem is not with inauthenticity;
the problem is with comparison.
And mind is a great effort to compare.
Mind goes on comparing;
it goes on comparing every moment
and that's how it goes on missing the glory.
The absolute glory is missed
because the mind goes on comparing.

You come across a rosebush and you see a rose;
the mind immediately compares:
you have seen bigger roses; this is nothing.
But this rose is *this* rose;
it has nothing to do with any other rose.
There may be bigger roses,
there may be more beautiful roses;
but this rose has its own beauty, has its own reality,
has its own authenticity, here-now.
Why are you missing this by bringing a comparison in?

Look at this rose.
No other rose can give that which this rose can give.
Watch it. Delight in it. Dance with it.
Sing a song near it. Open your heart to it.
Let it spread its fragrance towards your being.
Let it flow towards your heart
and let yourself flow towards it.
Why bring in comparison?

Once you learn the nonsense of comparison
you will miss all.
Then, another day, there is another rose —
you will miss that too.
And the ridiculousness is that you missed yesterday's rose
and you are missing today's rose.
When you look at today's rose
you will think of yesterday's.
And when you were near yesterday's rose

you were thinking of other roses.
You never looked at anything.

A comparing mind misses everything
and goes on thinking that others,
which are no longer present,
were more beautiful.

Be true to the moment.
And when you have lived it, don't carry it;
there is no need.
When you have crossed the river,
don't carry the boat on your head.
Leave it there. Now it is no more needed.
Otherwise it will become a burden.
And in the marketplace, people will laugh at you.

What is the most stupid thing Mulla Nasrudin ever did?

It is difficult to say, because he is still alive.
And one thing is certain —
he will not die before me.
So don't ask, because nobody can predict;
he is unpredictable.
And he will do more and more stupid things;
one grows through experience.

He is not going to die before me;
I cannot afford that.
So, I cannot say.
When I am gone, he will also be gone.
Then you can think about it.
Much research will be needed.

Mulla Nasrudin is not a person;
he is the whole humanity.
He is you; he is you, all together.

The True Sage

Whatsoever you can do, Mulla can do more stupidly.
He is perfect!
Whatsoever any human being can do,
he can do more perfectly.
He is your stupidity.
And if you can understand it
you will laugh and you will weep also.
You will laugh at the ridiculousness of it
and you will weep that that ridiculousness is yours.
When you laugh at Mulla Nasrudin, remember,
you are laughing at yourself.
He just brings you face to face
with whatsoever you are,
so that it can be encountered.

Mulla Nasrudin is not new; he's an old Sufi device.
There are stories which are one hundred, two hundred,
even three hundred years old, around Mulla Nasrudin.
He is an old device.

There have been many claims
to whom Mulla Nasrudin belongs.
The Russians say he belongs to them.
They have a gravestone
which proves that he belongs to them.
Iranians say he belongs to them.
Arabs say he belongs to them.
In Bukhara, they have a place
dedicated to Nasrudin's memory.

He has been all over the world.
In fact, wherever there is stupidity,
there is Mulla Nasrudin.
He belongs to all; nobody alone can claim him.

And I say that he is still alive.
He may have died in one country
but he is resurrected in another.

Many times, I myself have seen him dying
and the next day he knocks on my door.
It is impossible. It seems he cannot die.
He is human stupidity.

But if you look deep into the stupidity
you will see the wisdom also.
In all his stupidities
there is a germ of hidden wisdom.

Just the other day it happened. . . .
He was sitting at his grocery store
and I was by his side.

A tiny, fastidious woman came at rush-hour
and she upturned the whole grocery store.
For hours she bothered and bored Nasrudin.
Only after hours of struggle could he satisfy her;
she finally purchased what she wanted and was satisfied.

And then the woman said:
'Mulla, you may not be knowing,
but when I came to your shop
I had a very terrible headache —
and now it is absolutely gone.'

Mulla Nasrudin said: 'Dear madam, don't be worried.
Don't be worried!
It has not gone. It has come to me.'

He may look stupid, but he is wise also.
If you understand him
you will laugh and you will weep
because you will see yourself
and the whole humanity in it.

Don't ask:
What is the most stupid thing Mulla Nasrudin ever did?

The True Sage

He is always doing greater stupid things than before.
His every act is unique, incomparable.
If you look into it
you will think that this is the best;
but when the next act comes
it is something absolutely new,
something tremendously great.

Read about Mulla Nasrudin and try to understand him.
Make it a meditation.
It has been, for centuries, a Sufi meditation.

Sufi teachers used to give Mulla Nasrudin jokes
to their disciples to think and ponder and meditate.
Because whatsoever he says has meaning in it;
whatsoever he does has meaning in it.
They are not ordinary jokes — remember.
I don't tell them to you just to make you laugh.
No, they are not mere jokes; they are pointers.
You should not just laugh and forget them;
you should make them a part of your understanding.
And then you will see Mulla Nasrudin
arising many times within yourself — acting, behaving.
And then you will be able to laugh.
And if you can laugh at yourself,
you have laughed for the first time.

19th October 1975

One day
   the Rabbi of Zans
was standing at the window
   and looking out into the street,
Seeing a passer-by,
   he knocked on the window pane
and signed to the man
   to come into the house.

When the stranger entered the room,
   Rabbi Hayyim asked him:—
'Tell me,
   if you found a purse of ducats,
   would you return it to its owner?'
'Rabbi,' said the man,
'if I knew the owner
   I should return the purse
   without a moments delay.'
'You are a fool,' said the Rabbi of Zans.

Then he resumed his position
   at the window,
called another passer-by,
   and put the same question to him.
'I am not such a fool
   as to give up a purse full of money
   that has come my way,' said the man.
'You're a bad lot,' said the Rabbi of Zans,
and called in a third man.

He replied:—
'Rabbi, how can I know—

on what rung I shall be
when I find the purse,
   or whether I shall succeed
in fending off the Evil Urge?
   Perhaps it will get the better of me,
   and I shall appropriate
      what belongs to another.
   But perhaps God, blessed be He,
      will help me to fight it,
   and in that case,
      I shall return what I have found
   to its rightful owner.'
'Those are good words,' cried the zaddick.
'You are a true sage.'

True wisdom

Man is a machine.
He is born, lives, loves, dies —
but not as a man;
he is born, lives, loves, dies
just like a machine.
He is not conscious.

Everything happens; man is not the doer.
He has no will of his own.
But he believes that he is the doer,
he believes that he has a will-power,
a will of his own.
He believes that he *is*.
This is the greatest stupidity possible,
the base of all ignorance.
Because of this belief,
he never becomes aware of the true situation.

Man, ordinarily, is only in two states:
asleep, with closed eyes; and asleep, with open eyes.
And continuously, an undercurrent of dreaming goes on.

To say: 'I am'
is not true in the ordinary state of humanity,
because there are many 'I's' within you.

The True Sage

You don't have a single 'I';
you don't have a single center of reference.
One mood comes and goes;
another mood comes and goes.
And with each mood, a separate 'I' dominates you.

When you are angry, it is not the same 'I'
as it was when you were in love.
A totally different personality takes possession of you —
and many times you have suspected.
Many times you have been angry and have said:
'In spite of me, I was angry.'
What do you mean when you say: 'In spite of me?'
Then who was angry?
You have suspected rightly that the 'I'
which you are ordinarily identified with
was not in power.
Somebody else dominated you —
a vagrant 'I', a vagabond 'I', an unusual 'I'.

Just a few days before, a sannyasin came to me.
She was very happy that she had fallen in love
and that she had found a lover.
She was ecstatic.
And she asked if I would give her a Tantra technique
so that she could move
into deeper orgasmic states of love.

I looked into her and I said:
'Wait for seven days.
Next time you come, bring your lover with you.'

She came back after a week, but she said:
'We have quarreled and separated.'

So I asked: 'What about the Tantra technique?
I am ready to give it to you.'

True Wisdom

She said: 'But now I have no lover.'
And she was so sad and so depressed —
and not even suspecting what had happened.

When you fall in love, you believe that —
you think something permanent has happened in your being.
When you are sad, then you believe that that is true.
You are such a great believer.
You never suspect for a single moment
that these are moods,
and they pass just as clouds pass in the sky,
and they go on flowing just like a river flows.

Nothing is permanent in you.
How can you say: 'I am'? That will be a falsity.
To assert 'I am' is to say a lie.
You cannot say that; you are many 'I's'.
There are a thousand and one egos within you —
a crowd, a multiplicity. You are poly-psychic.
You are just like a wheel.
Think of a moving wheel of a bullock cart:
one spoke comes up; then it goes down.
Another comes up; that too is on the way down.
And the wheel goes on moving.
Every moment a different spoke comes up.
You are like a wheel — you go on moving.
And many spokes are there which you call 'I's'.
When one 'I' comes up, you get identified with it.

When you are angry you don't see
that anger is like a cloud surrounding you.
You become one with it.
The mood takes total possession of you;
you are possessed by it.
Then it is not good to say: 'I am angry.'
It would be better to say: 'I am anger.'

311

When love possesses you, you become love.
Don't say: 'I am in love.' You *are* love.
You get so identified with the mood
that your separate identity, your separate being,
is no more there.
And this goes on continuously
from the moment you are born to the moment you die.

You become young and you think you *are* young.
And you know that the body is changing every moment.
Then you become old and you think: 'I am old.'
In youth you were jubilant that you were young,
full of energy.
In old age you are sad and depressed,
because now the energy has gone.
While alive, you think you are the body,
and when death comes, then you say: 'I am dying.'
Whatsoever happens, you become identified with it.

This is the state of affairs
of a humanity which is fast asleep.
That's why it cannot be said that you are man yet;
you are a mechanism.
The man will be born within you
when you become conscious of the whole mechanism —
and yet don't get identified.

You can see anger coming,
you can see anger all around you,
and yet you remain a watcher on the hill.
You go on seeing. . . .
A cloud has come. There is a fog all around —
but you remain separate.
You know well: 'I am the knower and not the known.'
You know well: 'I am the witness and not the witnessed.'
You know well that infinite distance exists
between you and that which surrounds you.
It may be touching you, but infinite distance exists —

because the known can never touch the knower,
the seen can never touch the seer.
The seer transcends; the seer is the *very* transcendence.

Just a few days before, I was telling you
that there are three ordinary types of man.
Man number one is identified with his body.
Man number two
is identified with his feelings, emotions.
Man number three
is identified with his mind, thinking, thoughts.
And all the three are asleep.
Their sleep may be different.
One sleeps in the body;
another sleeps in the emotions;
the third sleeps in his thoughts.
But the sleep is the same:
the quality is of unconsciousness, stupor.

Then there is the fourth man, man number four.
He becomes alert.
He watches his body, but is not identified with it.
He uses his body, but is never lost in it.
He remains aloof, detached, distant.
He uses his feelings;
many times he is surrounded by his feelings,
but he is never overpowered.
He remains separate.
Thoughts are there;
the mind goes on functioning and creating thoughts,
but man number four remains alert.
Body, mind, heart — they all function.
They function even better than they function in you
because there is no disturbance
from the innermost being;
the innermost being remains aloof.
This is man number four.

The True Sage

Man number four is what I mean by a sannyasin.
There is no need to go anywhere;
wherever you are, become aware.
And there and then sannyas starts functioning.
It is not a question of changing places;
it is a question of changing the inner attitude.
You remain in the body,
but you know now that you are not the body.
And once number four is there, man is born.

You are born only with a potentiality to be a man;
you are not born as a man.
You are only born with the capacity to become a man;
you may become, you may not become.
You can miss the whole point.
You can go round and round,
and never reach and penetrate the center of your being.
But if awareness arises and you become watchful,
man is born.

Hindus have called this state *dwij*,
the state of the twice-born.
The first birth is through the parents,
the mother and father.
The second birth is through awareness —
and that is the real birth.
The first birth will culminate in death;
the second birth never culminates in death.
So the first birth is a birth in name only;
in fact, it is a way to death.
The day you were born was the day
you have been dying ever since.
One day, the whole process will be completed.
So your birth was nothing but entry into death.
You may take seventy or eighty years to reach,
but you have been walking towards death
every moment of your life.

True Wisdom

Only when you are twice-born, *dwij*,
only when the next birth has happened,
and man number four is born within you,
suddenly, you know there is no death.

Death exists only with identification.
If you are identified with the body, you will die.
The body is not you; it has to be left some day.
You cannot remain in it forever and forever.
It is a passing phase; it is just a milestone, not the goal.
You can rest a little while under the shade of a tree,
but one has to go.

You can get identified with the emotions,
but then there will be death — and you know it.
The body dies once in seventy years;
the emotions die every day, every moment.
You love a person and then there is death.
Or, you don't love, the mood has gone —
and you feel a subtle death happening.
You were friendly with a person;
now the friendliness has disappeared — a death.
Every moment you die in your emotions.

And thoughts are even faster in dying.
You cannot keep a single thought
for a few seconds in your mind;
it will try to escape.
Try it — just try to keep
one single thought for a few minutes.
It will not be there; it is already gone.
It is trying to escape.

The mind is dying continuously every moment.
The heart is dying continuously every hour.
The body is also dying continuously,
but a continuity remains for seventy, eighty years.
These three are the identifications.

The True Sage

The fourth consciousness arises
when you are not identified.

One thing more about this. . . .
There are four ways to reach God.
One is : to make an effort through the body to reach ;
that's what hatha yogis have been doing.
It is not a true way.
Something can be achieved through it —
because finally the body also belongs to God —
but it is not your totality.
Gurdjieff has called this 'the way of the fakir'.

You can see many fakirs in India.
You may be impressed by their attainments ;
they attain to certain powers.
For example, you can come across a fakir
who has been standing continuously,
for ten, twenty years.
He has never allowed his body to rest —
to sit down or to sleep. He has been standing.
Even if he has to sleep, he sleeps standing.
Now his body has become almost rigid, paralyzed.
Now it cannot move ; the flexibility is lost.
But you will see certain powers in him
because he has attained to the lowest kind of will ;
to stand for ten years continuously needs will.

Just try for ten days and you will know.
Just try for ten hours and you will know.
Just try for ten minutes —
not moving, just standing —
and you will know.
A thousand and one problems arise.
The mind says : 'What are you doing ?
Drop this whole nonsense.
Everybody is enjoying and what are you doing ? —
just standing like a fool ?'

Ten years, not moving, and a very low kind of will
concerned with the body happens.
It is very materialistic, but a will arises.
The man attains to a certain crystallization.
He can do a few things: he can heal.
He can touch your body
and a healing power will be possible
through his body to flow towards you.
He can bless; he can curse.
And whatsoever he says will come to pass.
Because a man who has remained standing for ten years
has attained to an intensity.
If he says something,
those words become very potential and powerful.
They are atomic; they carry energy.
If he curses you, the curse is going to happen.
If he blesses you, the blessing will be there.

But this man himself
will remain on a very low rung of being.
If you look into his eyes you will not see intelligence;
he will be a stupid type of saint.
Nothing of the higher,
but a crystallization of the lower will be there.
You can feel certain powerful vibrations around him,
not of intelligence, not of awareness,
not of meditation — but of concentration.
He can live a long time —
a hundred or two hundred years
will not be very difficult for him,
because his body will follow him.
Whatsoever he wants to do with the body, he can do.
But it is nothing of the spiritual;
it is nothing of the religious.
If you try through the body,
you are trying the lowest possibility within you.

If a fakir is fortunate,

then he may get the guidance of a Master
who can pull him out of his body.
Otherwise he will die, deep in his body.
And next life, everything will be lost again.

Unless something is attained in consciousness,
it cannot be permanent because the body will change.
Whatsoever you have attained with this body
will be lost with the next.
You may be a Mohammed Ali,
but you cannot carry the body to the next birth;
this body will be left here.
You may be a beautiful man;
you may be a beautiful woman, a Cleopatra —
but this body has to be left here.
All that has been attained
through the body and with the body will be lost.

Unless the fakir is fortunate enough
to come under the guidance of a Master,
he cannot be pulled out of his body.

In India,
it has been one of the compassions of the Masters. . . .
You must have heard,
there are ancient stories that in India
Masters used to travel all around the country
On the surface,
it looked as if they were great intellectuals:
a Shankaracharya, a Ramanuja, a Vallabha,
a Nimbark, a Buddha, a Mahavir.
On the surface it looked
as if they were going to convert people.
That was just a superficial thing.
Deep down, they were doing many things.
One of the most important things was
to go from town to town to look after fakirs —
because those fakirs could not come to you.

They were so deep-rooted in their bodies;
they had lost all intelligence.
They were not bad people;
they were ignorant, but powerful.
If their power could be released,
they could suddenly jump
to a higher rung of their being.

Meher Baba, in this age, did such a work.
He travelled all around the country for years,
just looking after fakirs.
Wherever he would hear that a fakir is,
he would go — to bring him out of his stupor.
A fakir is a good man, a very good man — but ignorant.

Then there is the second.
Gurdjieff has called it 'the way of the monk'.
You can call it the way of the devotee, *bhakti marg*.
The first is hatha yoga;
the second is *bhakti marg* — the way of the monk.

The way of the monk is to get to the divine
through feelings, prayers, crying, weeping —
in a deep love and affection,
in a deep thirst to move towards God.
But this type of man gets involved in the emotions.
He achieves a greater state,
a higher stage than the first, the fakir —
but still he is caught.
Somebody is needed to bring him out of that also.

Then there is the third way: the way of the yogi.
He works through the intellect,
he works through thinking.
It is the way of the philosopher, the intellectual.
He attains still a higher stage,
but then he gets caught.

All three get caught!

Only the fourth goes beyond, and is never caught.
That's why Gurdjieff has called his path 'the fourth way'.
And it is significant to understand,
because the Hassidic path is also the fourth way.

Hassidism, the Hassidic approach
also belongs to the fourth.
Body, feeling, mind — all have to be transcended.
One has to become just alert —
alert of all that happens within and without.
The only key for the fourth way is to be mindful,
to be aware, to witness, to see into things —
and not to get identified.

Now listen to this story.
This is a beautiful story;
it belongs to the fourth way.

One day
the Rabbi of Zans
was standing at the window
and looking out into the street.
Seeing a passerby,
he knocked on the window pane
and signed to the man
to come into the house.

When the stranger entered the room,
Rabbi Hayyim asked him:
'Tell me,
if you found a purse full of ducats,
would you return it to its owner?'

A very simple question, but not so simple.
The man was deceived by the simplicity.

'Tell me,
if you found a purse full of ducats,
would you return it to its owner?'

True Wisdom

The man must have thought
that the rabbi was asking a moral question;
that's how he was deceived.
The rabbi was not asking a moral question.

A really religious man is never bothered about morality,
because morality is nothing but a game.
One has to play the rules of the game
because one has to live with many people.
Morality exists because you have to relate
to so many people.
It has nothing to do with your essence;
it has something to do with your relations.

For example, if you are alone on the earth,
and you find a purse full of ducats
and gold and money,
will it be immoral to keep it?
Then the question of morality or immorality
does not arise.

If you are alone on the earth, can you be a thief?
It is impossible —
because to steal, you need somebody else to be there.
To rob, you need somebody else to be there.
If you are alone on the earth, you cannot be a thief,
you cannot be a robber.

If you are alone on the earth, can you lie?
It is impossible. To whom will you lie?
To lie, somebody else is needed.

Morality is always in relationship.
And religion is something
that you do with your aloneness.

So the rabbi is not asking a moral question;
he is asking a very important, significant question
about your inner being.

The True Sage

He asked:
'Tell me,
if you found a purse full of ducats,
would you return it to its owner?'

The formulation is moralistic;
that's how the man was deceived.

He said: *'Rabbi,*
if I knew the owner
I should return the purse
without a moment's delay.'

That's how everybody is.
If it is a theoretical question, there is no problem:
you are always moral.
In theory, everybody is moral.
The question arises only when a thing
becomes really real.
Sometimes, you even become immoral in theory.

I used to know a man in my village — he was a doctor,
but he had failed as a doctor.
His practice was not good at all;
he was always poor.
His whole personality was such
that nobody would think that he was a doctor.
A doctor has to look like a doctor;
his appearance is significant.
He was a very tiny man, ill-looking.

Sometimes I would send somebody to him,
but the people would think that he was not the doctor
but the compounder.
And they would ask:
'Mr. compounder, where is the doctor?'
Of course, he would get very angry.

It was certain that it was difficult for him

to succeed as a doctor,
so he used to waste his time on crossword puzzles.
And he was always enthusiastic that 'this time'
he was going to get one lakh rupees,
two lakh rupees, three lakh rupees. . . .
Every month it happened,
and when the contest was over,
he would forget about it
and start working on new crossword puzzles.

One day I was just joking with him.
I said: 'Look. You have been working so hard.
At least for one year I have been watching you —
and you have not won any prize.
It seems it is not in your fate.
Do one thing: join my fate with you.'

He said: 'How can it be joined?'

I said: 'Do one thing.
How much will you donate to me?
If you get one lakh rupees,
how much will you donate to me?'

He started thinking. He was a poor man.
He closed his eyes and he said: 'Okay. Fifty percent.'
It was hard to say fifty percent;
it was too much — fifty thousand rupees.

I said: 'Okay. Agreed.
Now it is certain; go ahead.
Now my fate also is aligned with you.
You are going to get it.'

In the night, near about twelve o'clock,
he knocked at my door, and he said:
'Listen, fifty thousand is too much —
I cannot sleep.
It seems that this time it is going to happen,
and you have hooked me.

The True Sage

It seems you have some idea
that this time it is going to happen.
It is not a question
of your fate being aligned with me;
it seems that you have some suspicion
that it is going to happen.
And I am also absolutely certain
that it is going to happen this time.
Please, fifty thousand will be too much.'

So I said: 'Okay, you suggest how much.'

He said: 'Ten thousand will do.'

I could see that even ten thousand was too much.
He was a poor man
who had never had ten thousand rupees;
it was too much.
I said: 'Okay. That will do.'

Next morning he was back again, very depressed —
feeling a little ashamed also.
He said: 'Please forgive me. Excuse me.
But I thought and thought and thought....
I am a poor man, you know....
Ten thousand is too much.'
He has not yet got anything!
This is just in his dream.

I said: 'Then what do you propose?'

He said: 'This time, let me have it completely.
Next time, whenever I will get it again,
whatsoever you say, I will give you.
This time it seems so certain.'

I said: 'Okay. You have it.
But don't complain to me later on
because now I am no more aligned with your fate.'

Then he became afraid.
By the evening he was back.
He said: 'Just as a token, you can have one rupee,
so that you are with me.
Otherwise, I have become afraid
that maybe I am not going to get it.'

The mind is so greedy; you don't know the greed.
When you are in thinking, just imagining,
you become absolutely moralistic.
Everybody is good.
You have been angry, and then you repent.
And in repentance, everybody is perfectly beautiful.
And you say: 'Never again will I do this.'
But you don't know what you are saying.
You don't know that this is what
you have been saying your whole life.
Every time you have been angry,
you have repented and you have said: 'Never again!'
Then it happens again and again and again —
and you have not been even watchful enough
to see the whole absurdity of it.

If you are *really* aware, you will drop repentance
because you know the foolishness of it.
You have repented many times. Nothing happens,

One man was here. . . .
He was a very angry man; he was continuously angry.
He told me: 'I don't want God.
I don't want any meditation.
Just bring me out of my angry state.
I repent, but nothing happens;
and I have taken all sorts of vows,
but nothing happens.
What to do?'

The True Sage

I told him: 'Do one thing. First, renounce repentance —
that from now onwards, you will never repent.
Be angry, but never repent about it.'

He asked: 'How is that going to help? —
because even repentance has not been of any help.
If I don't repent, I may become even more angry.'

I said: 'You leave it to me. First leave repentance.'

After a week he was back, and he said:
'It is impossible. I cannot leave repentance.
Whenever I become angry, it follows like a shadow.
It is automatic.'

The whole point to see is: you don't have any will.
The whole point to see is:
you have not been alert about yourself.
You don't know who you are!
All your promises are going to be false,
because you don't know who is the one who is promising.
How can you promise? How can you fulfill the promise?

One mood promises, and by the time fulfillment comes,
that mood is no more there; some other mood is prevalent.
And the other mood has not even heard about the first mood.

In the evening you decide:
'Tomorrow morning, at four o'clock,
I am going to get up.
And this time, I am really going to get up!'
But you don't know the mood that will be there
at four o'clock in the morning.
This is evening;
this is not four o'clock in the morning.
You can easily believe that you have a will.
Next morning at four o'clock,
somebody within you says:
'What nonsense. This is time to get up?

True Wisdom

It is so cold and it is raining . . .
and it is so beautiful to sleep.
Have a little more sleep, you are not feeling rested.'
You have completely forgotten your promise.
You turn over and have a good rest.
In the morning, when you are taking your tea,
now you are repenting,
now you are condemning yourself:
'What type of man am I?
I had decided to get up at four;
why did I change my mind?'
Now that is a third state, a third rung,
a third spoke on top.
You may again decide to get up at four o'clock,
because in the morning it is so easy to decide.
But again the thing will change.
And you have been doing this continuously
for your whole life
and you have not become aware yet!

The Rabbi said: *'Tell me,*
if you found a purse full of ducats
would you return it to its owner?'

A theoretical question; nothing is at stake.
You have not found the purse,
and you don't know about yourself at all.

The man said: *'Rabbi,*
if I knew the owner
I should return the purse
without a moment's delay.'

As if the question is only of knowing the owner.
The man said: 'If I knew the owner,
I would return it immediately.
But if I don't know the owner,
then it may take a little time to find the owner.'

The True Sage

In Mulla Nasrudin's town, this is the tradition:
if somebody finds something,
he has to go into the market
and loudly shout three times: 'I have found this thing.'
If it doesn't belong to anybody —
he can claim it, and it is his.

One day Mulla found a diamond.
He went to the marketplace;
he shouted thrice, then came back home.
His wife said: 'Where have you been?'

He said: 'I have found a diamond.
And the tradition says
that one has to go to the marketplace.
That's why I have been there.'

His wife said: 'Is this the time to go? —
in the mid of the night
when everybody is fast asleep!?
Did you really shout three times?'

Nasrudin said: 'Yes, I shouted, but very slowly.
In fact, I could not hear it myself.
I mumbled, because a beggar was sleeping there —
and I was afraid that he may jump and claim it.
But I have followed the rule; now there is no trouble.
We can have this diamond.'

'Rabbi,' said the man,
'if I knew the owner
I should return the purse
without a moment's delay.'

Just think — that's what you might have said.
Nothing is at stake; there is no purse, nothing.
You can be so cheaply moral.
And this man is saying:
'If I knew the owner, there would be no trouble.

True Wisdom

I would go immediately and give it to him.
If there was some delay,
it would only be because the owner was not known —
not because of me.'

Just think about it;
put yourself in the place of that man.
Would not the same answer have been yours?
Nothing is at stake.
And the rabbi would feel very good and blessed
that you are a moral man.

'You are a fool,' said the rabbi.

But why call such a moralistic man a fool?
Why does the rabbi say: 'You are a fool'?

The rabbi is saying:
'You are not aware what you are saying;
you are not aware of yourself.
Your whole life has passed,
and you don't know anything about your own being:
the greed hidden behind, the possessiveness,
the ambition, the ego, the lust.
You are a fool.'

Who is a fool? —
he who is not aware of himself.

*Then he resumed his position
at the window,
called another passerby,
and put the same question to him.
I am not such a fool,
as to give up a purse full of money
that has come my way,' said the man.*

The second man says: 'I am not a fool.'
But his definition of foolishness

is totally different than the definition of the rabbi.
And sometimes words deceive,
because they are the same.
The rabbi said to the first man:
'You are a fool because you are unaware of yourself.'

The second man says: *'I am not such a fool,
as to give up a purse full of money
that has come my way.'*

Now, for this second man,
foolishness has a totally different dimension and meaning.
He says: 'When you come across money,
if you are wise, you will escape with it immediately
so that nobody comes to know about it.'

He is saying: 'I am not a fool. I am not a simpleton.
And I am not deceived by all this moralistic nonsense
that you must give it to the owner,
that if it doesn't belong to you it is not yours,
that you will suffer in hell.
Or, if you give it, you will be rewarded in heaven.
I am not a fool.'

The second man is an ordinary worldly man,
but in a way, better than the first —
because whatsoever he is, he knows it.
At least he has a little glimpse of his own being,
and he knows: 'I am not a fool.'
He is a cunning man, clever, calculating.

The first was a simpleton.
The first was just like the second.
If the real situation was there,
the first would behave
just as the second would behave —
but the first believes that he is a moral man.

True Wisdom

This is the difference
between your so-called religious people
and irreligious people.
This is the only difference.

The religious man goes to the temple,
to the church, to the mosque.
He prays, talks about God,
carries scriptures, rituals —
and looks very religious.
But whenever there is an actual situation,
he behaves as irreligiously as anybody else —
sometimes even more.

Just look — India is a good example.
The whole country thinks it is religious.
In fact, India thinks
it is the only country which is religious.
They go on bragging about it.
They think that they are the religious leaders of the world
and that the whole world
should come and bow down to them.
They think that they should guide the whole world
as far as religion, God, spirituality, is concerned.
But if you look into their lives
you will not find
more materialistic people anywhere else.

This is my observation:
that people coming from the West
are less materialistic than people who live in India.
On the surface, they may look materialistic,
they may not have any pretensions
about being religious,
but they are less materialistic.
They cling less to things.

The True Sage

Indians are simply mad;
they cling to money, to a house, to things.
And, at the same time,
they go on pretending and bragging
that they are religious people:
they don't believe in matter; they believe in God.
They go on saying the whole world is illusion,
but you cannot get a single pai out of them;
it is impossible.
Why has this happened?

These are the two types.
The first type is the image of the Indian.
The second type is the image of the westerner.
The westerner knows that he is not a fool;
if he gets the money, he will take it —
it is simple.
The Indian will say: 'No, I will not touch it.'
But deep down he has already started to plan
what to do if he gets the money.
On the surface, one thing; deep down, another thing.
That's the only difference
between your so-called moral people and immoral people.
The moral people are hypocrites.

'I am not such a fool,
as to give up a purse full of money
that has come my way.'

In a way, the second man is more sincere
because he says the truth: 'I am not such a fool.
I am not going to give that purse to anybody.
If it has come my way, it is mine.
And I am going to have it.'
Maybe this looks immoral, but it is more sincere.
And finally, sincerity helps, not morality.
At least this man knows his cunningness!

The first man is absolutely unaware
of his cunningness.
He believes in his innocence.
When you believe in your innocence
and you are not innocent,
you are in great danger, you are a fool.
Because you are believing in something
which is not there.

It is better to be a plain worldly man
than to be a religious hypocrite.
It is good to be sincere —
even if your sincerity reveals things
which are not good.
Because once you know, you can transcend them.
If you don't know, they hide behind you;
your enemies are just in your unconscious —
and they can grab you any moment.
To know the enemy is better than not to know,
because then something can be done.

*'You are a bad lot,' said the rabbi,
and called in a third man.*

He said, *'You are a bad lot.'*
But he didn't say: *'You are a fool.'*
You are not good — that's true —
but you are not a fool.
The first man is not good, and he is a fool also,
because he does not know his own inner cunningness.
The rabbi called in a third man
and asked the same question.

The third man replied:
*'Rabbi, how can I know
on what rung I shall be
when I find the purse...?'*

The True Sage

This man is really aware of the whole situation.
He says he cannot promise.
He knows himself, he knows his own deceiver,
he knows his own cunningness,
he knows his evil moments,
he knows the inner conflict that will arise
when the purse is found.
He's really aware.

*'Rabbi, how can I know
on what rung I shall be
when I find the purse...?'*

'I may be in a religious mood; I may not be.
Because moods happen, and I am not the master.
I have no will of my own.
A certain mood possesses me,
and then I behave accordingly;
I am a machine.
What can I promise? How can I promise?
You are asking me an absurd question.'

*'How can I know
on what rung I shall be
when I find the purse
or whether I shall succeed
in fending off the Evil Urge?'*

'I know my evil urge also.
And I don't know! —
maybe the evil urge will be too much
and I won't be able to succeed in fending it off.
Maybe the urge won't be so great —
but I cannot say what will happen;
it is unpredictable.
I know my past:
many times similar things have happened
and the evil urge was very strong

and I could not be victorious; I had to give up.'

*'Perhaps it will get the better of me,
and I shall appropriate
what belongs to another.'*

Now is not the question;
it is a theoretical question.
But this man makes it real.

The question is not about the purse;
the question is about your own awareness.
Are you aware? What will you do?
One who is aware will know well
that nothing can be said.

The first was absolutely unaware.
The second was aware,
but identified with his cunningness.
The third was aware,
but not identified with his evil urge.
This is to be understood.

The first is in absolute unconsciousness.
The second is a little awake,
but he has not used his awareness to go beyond;
rather, he has used his awareness to become cunning.
He is identified with his evil urge.
He says: 'I am not a fool.'
What is he saying?
He is saying: 'I am clever and cunning, not a fool.'
He is identified with cunningness.
The third man is not identified with either.
He says: 'I don't know. Nothing certain can be said.'

*'Perhaps it will get the better of me,
and I shall appropriate
what belongs to another.
But perhaps God . . .*

— and this is the point to be understood,
the very center of this story —
*But perhaps God, blessed be He,
will help me to fight it . . .'*

'I know myself.
Alone I cannot fight; alone I will be defeated.
It is possible only through His grace.
If I am left alone, there is every possibility
I will be defeated by the evil urge.
I know myself. I know my strength. It is nothing.'

It is good if the question is theoretical.
But when the practical problem arises, he knows himself:
'I have been defeated many times when I was alone.'

*'But perhaps God, blessed be He,
will help me to fight it,
and in that case
I shall return what I have found
to its rightful owner.'*

What is he saying?
He is saying: Only if God helps,
then I will return it; otherwise, not.'
What he is saying is this:
'If I return it, I have not returned it —
God has returned it.
If it happens at all, it will happen through Him,
not through me.'

This is the quality of a religious man.
Even his virtues are not his.
Even with his virtues, he is not identified.
Even his virtues are through Him —
His grace, His gift.
Because otherwise, your virtues will become your ego.
And whenever a virtue becomes an ego,
you have already committed the sin.

Then it is no more virtuous.
It is already corrupted and poisoned.

'But perhaps God, blessed be He,
will help me to fight it,
and in that case
I shall return what I have found
to its rightful owner.'

'Those are good words,' cried the zaddik.
'You are a true sage.'

The fourth state of consciousness:
he is not identified anywhere,
not even with virtues.

Bodhidharma travelled from India to China.
The emperor came to see him.
He touched Bodhidharma's feet and said:
'I have made so many temples,
so many Buddhist ashramas,
and millions of bhikkhus, Buddhist sannyasins,
are fed by me, supported by me.
I have changed the whole country
into a Buddhist world.
All these virtues — what do you think, sir?
Am I going to gain through them?
What will be the benefit? What will be the award?'

Bodhidharma looked at this Emperor Wu and said:
'You will fall into the seventh hell.'

The emperor could not believe it
because all other monks,
so-called saints, were all saying:
'You are earning such virtue, *punya*,
that you are going to be received
into the ultimate nirvana.'
And this man says: 'seventh hell.'

The True Sage

Emperor Wu said: 'Have you gone mad?
What are you saying? Are you aware?'

Bodhidharma said: 'I am aware what I am saying.
And you can rely on me —
you will go to the seventh hell.'

'But why?' the emperor cried.
'I have not done anything wrong.'

Bodhidharma said: 'It is not a question
of doing wrong or right.
The question is of the very ego, that *you* have done something.
Thank God, thank the Buddha; blessed be His name.
It is through His grace something has happened.
Don't be the doer; please don't come in —
because the ego has to go to hell,
and if you are egoistic, you will have to follow it.
You are not going to hell,
but the ego has to go to hell.
And if you are identified with it,
you will have to go.
Nothing can be done about it. No virtue can save it.'

*'Those are good words,' cried the zaddik.
'You are a true sage.'*

And who is the untrue sage? —
he who thinks that he has been doing
so many virtuous acts,
so many austerities, fasting, chanting;
who thinks that he has been living a religious life,
and thanks himself: 'It is me.'
He is the untrue sage.

The true sage always feels that whatsoever happens,
happens through His grace.
He does not come in anywhere.

True Wisdom

The true sage is based in awareness,
rooted in awareness.
And this is what awareness should bring to you:
that you will not promise.

Who can promise?
You will not say with certainty:
'I am going to do this or that.'
You will say: 'Nothing can be said.
I know myself, how fragile my will is,
how weak my crystallization is.
I am a crowd; I have many "I's".'
One 'I' may promise, but by the time
the actual moment comes to fulfill it,
another 'I' may be dominant.
Then you become a liar.

I have seen lovers promising each other
that they will love each other forever and forever.
And not knowing anything about the next moment!
Not knowing anything —
what do they mean by 'forever and forever'?
If they are a little alert, they will say:
'It feels in this moment,
it is a truth of this moment, in this mood,
that I will love you forever and forever.
But nobody knows about the next moment.'
That's why lovers always prove
to be deceivers to each other.
In the end they think that they have been cheated.
They have both promised things
which they cannot deliver.

A man asked Buddha: 'Sir, give me some guidance.
I would like to serve humanity.'
Buddha looked deeply within him;
the man must have felt very uneasy

because Buddha went on looking and looking.
The man started perspiring, and he said:
'Sir, what are you doing?
If you can give me some hints, please give them.
Otherwise, why are you staring in my eyes?'

Buddha said: 'I was looking whether you *are* or not.
And you *are not*. Who will serve humanity?!
You don't exist at all! You are a momentary bubble.
You only have a momentary existence —
king for the moment, enthroned for the moment.
Next moment you will be gone
and somebody else will be the king.
Who will serve humanity?
It will be good if you first try
to find out where you are, who you are.
First be! And then there is no need to ask me.
Because whenever one *is*, compassion flows;
if you *are*, compassion follows.
To *be* is the only thing that has to be done!
How can you *be* if you go on being deceived
by your own egos, desires, moods, thoughts, feelings?'

The zaddik is right.
He says: 'You are a true sage
because you have simply stated the truth.
You are not trying in any way
to deceive me or yourself.
You simply stated: "I cannot believe in myself.
I have believed in the past
and the belief proved wrong.
I know my lust; the evil urge can be very strong
and I may not be able to fend for myself.
The only hope is, if God, blessed be His name, helps me.
I am corruptible;
only if the source which is incorruptible helps me. . . .
I am cunning;

only if the source which is innocent, virgin,
helps me, showers on me — then only is there hope.'

It happened:
One of the greatest women who ever lived —
Saint Theresa —
was going to build a church.
And she was a poor woman.
The whole town gathered, and she talked ecstatically:
'A great church has to be built here on this spot.'

The people said: 'Good. Your dreams are good,
but from where is the money to come?'

Saint Theresa pulled
two small coins from her bag, and said:
'Don't be afraid. Money I have got.'
There were just two small coins!

So the people laughed and said:
'We always knew that you are a little too innocent.
These two small coins —
you cannot purchase even a brick! —
and you are thinking to make a great church?'

Theresa laughed and said:
'Yes, my hands are small, my coins are small.
But you don't see: God is with me.
Two small coins plus God — everything is possible.'

And on that spot stands a great church —
one of the most beautiful.
Two small coins plus God.

God means infinity. God means all.

'Blessed be His name,' said the man.
'I cannot promise anything on my own,
but if He wills, then everything is possible.

The True Sage

I may be very small
and the evil urge may be very great,
but if He helps, then there is no problem.
My small strength is nothing.
In fact — plus all — that will do.'

Said the zaddik : *'You are a true sage.'*

So, the true sage
has to begin from the fourth state of mind :
that is consciousness.
Then the door opens.
Once you attain to the fourth,
God is available to you
and you are available to God.
Then the door opens.
Up to the third, the door is closed.
And you can do only one thing to become aware.
Up to the third, you cannot do anything;
beyond the fourth, you need not do anything.
This has to be remembered.

Up to the third, you are unconscious
and you cannot do anything;
your life is mechanical.
Beyond the fourth, you need not do anything;
God is available, He starts doing.
Then you ride on His tide. He takes you.

So the only thing that can be done
and that should be done
is to become more and more aware
and alert and conscious.

Walk, but make walking a meditation ; walk knowingly.
Breathe, but let your breathing
become a constant meditation ; breathe knowingly.
The breath going in : watch it.

True Wisdom

The breath going out: watch it.
Eat, but eat with full awareness.
Take a bite, chew it, but go on watching.
Let the watcher be there in every moment,
whatsoever you are doing.

Going to sleep? — lie down on the bed and watch.
Falling into sleep — go on watching, go on watching.
Many times in the beginning you will be lost
and the watching will disappear
and sleep will take possession of you.
One day by and by you will see sleep taking possession,
but your awareness is still there.
And when you can see your sleep,
you have seen the whole situation of humanity.
Then by and by sleep takes possession,
but you are still alert.
Deep down somewhere, a flame goes on burning.
The night may be dark all around,
but the flame goes on burning.
The whole night you sleep,
and still you are not asleep.
That's the meaning
of Krishna's saying to Arjuna in the Geeta:
Ya nisha sarvabhutayam tasyam jagriti samyami —
that which is a night to all,
even there, the yogi, the *samyami*,
one who has become a master of oneself,
remains alert, awake.

The body sleeps, the heart sleeps, the mind sleeps —
but you remain alert
because you are nothing else but alertness.
Everything else is a false identification.
Awareness is your nature.
The body is your abode. The mind is your computer.
Awareness is you, is your very being.

The True Sage

Satchitanand has been our definition
of the ultimate truth.
We have used three words: *sat, chit, anand.*
Sat means true, truth, being.
Chit means consciousness — aware, alert.
Anand means bliss.
Be — and the only way to be is to be aware.
And once you are aware, bliss follows.

Satchitanand is your innermost core of being.
And it is nothing to be attained;
it is already there.
It has only to be discovered, uncovered.
It is your hidden treasure.

The zaddik is right because the man is alert.
The first ray of alertness has penetrated his being.
He has become the true sage.

I would like you to become sages;
I would not like you to become saints.
Saints are virtuous people, good people.
They belong to the first category:
those who have been trying to be good,
moral, virtuous, righteous, pious.
I would not like you to be saints;
I would like you to be sages.

To be a sage has nothing to do with morality, virtue.
I'm not saying that a sage is not virtuous;
I'm saying he is not concerned with it.
It follows as a consequence;
he has not been practicing it.
A practiced virtue is not a virtue at all;
a practiced virtue is just on the outside, painted.
You may have practiced it so hard.
that it has created a crust around you,
but deep down you remain the same.

True Wisdom

The saint is against the sinner;
the sinner is against the saint.
The first man can become a saint,
the second man can become a sinner,
the third man can become a sage.

A sinner is one who is identified
with his bad qualities, wtih his evil urge.
A saint is one who is identified with his good urge;
he is virtuous, pious.
And a sage is one who is not identified.
The sinner thinks himself to be the devil incarnate.
He thinks in terms of sinning more and more;
he thinks that this is his cleverness.
The saint thinks that his cleverness is
to practice virtue, to become innocent —
not to do anything that is bad.
Then he gets more and more identified with good.

A sage is not identified at all.
A sage is a state of non-identification —
neither this nor that, *neti neti*.
He says: 'I am neither this bank nor that;
rather, I am the river.
I am neither the saint nor the sinner,
neither good nor bad.'

Sinners live in a sort of hell,
and saints imagine themselves in a sort of heaven.
And the sage? — for him it is moksha,
for him it is the absolute freedom.
He is freed from all duality.
The secret key, and the only key, is awareness.

For awareness you need not go to the Himalayas;
you need not go anywhere.
Your life gives you enough opportunities to be aware.
Somebody insults you — listen to it in full awareness.

And you will be surprised —
the insult is no more an insult.
You may even smile.
It does not hurt;
it hurts only when received in unawareness.
Somebody praises and appreciates you —
listen with alertness.
And then nobody can persuade you to do foolish things.
Nobody can bribe you; flattery becomes impossible.
You will smile at the whole nonsense.

Listen. Watch. Be aware.
And by and by
a different quality of being arises in you
which is neither the body
nor the feelings
nor the thoughts.
A different pillar of flame starts gathering within you
and becomes more and more crystallized.
As this awareness becomes crystallized,
for the first time you will feel
more and more that you are — the feeling of being.
And then moods will become more and more irrelevant.
They will come and go,
but you will remain unperturbed.
The climate will change around you,
but you will remain unchanged.
Whatsoever happens on the outside
will not in any way change you within.
The within remains absolutely pure and uncorrupted.

I will tell you one story.

One German thinker, Herrigel, was in Japan.
He was sitting with his friends
and he had invited his Master for dinner.
Suddenly there was an earthquake.

True Wisdom

They were sitting on the seventh storey of the building.
The whole building started shaking
and everybody started running down the stairs.
There was chaos.

Herrigel himself ran towards the door; it was automatic.
Nobody thinks about what to do in such situations;
everybody behaves like a robot.
That is the meaning: man is a machine.

But suddenly, he remembered at the door ...
because there was such a crowd
and he couldn't find the way ...
so he remembered for a single moment:
'What happened to the Master whom I have called?'
He looked back.
The Master was sitting in his chair in the same way,
but now he had closed his eyes.
Not a ripple of fear on his face, not a ripple of disturbance —
as if nothing had happened.
The presence of the Master was so magnetic ...
the uncorrupted presence,
the aroma that surrounded him,
the climate that he had created around,
the space in which he lived that moment ...
that Herrigel said: 'I was magnetized.
I don't know what happened.
I simply came back and sat by the side of the Master.
By his side I felt absolutely secure
as if nothing could happen.'

The earthquake came and went.
The Master opened his eyes
and started to talk from the same place
where he had had to stop because of the earthquake.

Herrigel said: 'I have completely forgotten
what you were saying before.

It seems centuries have passed . . .
and I am completely disoriented.
Please. Now I am not in a situation to understand
what you are saying.
Let us continue sometime later;
let me get settled.
But one thing I would like to ask:
when we were all running away,
why didn't you move?'

The Master said: 'I also moved,
but I moved in a different direction: withinwards.
You were running without;
I was also running, but within.
Because I know — without, there is no shelter.
The earthquake was all around —
where were you running?
Just running cannot help.
I entered into my being.
And *there*, no earthquake has ever penetrated.
I moved to a space within myself
where no disturbance ever penetrates,
where silence is absolute, stillness ultimate.
I also ran. I also sought a shelter.
But in the right direction.'

If you are trying to be aware,
you are moving in the right direction.
Sooner or later you will become the true sage.

Don't try to practice virtue.
Practice only one thing: awareness.
Virtue follows it, just as a shadow follows you.
Virtue is a consequence.
Once you enter into your own being
and become rooted there, centered there,
all happens —
because all the doors are open.

True Wisdom

God is open to you and you are open to God.

Let me repeat again:
up to the third stage, you cannot do anything
because you are not.
Beyond the fourth, you need not do
because God's grace has become available.
You do only the fourth.

Please be aware —
and you will be entering into the temple.
Let me repeat the whole story again.

*One day the Rabbi of Zans
was sitting at the window
and looking out into the street.
Seeing a passerby,
he knocked on the window pane
and signed to the man
to come into the house.*

*When the stranger entered the room,
Rabbi Hayyim asked him:
'Tell me,
if you found a purse full of ducats,
would you return it to its owner?'
'Rabbi,' said the man,
'if I knew the owner
I should return the purse
without a moment's delay.'
'You are a fool,' said the Rabbi of Zans.*

*Then he resumed his position
at the window,
called another passerby,
and put the same question to him.
'I am not such a fool
as to give up a purse full of money
that has come my way,' said the man.*

The True Sage

'You are a bad lot,' said the Rabbi of Zans,
and called in a third man.

He replied:
'Rabbi, how can I know
on what rung I shall be
when I find the purse,
or whether I shall succeed
in fending off the Evil Urge?
Perhaps it will get the better of me,
and I shall appropriate
what belongs to another.
But perhaps God, blessed be He,
will help me to fight it,
and in that case
I shall return what I have found
to its rightful owner'.
'Those are good words,' cried the zaddik.
'You are a true sage.'

20th October 1975

Questions and answers

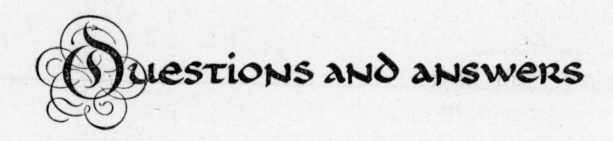

What is the difference between being passive and flowing with the river?

A lot of difference.
And not only of quantity, but of quality,
of direction, of plane, of dimension.
It has to be understood very minutely
because the difference is subtle.

The passive mind can appear
as if it is flowing with the river,
but the passive mind
also is not flowing with the river
because it has a certain attitude of passivity.

The passive mind is also a mind.
To flow with the river you need a no-mind.
But because of the similarity,
through the centuries many have been deceived.
And to cultivate passivity is easier
than to flow with the river.
To condition your mind into passivity is very easy.
That's why, in the past and even now,
monasteries, monks, sannyasins have existed —
people who have renounced the world.

The True Sage

What are they really trying to do?
They are trying to become absolutely passive.
But their passivity is negativity.
They have already chosen an attitude.
First, these persons were too active in the world:
running, desiring, ambitious.
The mind was active — excited with desire, future, hope.
Then they got frustrated,
because whatsoever you hope,
it is not going to be fulfilled.
All hopes are hopeless,
all desiring comes to frustration,
all expectations carry frustration as a seed within.

So, sooner or later,
everybody is bound to come to a point in life
when the active mind looks simply a hell.
Too much activity and no result out of it.
Running and running, and never arriving.
If you are intelligent, it happens soon.
If you are stupid, it takes a little longer time —
but it happens all the same.
If you are *very* intelligent,
then when you are young you will come to see it.
If you are not that intelligent — then in old age.
But sooner or later, everybody comes to feel
that a life with the active mind is frustrating;
it leads nowhere.
It promises much, but it never fulfills anything.
It leaves a distaste in the mouth,
a discontent in the being.
One simply feels tired and wearied, defeated.
One simply feels that the whole thing has been futile.

Whenever the mind feels this,
the mind immediately suggests: 'Try the opposite.'
Because the mind lives in polarity, in opposition.
It says: 'You have tried activity. Now try passivity.

You longed too much in the world. Now renounce.
You were clinging to money. Renounce money.
You had become too attached to the house.
Renounce the house.
You got too involved with a woman, children.
Now leave them and escape from all this.'

The mind suggests to try the opposite —
and it seems natural and logical.
You have done one thing and failed;
now do the opposite.
Maybe the opposite will succeed.

This is the pattern
of the old type of sannyasin, monk —
the monastery, the Himalayas.
They are born,
then they escape from activity.
They just try the opposite.
Then they try not to desire —
but to try not to desire is still a desire.
Then they try to leave the world —
but the very effort to leave the world
shows their attachment.

If you have really become unattached,
what is the point of renouncing anything?
You can renounce a certain thing only
because you are too involved in it.
Then you escape from a woman —
but that simply shows that your mind
is still fantasizing about women.
Wherever you go,
you may go to the opposite,
but still, you will remain the same.
This has to be understood:
through the opposite you never change.
You appear to have changed; your remain the same.

And this is one of the most important things
to be understood —
otherwise you will be in the trap again.
Now the trap will be of passivity, of *not* desiring,
renunciation, non-attachment, non-violence.
First, the world was your activity;
now, the world has become a passive thing for you.
But *you* are the same!
Now God, moksha, will become your activity —
a faraway world somewhere in the sky,
where everything is beautiful.
This world will be ugly —
now the beauty will be transferred
to the other world.
Your object of desire changes, but you don't change.
First you were asking for money,
now you ask for meditation —
but the greed is there.
First you were asking for things of this world,
now you ask for things of the other world.
But the asking is persistent, the same.

People who will be looking at you from the outside
may be deceived
because you will look totally transformed:
you don't touch money,
you don't have much to possess,
you live in a cottage or under a tree,
you are a naked fakir.
People who are in the world — they will worship you
because now they think
that you have transformed your being —
and they are still in the world.
When they come to you, they compare.
And they imagine that you must be very peaceful
because you look passive.

Passivity can give an appearance of peace.
It is not peace; it is just a deadness.
Peace is alive! Passivity is dead.

Just for example:
think yourself swimming in the river,
trying to go up current, fighting;
you are active.
Then, a dead body floating down the river:
not fighting at all, just floating down the river.
But dead! — a corpse that is passive.
Life is fighting. Death is passive.

And the man who I say really floats with the river
is neither alive in the sense of fight,
nor is dead like a corpse.
He floats with the river, but he floats consciously.
He floats with the river not because he is dead,
but because he co-operates.
He floats with the river not because he cannot fight,
but because he has come to know
that fighting is futile —
and has not moved to the opposite.

He floats.
He communes with the river,
he has become one with the river.
Sometimes you will see him active
and sometimes you will see him passive.
Passivity and activity
are not two polarities to be chosen —
he has accepted both.
That's what I mean when I say:
'floating with the river.'

Sometimes you will find him in the marketplace:
very active.

The True Sage

Sometimes you will find him in the temple:
very passive.
But now he has no fixed mode of his being.
He can move from passivity to activity,
he can move from activity to passivity.
There is no barrier,
he has not created a fence around him.
He is fluid, liquid, flowing.
Otherwise, passivity itself can become an imprisonment.

I have heard of one Hassidic story.
A man was going to see his friend.
The friend was a farmer
in a deep-hidden valley in the hills.
When the man came near the house of the friend,
he saw something which puzzled him very much.

He saw a small meadow, not more than one mile long.
But one thing was very special and disturbing:
in that meadow
thousands of birds and animals were staying together.
Thousands! It was difficult to count.
There was no space left; the place was very much crowded.
And the whole beautiful forest around this meadow
was empty of birds and animals.
He could not believe: 'Why are they huddled together?
Why are they not moving into the sky, to other trees?
The whole vastness is available.'
They looked very nervous, tense, worried —
not at ease at all.

Of course, everybody needs space,
everybody needs a certain space to live.
Whenever that space is encroached upon,
nervousness arises.
But nobody was preventing
the animals and birds from leaving,
there was not even a fence there.

When he reached his friend's house
the first question he asked was about these birds:
'What misfortune has befallen them?'

The friend said: 'I don't know exactly —
because I have not seen, but I have heard:
in the past, many many years ago,
there was a landlord —
a very violent and sadistic man.
He enjoyed this whole experiment.
He created a high fence around the meadow.
He placed guards all around the place,
and he ordered the guards:
"If any bird or any animal tries to escape,
kill him immediately."
He forced thousands of birds and animals
into the meadow, into that prison.
And for years this was the routine:
whenever any bird or animal tried to escape,
he was killed.

By and by, the birds and animals settled,
they accepted their prison.
They forgot about their freedom,
because freedom became associated with fear and death.

Then the landlord died.
The guards disappeared, the fence fell.
Now there is nobody to prevent them from leaving.
Neither the guards nor the fence is there —
but the birds and animals
have developed a fence mentality.
They believe that the fence is there.
They actually see the fence!
It has become deeply ingrained,
it has become a conditioning.'

The man said:
'Why doesn't somebody try to make them understand?

The friend said: 'Many good people have tried,
but the birds don't listen.
It is not only now ingrained in them —
their children are born with the idea.
It is in their blood and bones,
it has become a part of their blueprint.
The children are born with the idea of the fence.
Good people have tried, they go on trying.
And you will be surprised:
the birds have been very angry
and the animals have attacked good people.
They don't want to be disturbed.
In fact, they have created a philosophy
that they are in freedom
and the world beyond is the imprisonment.
Still, good people go on trying,
but it seems to be almost impossible
to persuade them that they are free
and that there exists no fence,
and that they can fly into the sky.'

I loved the story.

That's what Jesus, Baal Shem, Moses,
Mahavir, Buddha, Christ,
have been doing with you — the birds and the animals.
But you have developed a fence mentality;
you don't believe them.
Either you are active or you become passive —
but both belong to the same fence: the mind.

Think of a fence made of wood.
One board is white, another is black.
Then again one is white, another is black.
A fence made of wooden boards,
coloured in two colours —
one board white, one black: that is the mind.

One idea passive, one active;
yin, yang; right, wrong; good, bad;
the world, the nirvana —
all belong to the same fence.

And you go on choosing.
Sometimes you choose the white —
then you get fed up with the white.
Then you start loving and worshipping the black,
but the black is as much a part
of your imprisonment as the white.

Mind is active. Mind is passive.
Both are part of the mind.
And what I mean when I say: 'flowing with the river'
is to go beyond passivity and activity, white and black,
day and night, love and hate, the world and the god.
Go beyond it.
Just see the whole point:
that the active becomes the passive,
then the passive will again become the active.
This I have seen.

People who are in the world are very active.
They are always thinking deep down
to renounce all nonsense.
And I know monks
who have lived their whole lives in the monasteries,
and whenever they have confessed to me,
they have always said that they always think
that they have missed life.
They are always fantasizing to come back to the world.
The active wants to become the passive,
the passive wants to become the active.

Choice is of the mind!
To be choiceless is to flow with the river.

That's why Hassidism and I
insist not to leave the world.
Renounce it and be in it!
That looks difficult,
almost impossible for the mind to conceive.
The mind can conceive the world, the renunciation —
because both belong to the same pattern.
When I say: 'Be *in* the world and not be *of* the world,'
then the mind becomes uneasy.
It cannot understand: 'What are you saying?'

People come to me
and they say they would like to become sannyasins
but they are in the world:
'And how is it possible to be a sannyasin in the world?'
Particularly in India, it looks absolutely absurd.
The sannyasin is one who leaves the world.
But I tell you, a sannyasin is one
who lives in the world, and yet is not of the world.
When I say these things to people, they look confused.
They say: either this or that. I say: both together.

When you take both, negative and passive together,
they cancel each other; you become neutral.
Then you are neither man nor woman,
neither yin nor yang, neither body nor soul.
You have gone beyond the duality,
you have become transcendental.
That transcendence is flowing with the river.

Flowing with the river is the greatest art.
That is: to be active and passive both,
in deep co-operation with existence.
You have to do something.
You will have to live, you will have to earn.
At least you will have to breathe,
at least you will have to move.

Activity has to be used.
And you have to relax also.
Otherwise, activity will become impossible.

So sometimes be active, sometimes be passive —
but don't get identified with either.
Remain aloof.
Use activity, use passivity — but remain the third.
Just like when you put on clothes :
sometimes white and sometimes black.
Just as in the day you work and in the night you rest.
Just the same. Use both the dualities.
They are means; don't get identified with them.
Then you will be flowing with the river.
And this is the message of Hassidism.

Hassids are the greatest people
who have lived in the world,
yet have not allowed the world to corrupt them.
It is very easy to go to the Himalayas
and become uncorrupted.
Very easy!
Because who is there to corrupt you?
To live with the mountains,
you will become innocent,
but that innocence may be just an appearance.

Come back to the world.
The test is in the marketplace.
There you will come to know
whether you have really become innocent,
because when the opportunity
to become corrupted arises,
then only will you be able to know :
are you still corruptible or not?
The Himalayas, their silence, can deceive you.
It has deceived millions of people.

THE TRUE SAGE

Hassids say: 'Live in the marketplace.
Move with people,
because people are your environment.'

Somebody asked Socrates:
'Why don't you go to the mountains to study? —
near the rivers, trees, birds, animals.'
The man said: 'We have heard of ancient wise men
who used to go deep in the mountains
to live and study nature.'

Socrates said: 'My nature is people.
What can trees teach me?
They are good to look at, but what can they teach me?
What can mountains teach me? Good to relax.
What can rivers teach me?
My rivers, my mountains, my trees, are people.
People are my environment.'

He lived his whole life in Athens —
lived and died there, *in* people.
And he's right.

The true sage will not be an escapist.
He will live *in* people
and learn how to remain uncorrupted
where everything is a temptation to corrupt you.
Then you attain to the highest peak.

And that highest peak uses both the dualities of life.
And that highest peak is going to be very rich.

I have come across a few people
who have lived their whole life in the forest.
They are very saintly, but a little silly also,
because with the trees you will become silly —
that is natural.
You cannot have that intelligence
which a Socrates has.

You will become a tree. You will vegetate.
You will look very pure,
but that purity is not of a higher revelation;
that purity is of a regression, you have fallen back.
You have been trees in your past lives,
you have transcended that.
Now you are falling back.

Just think
you are thirty years, thirty-five years of age —
you can attain to innocence in two ways.
One is to somehow become a child again —
but then you will be foolish also.
Innocent you will be, but foolish also —
because a child is a fool.
Then there is another possibility:
to grow and become wise through experience.
You mature, you learn.
And at the very end,
when you have become almost an ancient,
you attain to your childhood.
But you do not attain through regression.

Go ahead. Let the circle be complete.
Don't fall back! Go on and on!
And one day you will see: the circle is complete.
You are old and yet you are a child.
Then you will not be foolish.

A wise man is like a child,
but also is not like a child.
A wise man is both.
He is a grown-up —
really grown up, mature,
lived the life, experienced it, enriched by it —
and yet has come to understand
that innocence is the only way to be,
is the only way to be divine.

The True Sage

An old man is again in a second childhood,
but the childhood is a second childhood.
He is reborn.

When I say to flow with the river,
I don't mean to become a driftwood.
I don't mean to become a corpse
and flow with the river.
All corpses flow;
there is nothing much to say about it.
If you are dead you will float with the river —
because you cannot fight!
First, you were encaged in activity.
Now you are encaged in passivity.

Never move to the opposite.
Always remain in both, and yet beyond.
Always remember never to go to the extreme,
because the way is just in the middle.
Buddha has called his way 'the middle path' —
majjhim nikaya.
And he is right.

One day in the afternoon it happened:
a parrot, a beautiful parrot
was allowed to air himself every day.
It was hot, and the whole house was fast asleep.
The servant came and allowed the parrot
to move around the room.

The dog of the house was also fast asleep.
The parrot came near the dog,
near his ear, and said: 'Rex!'
Of course, the dog became alert — 'Rex!'
He went round and round, looked around every corner.
Finding nothing, he again went to sleep.

The parrot waited.
The trick had succeeded: he befooled the dog.
So again he came near and said: 'Rex!'
Again the dog opened his eyes,
looked around, went around the house,
and was very much frustrated.

Then he felt the trick:
that there is nobody,
everybody is fast asleep —
no rat, nothing —
only this parrot.
Maybe he is doing something.
He again pretended that he was asleep,
with one eye cocked.

The parrot came again,
he tried the trick a third time.
The dog jumped on him.
Later on, the parrot was heard saying:
'The difficulty with me
is that I don't know when to stop.'

And that is the difficulty with you, with all parrots.
Where to stop?

From active you will go to passive.
From passive you will go to active.
And you don't know where to stop.
If you know where to stop, if you know the middle. . . .
Because the middle transcends both.
There is a point that you cross every day
again and again —
but you don't know where to stop.
There is a point when you move from love to hate.
You must be moving past the point
where a Buddha remains.

Just in the middle —
where love is no more and hate has not yet appeared,
when you move from compassion to anger —
you pass the point where a Buddha remains.

If you watch for twenty-four hours,
you must be passing that point
at least twenty-four thousand times —
where a Buddha is sitting, where Buddhahood is.
You go fast, you swing fast —
from one extreme to another you go.
You are not even aware
when you pass the point of Buddhahood:
the middle way, the middle path, the absolute middle.
There, suddenly you are neither a man nor a woman,
neither alive nor dead,
neither active nor passive.
And to know that point is to know all.

To know that point
is to know all that religion can give you.
It is not in the scriptures.
It is crossed by you every day.
You come on that crossroad every moment.
Whenever you are moving from one polarity to another,
you have to pass it;
there is no other way to go to the other polarity.
But you move so fast
that you are not alert when you cross that point.

When I say: 'flowing with the river,'
I mean: drop out of polarities
and just choose the river in between.
Co-operate with it, commune with it.
Be the river.

This is what sannyas is all about —
at least *my* sannyas.

Is it lonely up there?

It is not lonely, but it is alone.

Whenever you say 'lonely',
you show a desire for the other;
you are missing the other.
The word 'lonely' is indicative
that you are not happy with yourself,
that this loneliness hurts,
that this loneliness is getting a little boring,
that you would like to move away
from his state of loneliness.
When you say 'lonely,' you have already condemned it.

Loneliness means absence of the other —
not *your* presence.
You are missing the other
and your eyes are focused on that missing,
on that absence.

Up there, it is absolutely alone.
That's why Mahavir has called it 'kaivalya'.
'Kaivalya' means absolute aloneness.
But the quality of aloneness
is totally different from loneliness.
In the dictionaries they may both mean the same;
I'm not talking about the dictionary.
But in life's experience they are absolutely different.

Aloneness means presence of your being —
so full of yourself, so totally in yourself
that the other is not needed.
Aloneness is sufficient unto itself.
Loneliness is missing something,
loneliness is a gap — where the other was
or where you would like the other to be.
Loneliness is a wound. Aloneness is a flowering.

The True Sage

You are so happy to be yourself;
you are not missing anything.
You are totally yourself — settled, content.

Yes, up there it is very very alone.
And that is the beauty of it.

You alone exist — but you exist as a god,
you exist as the universe,
you exist as existence itself.
Stars and suns and moons move within you.
Trees and clouds exist within you.
Rivers and oceans flow within you.
You become the whole —
that's why you are alone.
Your own ego has disappeared,
so you cannot be lonely.

The ego always feels lonely.
That's why the ego always seeks the society,
the club, the movie-house, this and that.

The ego is always seeking the other,
because without the other, it cannot exist.
The other is a must — remember this.

'I' and 'thou' exist together.
If the 'thou' disappears, the 'I' will disappear —
it cannot be.
If *you* are there, I can be.
But if you are not there, how can I exist?
'I' and 'thou' are just two poles of the same phenomenon,
two poles of one thing.
If 'I' disappears, the 'thou' disappears.
If the 'thou' disappears, the 'I' disappears.

In aloneness
neither the 'thou' is there nor is the 'I' there.
It is absolute.

It has no center in it, in fact.
The whole is involved.
You cannot say where you are in that state —
you are not.
The whole is and you are not.
The ocean is, the drop has disappeared.
Or, you can say the drop has become the ocean —
which is the same.

Up there, the first thing to be understood:
loneliness is impossible; aloneness exists.
Aloneness has nothing of the quality of loneliness.
Loneliness is sad. Aloneness is blissful.
Loneliness is always dependent.
It is a slavery, a wound, a thorn in the heart.
Aloneness is a flowering, a fulfillment,
coming to the goal, reaching home.
Loneliness is a sort of illness.
Aloneness is health. Aloneness is wholeness.
Loneliness is something of the world
of disease, tensions, anguish, misery.
Aloneness has nothing to do with that world —
it is a transcendence,
it is absolute blissfulness, *satchitananda*.

And the second thing: don't call it 'up there' —
because it is not up.
It is neither down nor up.

Down and up are meaningless for the whole.
The whole simply is.
There is no up to it, no down to it.
Those words become meaningless.
But in the childish mind of humanity
God has always existed 'up there'
and the devil always 'down there'
and man always in between.

The earth, in between; hell, down; heaven, up.
This is a classification of the mind.
God is all: neither up, nor down, nor in the middle.

Only God is.
In fact, to say 'God is' is to repeat,
because God means *isness*.
Isness means God.
To say 'God is' is to repeat the same thing.
Just *God* will do, or *isness* will do.
This boggles the mind,
because then the mind feels uneasy.
It cannot categorize.
It cannot categorize
that which is impossible to categorize.

God cannot be defined in any way.
All definitions are false.
So whatsoever is said about God
is bound to be wrong,
God can only be showed in deep silence;
it cannot be said through words.

So please don't use 'up' and don't use 'there'
because He is always here.
'There' is just a fantasy. 'There' does not exist.
Everything is here.
This moment, here-now,
the whole culminates, joins together.
And it never moves from here, remember.
And it never moves from now.
That's why I use 'here-now' as one word.
I don't use them as two words.
Here-now — one word.

And that's what Einstein came to realize
through his whole life's research work.
He stopped using time and space as two words.
He created a new word, 'spacio-time'.

Time is now. Space is here.
If 'spacio-time' is true,
then 'here-now' should be one word.
And I use it as one word.
God is here-now.

I have heard a beautiful story —
Swami Ram used to tell it again and again.
He used to say that he had a friend,
a very famous lawyer, a supreme court advocate.
But he was an atheist.
He had written on his wall
where he used to sit and work in his office:
God is nowhere.

Then a child was born to him.
And the child started growing and learning language.
One day the child was trying to read the sentence:
God is nowhere.
But 'nowhere' was too big a word for him,
so the child divided it in two.
He said: 'God is now here.'
Suddenly, the father heard it.
He looked at the sentence: 'Yes, it can be that too.'
'God is nowhere' can be read as 'God is now here.'

And it is said
that that disturbed the father too much.
He pondered over it again and again,
it became a constant meditation.
And after that day
he could not read the sentence in the old way:
God is nowhere.
It got stuck.
The child opened a new door.
And whenever the father looked,
he read it just like the child: God is now here.
And it became a mantra.

The True Sage

It is said that the father was transformed,
because repeating that: God is now here,
again and again,
he started feeling a certain tranquility
arising in his heart.

So he used that as a mantra,
not saying it to anybody.
He would just look again and again.
And whenever he had time,
he would repeat inside: God is now here.

He became a theist.
The vision of a child transformed him,
the innocence of a child transformed him.

So don't say 'there'. 'There' is non-existential.
The 'there' does not exist, cannot exist.
All that exists is here-now.
That's all there is to life: now here.

Once you move from the now and the here,
you are in misery.
Once you move in your desire
you move from now and here,
and you create
a thousand and one miseries for yourself.

Be here-now.
And forget about God.
If you are here-now, you are in God,
and God will reveal Himself to you.
There is no need to search Him,
because the very search is basically unsound.
You cannot search Him because He is all.
He cannot be sought in any direction
because all directions are His.

You will not find Him anywhere,
because He is everywhere.
So from the very beginning,
all search is bound to fail.

Don't seek and search. Just be here-now
and He will search you, He will seek you.
That's what Hassids say.

One of the greatest contributions of Hassidism
is that you cannot seek Him; He seeks you.

How can *you* seek Him? You don't know the address.
You don't know the face.
You will not be able to recognize Him.
If He suddenly meets you on the street,
you will not even say: 'Hello.'
You will not recognize Him.
He will be so strange that you may get scared.
Or, you may not be able to see Him at all,
because we tend to see only that which we know.
That which we don't know, we tend not to see.

Scientists say that only two percent of impressions
are delivered to the mind through the eyes.
Ninety-eight percent are not delivered.
If all hundred percent
of the impressions are delivered,
you will be in a mess, you will go mad.
That will be too much.
You will not be able to cope with it.
So only a few selected informations
are given to the mind.
Ninety-eight percent are dropped out.

And I know well: if God meets you —
and I know that He meets you every day,
millions of times. . . .

The True Sage

But the mind drops
because it is known, strange;
you cannot fit Him anywhere with your mind.
He will be a disturbance.
So you simply don't see Him.
How can you seek Him? Where you will seek Him?

Hassidism says: 'You cannot seek Him. He seeks you.
You just be available and ready.'

I was reading an anecdote yesterday:
A medical student failed in his final examination.
He was very much afraid of his father,
so he sent a telegram to his sister at home:
'I have failed. Prepare father.
It may be too shocking to him.'
The sister tried, but the father became very angry.
Then she telegrammed to the brother:
Father is ready. You prepare yourself.'

And that is the case:
father is always ready; you prepare.

God is always ready to meet you;
you prepare, you be ready wherever you are.
He will seek you.
He will rush from everywhere, from all directions.
He will penetrate you in a thousand and one ways
and reach to your heart.

Do you ever despair of us and your work?

   You do your level best,
but I do not despair because I cannot.

Despair exists with expectation.
Nothing can despair me —
I am not expecting anything from you.
If it happens, it is beautiful.
If it doesn't happen, that too is beautiful.
To me, it is not a desire
for you to become enlightened.
If it is a desire and you go on missing,
then I will be in despair.
But it is not a desire at all.

It is my happiness to share
whatsoever I have attained.
I share it because I have it.
If you take it, good.
If you don't take it, that too is good.
Because basically
enlightenment cannot be anything else
than *your* freedom.
This is part of your freedom:
if you want to take, you take;
if you don't want to take, you don't take.
Whatsoever I say, if you do it,
that's your freedom.
If you don't do it, that's your freedom.
And I am here to free you!
So how can I have any expectation? —
because any sort of expectation
becomes a sort of slavery, a bondage.

If I expect you to become enlightened
and you are not becoming,
then there will be despair.
And a man who is in despair himself —
how can he help you to become enlightened?
No, that's not possible.

The True Sage

I can help you only
because you cannot force me into any sort of despair.
I will remain happy
whether you are in heaven or hell.
I will remain happy whether you remain ignorant
or whether you become enlightened.
To me, your misery is your choice.
It exists nowhere except in your choice.
If you choose, good! If you love it, good!
Who am I to distract you?
It is your choice.

What am I doing here then? —
I am simply sharing my understanding.
That is my happiness: to share it.
It is your happiness whether you take it or not —
that is irrelevant to me.
Even if you are not here, even if nobody is here,
even if I am sitting alone,
I will be still sharing my happiness
with the trees and the rocks.
In fact, to say that I am sharing it is not right.
It *is being* shared.
To say that *I* am sharing it, makes it wrong —
as if I am doing something to share it.
No, it is being shared.

A flower has bloomed and the perfume is spreading.
Not that the flower is sharing it;
the flower cannot help but share.
The fragrance is on the wings,
moving, going far away.
Whether somebody will be able to fill his being
with that fragrance or not
is not a question for the flower.
It has flowered, and that's all.

Questions And Answers

The flower is happy that it has bloomed.
The flower is happy because it is fulfilled,
and fulfillment spreads a fragrance all around.

It is just like when you kindle a lamp
and the light spreads.
Not that the lamp is trying to share its light —
what else can it do?
It has to be so.
Not that the light is waiting
for somebody to come and enjoy it.
If nobody comes, it is all the same.
If many come, that too is the same.

I am not sharing, in a way;
rather, I am being shared.

Ordinarily you think you breathe.
When you become awake someday, you will see:
you are breathed, you are not breathing.
Ordinarily, you think that you are.
When you become aware, you will say: 'God is.'

And don't call it work.
I'm not doing anything.
At the most, you can call it play,
but don't call it work.
Playing.

If it is a work it will be serious.
If it is a work there will be a desire
to attain to certain results.
If it is a work it will have a burdensome quality
of a duty to be performed.
If it is work there will be a reluctance.
And if you don't follow me,
there will be frustration.

The True Sage

It is just a play.
I don't even call it a game,
because a game starts moving
in the direction of work.
It is just like children playing.
There is no end to it. It itself is the end.

I love to tell stories to you, I am a storyteller.
And the result is not anywhere there
in my consciousness.
If I have told you a beautiful story — finished.
It was beautiful. I loved it. I enjoyed it.
Whether you enjoyed it or not is for you to decide.

One of my teachers was a very rare being.
He was a little eccentric as philosophers tend to be.
He was one of the greatest philosophers
of this century in India.
Very rare, not much known —
a real philosopher,
not simply a professor of philosophy.
He was very much eccentric.

Students had long dropped coming to his classes
when I came across him.
For many years nobody had entered into his class
because sometimes he would talk continuously
for three, four, five, six hours.
And he used to say:
'The university can decide when the period starts,
but the university cannot decide when it stops,
because that depends on my flow.
If something is incomplete, I cannot leave it.
I have to complete it.'

So it was very disturbing.
He would take the whole time sometimes.

And sometimes he would not say a single thing for weeks.
He would say: 'Nothing is coming. You go home.'

When I entered his class,
he looked at me and he said:
'Yes. You may fit with me.
You also look a little eccentric.
But remember: when I start talking,
whenever it stops, it stops.
I never manipulate.
Sometimes I will not be talking for weeks;
you will have to come and go.
Sometimes I will talk for hours.
Then if you feel uneasy,
if you want to go to the bathroom or something,
you can go —
but don't disturb me.
I will continue.
You can come back. Silently, you can sit again.
I will continue because I cannot break it in between.'

It was a rare experience to listen to him.
He was completely oblivious of me, the only student.
Rarely would he look at me.
Sometimes he would look at the walls and talk.
And he was saying profound things
with such a deep heart
that it was not a question of addressing someone;
he was enjoying.
Sometimes he would chuckle and enjoy,
his own thing he would enjoy.
And many times I would go out and talk to people.
After minutes, after even hours sometimes,
he was there.
And he had been talking.

A play — not even a game.

The True Sage

I am talking to you; it is not a work.
It may be work for you; it is not work for me.
That day will be a blissful day
when it is not a work even for you,
when it has become a play,
when you delight with me,
when whatsoever I have to share,
you delight in, you participate in.
In those rare moments of participation
you become one with me.
And the work is done.
That is the way to do it.

Gurdjieff's people called their discipline 'the work'.
I call my discipline 'the play'.
Gurdjieff's disciples are very serious, doing great work.
Please, don't be serious here around me.
Seriousness is a disease, more dangerous than cancer.
Someday cancer will be curable,
but seriousness is incurable.

Be light, weightless,
happy in this moment to be here with me.
Participate. Enjoy.
The work will take its own care.
The work happens by the side;
you play and the work happens by the side.
My whole emphasis is to be playful.
If you can be playful,
everything will come on its own accord.

So it is not a work to me.
I love you. I enjoy you.
I am simply delighted in your being.
I am happy that you are here.

This moment is the end.
In this moment everything is fulfilled.

I don't look beyond it,
because to me, this moment is eternal;
it always remains there.
No other moment is coming.
This is the moment. It is eternity.

When you understand how to play,
how to be playful with me, around me,
you have opened the door.
That door opens automatically—
you never open it.
You simply play, and it opens.
That is the secret formula to open it.
Life's door, love's door, God's door —
they all open when you are playful.
They all become closed when you become serious,
when you become work-oriented.
Then you miss God.

God is a love, a song, a dance.
God is not a commodity; He is absolutely useless.
What can you use? What use can you put God to?
He is non-utilitarian.

I am here — absolutely useless.
To what use can you put me?
You can enjoy me —
just like you enjoy flowers in the morning,
or you enjoy clouds in the sky,
or you enjoy the songs of the birds.
These things cannot be sold in the market,
they are not commodities,
but they have a tremendous beauty in them.

Anything that you transform into a commodity
becomes profane.
Anything that you love for its own sake
immediately becomes holy, sacred.

The True Sage

This is from Somendra.
Recently, sitting before you,
I have become bathed in sweat.
What is happening?

By jove, Somendra, love is happening!
And whenever love happens, you feel very nervous
because you are moving in the unknown.
You are moving into something
which you cannot manipulate,
something which is beyond you,
in which you can be lost — lost forever.
It may be a point of no-return
and you never come back.
That's what is happening.

The whole personality:
shivering, afraid, sweating, nervous.
A death is happening!
That's what I mean when I say love is happening.

Love and death are two names of the same phenomenon.
On the edge of love one feels so scared
that one can be absorbed into it
and there may be no possibility to come back.
It is death, dawning before you.
Love is death,
and if you have known love as death
you have opened a secret chamber of life.
Then you will know death also as love.
Then death becomes God.

Before I know it
my watcher turns into my judger.
What to do?

384

Questions And Answers

Don't judge it.
If your watcher becomes a judger, okay.
Don't judge the judger — watch it.
If again the judger comes, watch it.

Always go on falling back on the watcher;
don't be defeated by the judger.
And don't be disturbed.
It is not a question that you have to not judge.
If you force it you will not be happy —
you will be suppressed.
And whatsoever you will do, the judger will be there —
no matter how you force, suppress.
No! Release it!

If a thought comes,
and another thought follows and becomes a judgment,
watch the judgment also.
Always go on falling into the watcher —
that's the whole thing.
If again the judger comes, let it come.
Don't be afraid.
You are always free to become a watcher again.

The whole method of watching is not to be deceived
and not to be distracted by the judger.
Let it be there, there is no condemnation about it.
What can you do if the judger comes? What can you do?
There is nothing to do.

You can again become a watcher.
Let it go on and on.
The judger is going to be lost somewhere,
and then the watcher will be centered.

It is going to be a long process
because you have always been helping
the judger to come in.
For many lives, for thousands of years,

The True Sage

you have always been getting identified
with the judger.
So the judger does not know
that you have changed your mind.
It will still be coming for a few years.
It depends on you.

If you go on falling to the watcher,
sooner or later, the judger will understand
that it is no more needed — an unwelcome guest.
It will knock at your door a few times,
but the knock will become
feebler and feebler and feebler.
One day,
seeing that you are no more interested in it,
the judger disappears.
You cannot suppress it.

*How is it possible
that you always and always, without exception,
talk about those things I have just thought about
or that came into my mind a day or a minute before?*

When I am talking, you are part of me.
You are not just the audience,
you are also talking through me to yourself.
And I am also not only the talker,
I am also part of the audience,
I am also listening.
It is a deep participation.
That is what is the meaning of communion.
It is not a communication only, it is a communion.

If you really listen to me, I am talking —
and you are also talking through me.

You create many things that I would not have spoken
if you were not there.

Somebody enters, a stranger — the audience changes.
I will have to talk about something else.
I may not know the man — that is not the point.
When the audience changes, the talker changes —
if it is a communion.
If it is a ready-made talk, then nothing matters.
Whoever you are doesn't matter.

I am not saying anything which is ready-made.
I am just here-now, responding to you and your being.
So if you have a certain thought,
it is bound to be reflected in my talk.
If you have a certain question,
somehow or other, it will synchronize;
it will bring its own answer.
That's how it happened. There is no miracle.
It is simply the miracle of communion.

If you are in deep love,
then you reflect in me and I reflect in you.
Then you are a mirror to me and I am a mirror to you.
My mirror reflects in you;
your mirror reflects in me.
And this goes on and on.
Two mirrors facing each other
can reflect infinitely, again and again.

The more you come closer to me,
the more there will be no need to ask.
There the question arises, and *here* is the answer.

Questions have to be asked
because you are not yet certain of the communion.

So don't be puzzled!
It is simply the miracle of communion,

it has nothing to do with me.
I am not trying to read your mind, remember;
I am not a mind-reader. I never do such foolish things.
I never read your mind.
But I am here, just like a mirror —
and you are reflected.

If you love me, your questions will be answered.
If you deeply participate with my being,
you will hear your own being revealed through me.
You are also talking through me,
I am also listening through you.
The talker and the listener disappear;
a circle of energy is created.
This is the difference
between communication and communion.

In communication
you may be a student, I may be a teacher.
In communion
I become the Master, you become the disciple.

One needs only a little trust
and everything will be answered —
not only answered, eventually solved.

By the time I see my moods, I am knee-deep in them.
Then it is not so much a question of watching,
but of riding on the wave until it subsides.

   So ride on it. But still watch.
You can ride on the wave.
How does it come in the way of the watcher?
In fact, when you are riding on the wave,
you can perfectly watch the wave.

The only thing to remember:
don't allow the wave to ride on you.
Ride on the wave — there is no problem.
Ride on the wave of anger and watch it.
The problem arises when anger rides on you
and the watcher is lost.
Then you get identified.

Nothing is wrong in anger.
Just don't get identified; watch it.
It is a beautiful experience, an energy experience.
Anger is pure energy.
I call it white petrol — the purest form of energy.
It becomes destructive because you get identified with it.
It is inflammable because it is pure.

A man who cannot be angry will be impotent
because he has no energy.
A man who can be angry has a potentiality,
a great energy in him.
But it has to be used rightly,
because the more energy you have, the more dangerous.
With more energy,
there is more possibility of exploding.
So you need to be more alert and aware.

Once you are aware,
the energy is there, but it never becomes destructive.
And to have energy is to have a depth,
to have energy is to have a height,
to have energy is to have a reservoir.

You can see two types of people who are not angry.
One: those who have no energy; they are empty shells.
You can see: shrunken beings.
They will not be angry,
but they will not be able to love either —

The True Sage

because one who has no energy to be angry
will not have energy to love.
Shrunken beings, already dead.
Only a part of them lives — ninety percent gone.
Only a little part still throbbing. Partially alive!
Then you will find another type of being
who is so full of energy that he is a reservoir.
He's also not angry because he knows how to be aware.
His no-anger is not absence of the energy of anger;
his no-anger is because of awareness.
This man can love, and love tremendously.
This man can become a great compassion.
The whole world can be filled by one man's compassion.
The world is not big enough:
a single man's compassion, if it explodes,
can fill the whole universe.
When a Buddha moves on the earth,
when a Jesus moves on the earth —
that's how it has happened.
A single man's energy —
purified, absolutely purified, with no identification —
becomes a soothing shower on the whole of existence.

It is said about Buddha and Mahavir. . . .
These stories are beautiful.
A Buddha moved in a forest —
don't take it literally, these are beautiful stories —
and trees started flowering out of season.
When he attained to enlightenment
the whole forest surrounding the area
bloomed in the morning.
The trees completely forgot that it is not the season.
Sometimes one has to forget when such a miracle happens.
Buddha showered on those trees.
They were happy. How else can a tree show its happiness?

It is said about Mahavir: whenever he would walk —
and he was a naked man, with no shoes, with no clothes —
thorns would be on the path
but they would turn upside down.
Thorns turning upside down so that Mahavir is not hurt.
Beautiful stories, indicating great phenomena.

Yes, it should be so.
I know thorns won't do that. I know it well.
But it should be so.
When Mahavir passes by,
even a thorn *should* become a flower.

Energy is good. Identification is bad.

Mahavir must have been potentially a very sexual man.
Otherwise, from where does this non-violence
and love come?
The same energy is released.
In awareness it becomes love;
in identification, unconsciousness, it becomes sexuality.

Buddha must have been a very very angry man —
very violent.
I *know it* intrinsically.
Whatsoever the scriptures say is irrelevant.
He must have been intrinsically
a very angry and violent man.
Otherwise, from where does the compassion come?

And that is the meaning of the historical fact that in India
the twenty-four teerthankaras of the Jains,
Buddha, Ram, Krishna —
they all were kshatriyas, warriors.
All the Hindu avataras
except one man, Parashuram,
were kshatriyas, warriors: angry people, violent.
The twenty-four teerthankaras of the Jains — all kshatriyas.

391

Not a single brahmin.
Buddha himself was a kshatriya.
In India, the whole history indicates something.
Why has it happened to kshatriyas? —
that they became the greatest openings
of compassion in the world? —
they had anger, they were fighters.
They could have been violent.
Once the energy is released and awareness arises,
the awareness rides on the energy and uses it.

Only one brahmin, Parashuram, was one of the avataras.
But he was not a brahmin at all.
It is said that you could not find a more violent man
in the whole history of the world.
He was so against the warriors, the race of kshatriyas,
that it is said that thirty-six times
he killed all the kshatriyas in the world.
He wanted to uproot all the kshatriyas in the world.
He was not a brahmin at all.
The world has never known such a great warrior.
Why?

The fact is simple and scientific.
If love is released, sex must have been there.
If compassion is released,
anger, hatred, violence, must have been there.
If non-attachment is released,
greed must have been there,
jealousy, possessiveness, must have been there.

You can know a tree by the fruit.
And you can know a man:
whatsoever happens in his enlightenment is his fruit.
You can know from where that fruit comes.

A lotus flower comes from the ordinary mud.
You cannot conceive by seeing the lotus flower
that it comes from the ordinary mud.

They seem so contradictory.
But life joins contradictions.
The most beautiful flower in the world,
the most delicate,
comes out of ordinary mud, dirty mud.

Love comes out of the mud of sex.
Compassion comes out of the mud of anger.
And nirvana? — comes out of the mud of this world.

Bhagwan,
I wonder . . .
what is Hassidism?

I also wonder.

by Bhagwan Shree Rajneesh

The Ultimate Alchemy Vols. I and II
(discourses on the Atma Pooja Upanishad)

The Book of the Secrets Vols. I, II, III and IV
(discourses on Tantra)

The Supreme Doctrine
(discourses on the Kenopanishad)

YOGA : the alpha and the omega Vols. I, II and III
(discourses on Patanjali's Yoga Sutras)

VEDANTA: Seven Steps to Samadhi
(discourses on the Akshya Upanishad)

The Way of the White Cloud
(talks based on questions)

Roots and Wings
(talks based on questions)

The Empty Boat
(discourses on Chuang Tzu)

No Water, No Moon
(discourses on Zen)

The Mustard Seed
(discourses on the sayings of Jesus)

When the Shoe Fits
(discourses on Chuang Tzu)

Neither This Nor That
(discourses on Sosan — Zen)

. . . and the flowers showered
(discourses on Zen stories)

Returning to the Source
(discourses on Zen stories)

The Hidden Harmony
(discourses on the fragments of Heraclitus)

TANTRA: The Supreme Undertaking
(discourses on Tilopa's Song of Mahamudra)

The Grass Grows by Itself
(discourses on Zen stories)

Until You Die
(discourses on Sufi stories)

Just Like That
(discourses on Sufi stories)

TAO: The Three Treasures Vols. I and II
(discourses on Lao Tzu)

Hammer on the Rock
(darshan diary)

Above All, Don't Wobble
(darshan diary)

Come Follow Me Vol. I
(discourses on the life of Jesus)

I am the Gate
(talks based on questions)

The Silent Explosion
(talks based on questions)

Dimensions beyond the Known
(talks based on questions)

translations

La Rivoluzione Interiore
(Italian—published by Armenia Editore)

Hu Meditation of Kosmic Orgasme
(Danish—published by Borgens Forlag A/S)

Rajneesh Meditation Centers

SHREE RAJNEESH ASHRAM, 17 Koregaon Park, Poona 411 001, India. TEL: 28127

SAGAR DEEP, 52 Ridge Road, Malabar Hill, Bombay 400 006, India. TEL: 364783

ANANDA, 29 East 28th St., N.Y.C., 10016, U.S.A. TEL: 212 686-3261

NEELAMBER, Blackmore Lane, P.O. Box 143, East Islip. N.Y. 11730. U.S.A. TEL: 516 581-0004

ANAND TARU, 12 Hearn St., Watertown, Boston, Mass., U.S.A.

BODHITARU, 7231 SW 62nd Place, Miami, Florida, U.S.A.

SATSANG, 887 North La Salle, Chicago, Illinois, U.S.A. TEL: 312 943-8561/8549

PARAS, P.O. Box 22174, San Francisco, Calif., 94122, U.S.A. TEL: 415 664-6600

ARVIND, 1330 Renfrew St., Vancouver, B.C., Canada

KALPTARU, Top Floor, 10A Belmont St., London NW1, England Postal Address: 28 Oak Village, London NW5. TEL: 267-8304

NIRVANA, 82 Bell St., London NW1, England. TEL: 262-0991

SURODAYA, The Old Rectory, Gislingham, by Diss, nr. Eye, Suffolk, England

GOURISHANKAR, 9 Ravensdeen Gadns, Penecuik, nr. Edinburgh, Scotland. TEL: Ponecuik 73034

PRASTHAN, 21 Wilmot Road, Glasgow C13 IXL, Scotland

PREMNATH, 45-390 Desmonts, France

SHANTIDWEEP, 25 Avenue Pierre, Premier de Serbie, Paris XVIe, France. TEL: 700-7930

ANAND NIKEAN, Kobmagergade 43-1150, Copenhagen K, Denmark

ARIHANT, Via Cacciatori delle Alpi 19, 20019 Settimo, Milanese, Milan, Italy

SATYAM, 15B Route de Loex, 1213 Onex, Geneva, Switzerland. TEL: 022 93-19-46

AMITABH, Korte Prinsengracht 9, Amsterdam, Holland. TEL: 238966

PURVODAYA, D-8051 Margarethenreid, Munich, West Germany

SHREYAS, 8 Munich 60, Raucheneggerstr. 11, West Germany. TEL: 809 882662

ANANDLOK, 1 Berlin 61, Luckenwaldstr. 11, West Germany

SHANTI SHILA, P.O. Box 358 MCC, Makati Rizal, Philippines. TEL: 70-33-14

ASHEESH, c/o Oda, Kangawa-Ken, Chigasaki-Shi, Tomoe 2-8-23 Japan

ANAND NEED, P.O. Box 72424, Nairobi, Kenya, East Africa

PURNAM, Caixa Postal 1946, Porto Alegre — R. G. Sul, Brazil. TEL: 21888

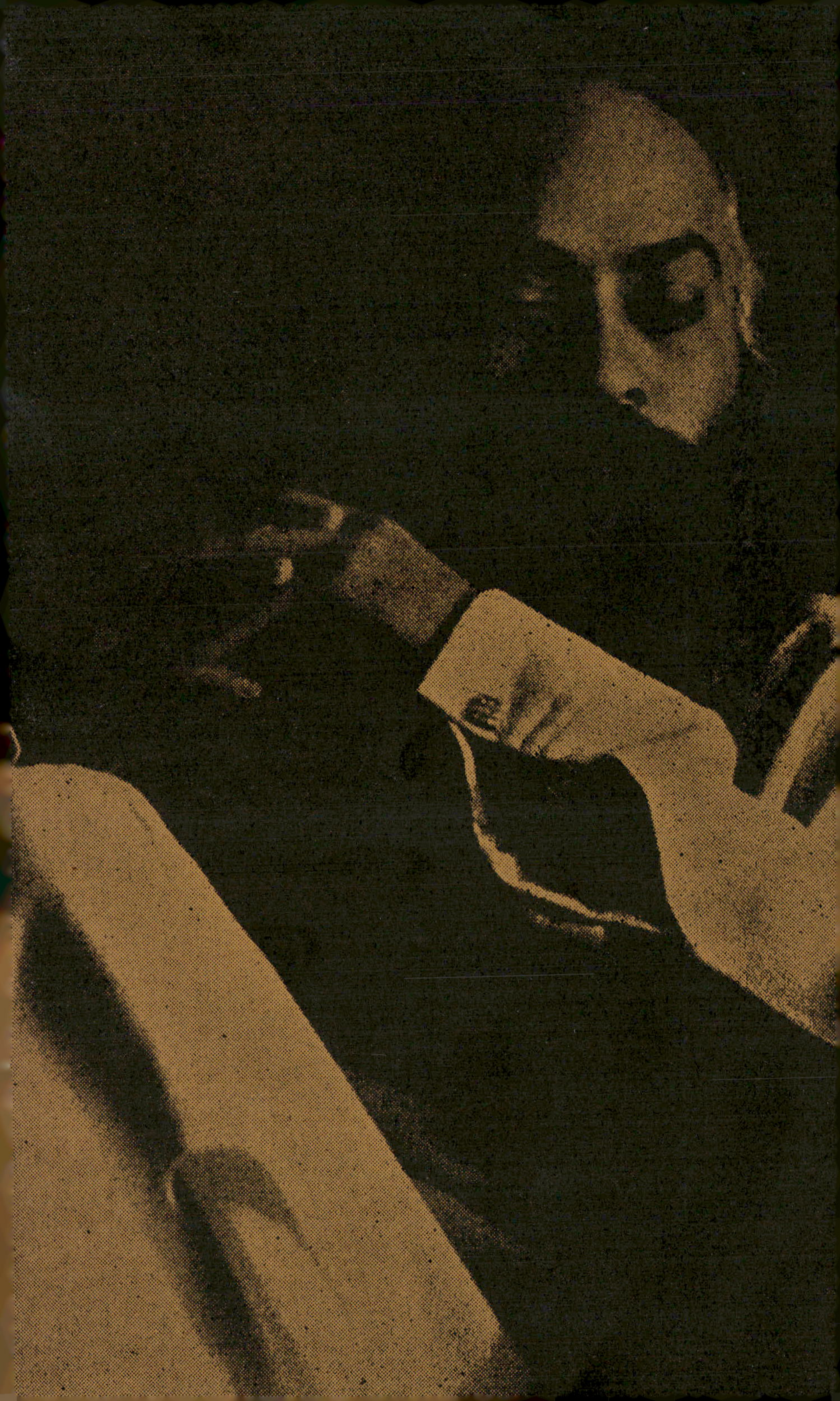

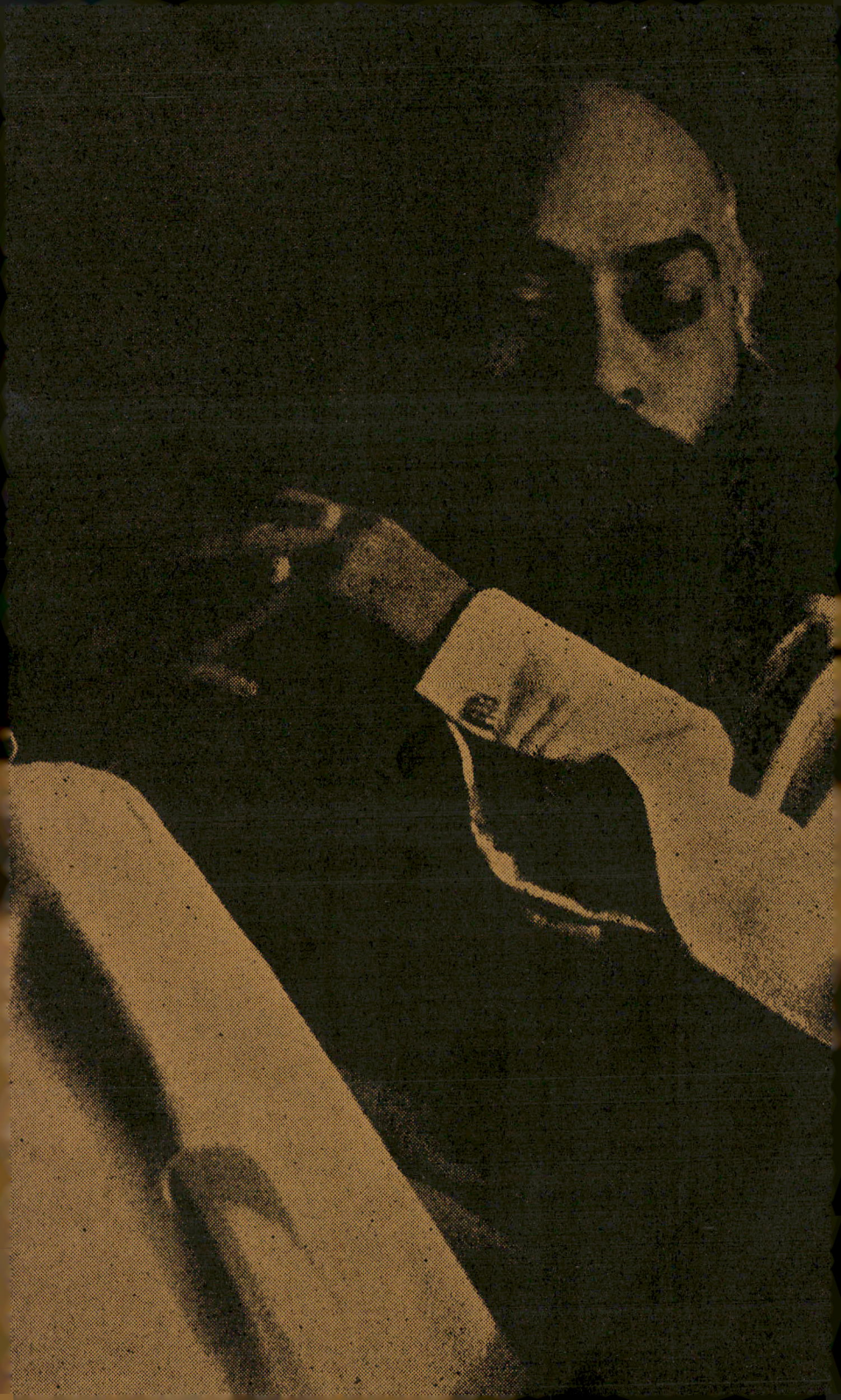